The Fall of the House of
BEAVERBROOK

The Fall of the House of
BEAVERBROOK

Lewis Chester
and Jonathan Fenby

WITHDRAWN

ANDRE DEUTSCH

First published 1979 by
André Deutsch Limited
105 Great Russell Street London WC1

Copyright © 1979 by Times Newspapers Limited
All rights reserved

Printed in Great Britain by
Ebenezer Baylis & Son Limited
The Trinity Press, Worcester, and London

ISBN 0 233 97161 0

Contents

Illustrations

Acknowledgements

This book deals with matters which some people would prefer not to be disclosed. We are, therefore, more than usually grateful to those who provided us with information. Fortunately for us, most journalists are compulsive talkers even when the stories they relate display them in a less than heroic light. Without this attractive foible the book could scarcely have been written.

Some chose to talk to us on a confidential basis and we respect their wish for anonymity. Others we can thank openly. They are in alphabetical order: Maxwell Aitken, Lord Barnetson, Sheila Black, Peter Caney, John Coote, William Deedes, Nigel Dempster, the late Olga Deterding, Les Dixon, Tony Dyer, William Ellsworth-Jones, David English, Robin Esser, Stephen Fay, Michael Foot, MP, Sir James Goldsmith, David Gordon, Sir Denis Hamilton, Bert Hardy, Alan Hare, Roger Harrison, Roy Hattersley, MP, David Henshall, Peter Hetherington, Anthony Holden, Marmaduke Hussey, Richard Ingrams, Simon Jenkins, the late David Karr, Louis Kirby, Phillip Knightley, David Lawday, David May, Alison Miller, Ken Morgan, Rupert Murdoch, Brian Nicholson, Owen O'Brien, Bruce Page, Sir Edward Pickering, Tom Pocock, Percy Roberts, Mike Rothwell, Lord Robens, Frank Rogers, Ted Simpson, Jocelyn Stevens, Sam White, Max Wilkinson, Charles Wintour and Roy Wright.

Thanks are due to Lord Rothermere, the proprietor of Associated Newspapers, for permission to reproduce two of his letters in full, and to the Economist Intelligence Unit for permission to reproduce extracts from its Survey of the UK National Newspaper Industry, published by the Joint Board for the Newspaper Industry in 1967. The report is now out of print.

Acknowledgements

We also thank Harold Evans, the editor of the *Sunday Times*, who initiated this project and supported it throughout. For detailed advice on the text we are grateful to Mimi Chester, Faith Evans and Vivienne Menkes. For aid and comfort we are indebted to Renée Fenby. The manuscript was expertly typed by Angela Price and Carole Serra.

Some people who are important characters in our book chose not to be interviewed. They include Sir Max Aitken, the last proprietor of Beaverbrook Newspapers, Nigel Broackes and Victor Matthews of Trafalgar House, which now owns *Express Newspapers*, Lord Goodman, John Junor, editor of the *Sunday Express*, and Lord Rothermere. This book is dedicated to them, in the hope that they will be more forthcoming when the newspaper industry experiences its next crisis.

Lewis Chester
Jonathan Fenby
July 1979

ONE

The Crippled Crusader

LA CAPPONCINA WAS a good place to escape to when the
English climate became too depressing: a red-roofed villa
perched 100 feet above a rocky strip of French Riviera coast,
with a magnificent view across the Mediterranean. Its five
bedrooms provided ample accommodation for the owner's
frequent and famous guests. Between meals they could sit on
the sun terrace and look out at the calm sea and the palace of
Monaco on a headland in the distance. The more active could
walk among the groves of olive and cypress trees in the garden
or swim in a pool flanked by marble columns. It was a most
pleasant house to own and it was not surprising that Lord
Beaverbrook loved it. The newspaper proprietor demonstrated
his attachment to the area by ordering a marble figure entitled
'Bel Amour' to be brought out from England and placed in the
central square of the surrounding village of Cap d'Ail. Regret-
tably, vandals tore the arms off and the statue had to be
removed, leaving its plinth standing empty.

Much as Lord Beaverbrook loved his villa on the Riviera it
had unhappy medical associations for some of the prominent
people he invited there. His most famous friend, Sir Winston
Churchill, had his first stroke in La Capponcina in 1949 after
sitting up past midnight playing gin rummy. Seven years later
his greatest editor, Arthur Christiansen of the *Daily Express*,
suffered a heart attack at Cap d'Ail.

Medical problems were on the mind of Beaverbrook's son
and successor, Sir Max Aitken, when he decided to go to La
Capponcina in January 1977. The visit meant that he would
miss the final stages of the annual London Boat Show at
Olympia, one of his favourite events. The show was sponsored
by the *Daily Express* and Sir Max, an enthusiastic sailor, always

took an active part. The 1977 show, however, failed to lift the depressed spirits of the 66-year-old proprietor.

Sir Max was still suffering from the after-effects of two mild strokes sustained the previous year and his doctor had told him that he must rest. The information about his poor health had been kept secret from all but his most senior employees. Apart from the family's natural discretion, business considerations made it advisable to avoid broadcasting news of Sir Max's condition outside the most restricted circle. On 6 January, while the proprietor was still in London, the circle widened considerably. Sir Max arrived uncharacteristically late for the opening day of the Boat Show, looking pale and leaning heavily on the arm of his wife, Lady Violet. The men who ran his newspapers, already concerned about the financial state of his empire, could see that their chairman was a sick man.

Ten days later, Sir Max set off with a young lady friend for La Capponcina. He left orders for a new Jaguar car with white wall tyres to be driven to Cap d'Ail for his use there. The order was to be countermanded before the car could be delivered.

At La Capponcina, Sir Max and his friend were looked after by an old family retainer, Madame Franco, a fixture at the villa from the days of Lord Beaverbrook. Despite her long service for Sir Max and his father, she spoke little English. Her cooking, however, made up for any communications problems, though guests could run into some unexpected expense through the tradition that visitors paid for the meals which Madame Franco and her family ate. As a result, one visitor recalls, 'you got splendid fare but it came very expensive'.

On 21 January Sir Max had another stroke. It was a major attack which paralysed his right side. The two women at the house were clearly in no position to cope. The Aitken family in London was alerted and Lady Violet and Sir Max's daughter Laura flew out to Nice in a chartered jet. She collected her sick husband and promptly flew back.

While they were still airborne, Sir Max's 26-year-old son and heir, Maxwell, and Beaverbrook's chief executive, Jocelyn Stevens, boarded another chartered plane *en route* for Paris, where they were scheduled to meet a businessman to discuss the destiny of the Beaverbrook empire. As they flew over the English Channel, in the direction of the plane bearing Sir

Max, Lady Violet and Laura Aitken back to London, Stevens remembered thinking: 'Just one midair collision and all Beaverbrook's problems would be over.'

The problems of Beaverbrook Newspapers in January 1977 were of a spectacular order. Less than two years earlier the company had increased its borrowing to £14 million, to pay for a programme drawn up in the early 1970s to replace antiquated pressroom machinery and to develop property in London and Bristol. The Finance Corporation for Industry, a bank consortium, had put up £8 million and £3 million had come from the First National Bank of Boston. Lloyd's, the group's British bank, was already sufficiently concerned about Beaverbrook's future to limit any further lending. By the summer of 1976 the annual interest payments alone had reached £1·9 million, and the group's ability to keep up the repayments became more problematic with each passing month.

Unlike other national newspaper companies Beaverbrook was not structured to weather the lean years. Most groups had extensive interests outside British national newspapers, which helped as a buffer against the notorious fluctuations of fortune in Fleet Street. Beaverbrook, in contrast, was almost totally dependent on the profitability of its two London word factories – one in Shoe Lane, just north of Fleet Street, where the *Evening Standard* was produced in charmless Dickensian conditions, and the other in a swanky black glass building in Fleet Street (sometimes known as 'the Lubianka') which housed the *Daily Express* and the *Sunday Express*.

The *Daily Express*, once the group's proud flagship with a circulation of about 4 million, presented the central problem, selling almost 2 million copies a day fewer than in its heyday. Asked where the old *Daily Express* readers had gone, one editor plaintively replied: 'Largely to the cemetery.' Most of the readers it retained were also well on the way there.

Readership surveys showed that 58 per cent of the *Daily Express*'s readers were over 45, and 22 per cent were drawing their old-age pension. Nor were they the kind of readers advertisers most wanted to reach. A lot of *Express* readers were poor. Commercial television, the *Sun* (circulation 3·7 million) and the *Daily Mirror* (circulation 3·8 million) all offered better

13

ways of reaching the lower-income groups. Demoralization in the advertising department was matched by the mood on the editorial floor. Expressmen were no longer the envied aces of Fleet Street. *Private Eye*, the satirical magazine, underlined the general slide in the paper's reputation as editor after editor failed to arrest its decline. In the *Eye* the *Express* was the 'Daily Getsmuchworse' and its stock character, 'Lunchtime O'Booze', was based on what was regarded as the quintessential *Express* hack, operating on reflexes blurred by alcohol and the memory of a vanished golden age of cheque-book journalism.

The *Evening Standard*, more respected editorially, had also been going through a bad spell as a result of the slump in advertising. It was thought that an increase in the retail 'cover' price might restore its position, but there was no way the evening paper alone could turn the company round. The group as a whole was displaying an unhealthy dependence on one product, the unchanging *Sunday Express*.

As if to remind the Beaverbrook men of their group's fragility, 1977 began with the newsprint manufacturers announcing a £40 per tonne increase in prices. Holding costs by simply cutting back on manpower was not a realistic option, despite the many well-documented instances of overmanning in the industry.

Long-term hopes of a resolution of the industry's problems were pinned on the new technology, introducing computer-linked methods to displace the traditional hot metal setting operation. The problem in Fleet Street was that the new techniques cut directly across the interests of the most entrenched craft skills in the country. Beaverbrook, along with the other Fleet Street managements, was involved in talks with the leadership of the print unions, trying to reach a solution, but there was no possibility of one being found in time to have any impact on the group's immediate crisis.

Losses for the last half of 1976 were running at £1·45 million. At a time of general unrest throughout the industry Beaverbrook had virtually no margin of safety. The loss of two issues of the *Sunday Express* could reduce the group to insolvency. Lloyd's Bank had already indicated that it would be unwilling to renew the Beaverbrook overdraft facility when it expired in April 1977. 'We were headed for the knacker's yard,' Jocelyn Stevens recalled, 'facing a complete break-up.'

The plight of the once famous and flourishing house of Beaverbrook was rendered the more poignant by the still-potent legend of its founder, who had died less than 13 years earlier. The Canadian-born Lord Beaverbrook, who became an intimate of prime ministers and kings, had established what seemed to be one of the century's most unassailable press empires. Few public figures were more controversial, but there was no disputing his extraordinary success as a popular newspaper proprietor.

During his lifetime 'The Beaver', as he was called, attracted a wide variety of opinions. His impulsive energy, both as a press proprietor and as a politician, was reflected in the depth of his friendships and enmities. His principal biographer, the left-wing historian A. J. P. Taylor, said quite simply that he loved Lord Beaverbrook. Lord Reith, the first director-general of the BBC, thought he was evil, disgusting and loathsome, confiding to his diary the judgement: 'To no one is the vulgar designation shit more appropriately applied.'

'The Beaver' certainly had some strange habits that were not normally considered appropriate to his high station in life. He once received an employee in Cherkley, his Surrey country home, walking up and down naked except for his panama hat as he dictated to his male secretary. Other minions reported being given instructions while he cradled a girlfriend on his lap. The writer Harold Nicolson, who worked on the *Evening Standard* during the 1930s, told a colleague of a conversation carried on while Beaverbrook sat on the lavatory drinking liquid paraffin to combat constipation. He liked his key employees to have big heads. On one occasion a Beaverbrook editor introduced a promising young journalist to him. Beaverbrook's comment after the young journalist left the room was: 'Small head. Big feet. Won't do.'

The pungency of his telephone manner could be alarming. One of his assistants, instructed to send a cable, queried the spelling of the name of the addressee. After an impatient pause the proprietor's voice came rasping down the line: 'G for God Almighty, L for Lunatics, A for Atlantic Ocean, N for Nancy, C for Cunt and Y for You.'

* * *

Lord Beaverbrook was born William Maxwell Aitken in Maple, Ontario, on 25 May 1879. His father was a Church of Scotland minister who had emigrated to Canada 15 years earlier.

As a child he was a dullard. Late in life Lord Beaverbrook attributed his remarkable abilities to having his head cracked by a mowing machine as a small boy: 'The crack which the wheel gave to my skull,' he reasoned, 'gave my brain room to expand, which it needed. Doctors can make what they like of the incident. I have made a lot of it.'

In his youth Aitken worked through a classic series of jobs for tycoons-to-be. He was a clerk in a lawyer's office, sold newspapers, worked in a drugstore, ran a bowling alley and peddled insurance. He also started a newspaper in his home town, but production stopped abruptly when his father found him working on Sunday.

Relations between father and son subsequently improved. The Reverend Aitken confessed to his son on a Canadian railway station platform that he did not really believe the gospel he expounded so vehemently for a living. Years later, in comfortable retirement, he said: 'I am grateful beyond telling that I will never have to preach another damn sermon.'

Max Aitken's first fortune in Canada came from a profitable new field which had opened up for young men in a hurry – selling bonds and promoting companies and company mergers. In 1906 he married Gladys Drury, a colonel's daughter, and spent part of his honeymoon looking into business possibilities in the Caribbean. By 1907 he had become a dollar millionaire. His success with a dazzling series of mergers in the cement business, bringing together most of the firms in Canada, put him in the multi-millionaire class. Aitken boasted that he could not be compared to the American plutocrat J. P. Morgan because: 'Morgan had failures, I have none.' He was ready for London.

Aitken set up in Britain in 1910 with a reputation as a businessman, company promoter and high-class bond salesman. His first activities were, not surprisingly, financial. One early deal brought him into contact with Alfred Harmsworth, Lord Northcliffe, the dominant figure in the development of the popular press in Britain. The rivalry between the Northcliffe and Beaverbrook newspapers would rage on from the 1920s into the 1970s, but Aitken's first contact with the 'chief' of Fleet Street was about motorcars, not the press. It arose when Aitken bought heavily into Rolls-Royce and wanted the firm to go over to mass-production. The management of Rolls-Royce objected and got the backing of Northcliffe, who took a non-financial interest in the firm. He wrote to Aitken asking him not to interfere with the 'delicate orchid' of Rolls-Royce. Aitken sold out his shares and received from Northcliffe the accolade of being 'one of the straightest men in the country'.

Aitken's main ambition was political. Throughout his life his political involvement was to take two main forms: either he was deep in behind-the-scenes manoeuvres within a small circle of leading figures such as Lloyd George, Bonar Law or Winston Churchill; or he was conducting strident public campaigns through the press. Sometimes, he combined the two. Parliamentary debate and party organization were not the kind of activities which the impatient, domineering William Maxwell Aitken ever found congenial, though he was elected Unionist MP for Ashton-under-Lyne in Lancashire soon after his arrival in Britain.

The public campaigns were not to become possible until he had acquired newspapers and built them up as mass-circulation vehicles for his views. The backstairs role, on the other hand, was played out for all it was worth during Aitken's early years in Britain, particularly in the 1916 crisis which saw the overthrow of Asquith as Liberal prime minister and his replacement by Lloyd George at the head of a wartime coalition. He was equally close to the centre of the action when Law supplanted Lloyd George in 1922. But on each occasion his role was that of a fixer, a go-between, rather than that of a kingmaker which subsequent demonology was to ascribe to him.

That demonology was to be helped by the popular physical picture of Aitken. He was in fact a man of average height, but the general image of him, fostered by cartoonists in his own newspapers, was of a small, hobgoblin figure, with a disproportionately large head and a huge, mischievous grin. It was an image which fitted in with the idea of Aitken as a political power behind the scenes and formed part of the persona he built up for himself.

When Lloyd George and Law proposed him for a peerage in 1916, King George v replied that he did not consider Aitken's public services called for such recognition, but it was too late for a royal refusal. Aitken and his constituency had already been told about the honour. The king gave way and Aitken became Baron Beaverbrook, taking his title from a stream in Canada where he had fished as a boy. He was 37 years old. In the same year he acquired his first national newspaper, the *Daily Express*. The paper, under its American-born editor Ralph D. Blumenfeld, had been in difficulties for some years and the biggest private shareholder, Sir George Lawson Johnston, who had made a fortune out of Bovril meat extract, was anxious to sell out. Beaverbrook paid £17,500 for the Johnston holding.

Disregarding a dismal welcome to Fleet Street from Northcliffe, who told him he would lose all his money there, Beaverbrook radiated the verve and optimism which were to be his trademarks as a press proprietor. 'The *Daily Express* is rapidly changing its character,' he wrote in 1918. 'It was originally a paper with a small, but firm clientele, representing a pretty strong, if limited view. It is now becoming a paper with an enormous and infinitely varied circulation.' Even given Beaverbrook's expansionist view of life, 'enormous' was still only a relative word at that stage in the life of the *Daily Express*: it had a circulation well below that of Northcliffe's *Daily Mail*, which sold four times as many copies.

To go with the *Daily Express* Beaverbrook wanted a Sunday paper. After a bid for the *Sunday Times* had failed for political reasons, he started the *Sunday Express* in 1918. Originally, as its name implied, it was conceived of as a seventh-day extension of the *Daily Express*. But it quickly generated more than one-day-a-week problems.

While his daily paper forged ahead, Beaverbrook's *Sunday Express* lost money. Circulation fell from an initial 300,000 to 180,000. In the first two years losses totalled nearly £500,000. Beaverbrook later referred to his 'adventure' in launching the *Sunday Express* as a folly. 'I sometimes used to go out into my garden and shake myself like a dog. Had my right hand lost its cunning?' he recalled. In his own mind he wrote off his investment as a total loss. Then the paper pulled round.

Success was the title of one of Lord Beaverbrook's earliest books, in 1921, and it was something he could soon boast of in his newspapers. In 1923 he added the *Evening Standard* to his burgeoning empire. In an industry in which strong men were still able to mould enterprises in their own image Beaverbrook used his three newspapers to project everything in his character, good and bad, on to millions of readers every day. Gloss and energy, a highly personal view of events and people, a refusal to take life too seriously, mischief and ruthlessness allied with charm and optimism – all shone from the pages of his newspapers.

The owner's bouncy philosophy was put into words and pictures by a line of editors whose different personalities reflected the various stages of the development of the *Express*. Blumenfeld, who remained as editor for a while after Beaverbrook took control, was a political figure as well as a newspaperman. For all his experience in the pre-Beaverbrook years of the *Express*, he used to say that he learned the business of journalism from Beaverbrook. His successor, Beverley Baxter from Canada, gave the paper a lot of its sheen and smartness, reflecting his own way of life, which led to his occasionally turning up in the bustling *Express* office in white tie and tails after attending the opera or a smart party.

While Beaverbrook concentrated on editorial issues his principal manager, E. J. Robertson, made sure that the business actually worked, that the printing plant was efficient, that paper supplies were bought for the lowest possible cost, and that the paper's distribution arrangements would get the sparkling editorial product into as many newsagents' shops as possible. Like Beaverbrook, Robertson had been an outsider to the newspaper business when he first became involved with the *Daily Express*. He had met Beaverbrook in a Canadian hotel where he was working during a university vacation. Beaverbrook asked if he wanted a tip; Robertson replied that he would prefer a job. When linked with Beverley Baxter's brief career as a piano salesman, this enabled Beaverbrook to proclaim that he had carried the *Daily Express* to greatness with the help of a bell-hop and a piano tuner.

Baxter thought the *Express* could not live without him. His successor proved how wrong he was. Arthur Christiansen, appointed editor in 1933 after working as Baxter's assistant, was a very different proposition from either his worldly predecessor or the political Blumenfeld. An expert newspaper technician, he spent his time making up pages in the new black glass *Express* building in Fleet Street rather than talking to prime ministers or attending fashionable first nights. Under Christiansen the *Daily Express* pioneered the modern style of popular newspaper layout, with pictures and text displayed in an elaborate jigsaw. The regimented system of strict vertical columns lined up across the page became a thing of the past. Pages were frames in which almost anything could be done to achieve an effect. Big photographs and a muscular new typeface called Century reflected the energy and zest of the paper. Christiansen described his approach to journalism in the following terms: 'When you looked at the front page you said "Good Heavens", when you looked at the middle page you said "Holy Smoke", and by the time you got to the back page – well, I'd have to utter a profanity to show how exciting it was.'

The editor looked after the presentation, while the proprietor imposed the ideology of the radical Right. Moving between his homes in Britain, the Bahamas, Canada and the French Riviera, Beaverbrook constantly bombarded his executives with suggestions. A characteristic injunction to his staff was: 'People do not read to be bored. Unless a newspaper can make its material in every department interesting it simply is not read. Be sure that when you read your *Daily Express* you will not be bored.'

Sometimes the messages came by telephone, sometimes dictated on reels of tape, sometimes written out on narrow strips of paper, to encourage thrift. Beaverbrook delighted in catching people out and in pointing to mistakes. He watched the length of editorials and news stories to see that they did not get too long – 400 words was the usual maximum. His own fondness for gossip was reflected in the suggestions he sent to build up two of the most enduring features of his newspapers – the William Hickey and Londoner's Diary columns in the *Daily Express* and *Evening Standard*. He castigated editors for paying too much attention to people he disliked, or for mentioning them at all. He issued instructions to book reviewers which are still pertinent: '(1) Name – author – publisher (2) What the book is about. The story if possible (3) The author and his idiosyncracies (4) Is it worth reading? (5) Wisecracks if good. But not any clever quips if commonplace.' A lavish host himself, he warned his editors against too much socializing and told them on one occasion: 'All good journalists dine at Lyon's Corner House.'

From the start, Beaverbrook aimed not only for large circulations but also for social variety in his readers. For all his wealth and connections he was in many ways a classless person, an intruder from Canada who never settled into the British establishment. He wanted his newspapers to be the same, and he succeeded to an extraordinary degree. It was said, Beaverbrook wrote, that the *Daily Express* appealed to a middle-class mind.

> That is not so [he went on]. It appeals to a particular kind of mind in every class. Having begun in a small way it appeals to those who are not ashamed of small beginnings but who look forward to dealing with the events of life on a larger scale. We appealed to the character and temperament which was bent on moving upwards and outwards and which was not to be trammelled by any doctrinaire conceptions in its views of national needs and opportunities.

And which, he might have added, corresponded to the temperament of the owner.

He once summarized his aims as: 'More life – more hope – more money – more work – more happiness', and was delighted when the *Manchester Guardian* described him as 'The Pedlar of Dreams'. (The author of the phrase, Howard Spring, was later employed as a book critic on the *Evening Standard*.)

By the mid-1930s Beaverbrook could claim that he had achieved the world's biggest daily newspaper sale: in the 15 years after Northcliffe's death the circulation of the *Daily Express* rose from 790,000 to 2·2 million, while the *Mail*'s stagnated at around 1·7 to 1·8 million. Leadership in the popular newspaper field was now contested by the left-wing *Daily Herald* and the *Daily Express*.

The leap ahead of the *Herald* and *Express* took place on the back of a frantic give-away campaign in which prospective readers were offered sets of Dickens, encyclopedias, cutlery, clothes, china and dozens of other gifts if they would subscribe to a newspaper. The idea of gifts in return for subscriptions was an old one. Insurance offers had been a favourite come-on earlier in the century and during the First World War readers of the *Daily Chronicle* had even been extended cover against bombardment by Zeppelins. But the gift campaigns of the 1930s reached new peaks and ended only when circulations had been pushed up so far that additional give-aways would have been a waste of money.

Beaverbrook's main political concern in the early 1930s was the cause of 'empire free trade'. He founded a United Empire Party dedicated to the idea of free trade within a British Empire sealed off from the rest of the world by tariff barriers. For a brief time it seemed that the crusade might have a real impact. United Empire Party candidates won two by-elections in London before the orthodox Conservative Party reasserted its authority. The movement fell apart, bequeathing its emblem of a red crusader with drawn sword to live on symbolically on a corner of the *Daily Express* front page.

During the late 1930s Beaverbrook used his newspapers to campaign for a strong Britain free of European entanglements. His historical view of such connections was reflected in a *Daily Express* article addressed to First World War veterans, which was surrounded by rows of white crosses and had the words 'All in Vain' repeated throughout the text. After the Second World War had started Beaverbrook wrote to a friend: 'I am convinced that Britain can stand for ever. It is only necessary for us to produce at home for our requirements. To give up coffee and drink beer. To smoke our own tobacco. To build aeroplanes. To train men and love the neutrals.' One cannot be sure how serious he was, any more than one can know how seriously Beaverbrook intended many of his other expressions of opinion at the time, such as his statement in a 1938 letter that the Jews were drawing Britain into war with Hitler. Twenty years later, in an article which he wrote himself but published under the name of the *Daily Express* editor, he described the Second World War as 'The Unnecessary War' and gave his judgement: 'If Chamberlain's will to peace had held strong and firm, those dictators [Hitler and Stalin] would have destroyed each other without any sacrifices by Britain.'

During his 24 years as editor of the *Express* Arthur Christiansen perfected a style which dominated British popular journalism. It blended information, tightly but attractively written, strong feature articles, a constantly inquiring approach to people and events, a concentration on the personal and the concrete rather than the abstract and a big reporting service which ensured that an *Express* man was always present at any significant event at home or abroad.

Once found, the news was to be aimed at a clearly defined audience, personified in Christiansen's daily bulletins to his staff as the 'Man on Rhyl Promenade', who was made to ask questions like: 'What's this Château Yquem and garlic stuff in the *Express* today? My champagne's a bottle of Guinness and a plate of winkles.' In another bulletin Christiansen laid down in 24 words the basic *Express* approach to news: 'In the handling of every single story, whether it be high politics or broad humanity, we should never fail to have the COMMON TOUCH.'

Yet there was never any doubt about who was in charge. A rare occasion on which Christiansen thought of revolt showed clearly the relationship between proprietor and editor in the Beaverbrook world. 'I remember feeling sick when Neville Chamberlain described Czechoslovakia as "a far-away country" and I remember expressing my revulsion to Lord Beaverbrook over the telephone,' Christiansen recalled in his autobiography, *Headlines all my Life*. 'But when he said, "Well, isn't Czechoslovakia a far-away country?" I agreed that it was and got on with my job of producing an exciting newspaper.' The *Daily Express* headline after the Munich agreement came to symbolize the political pitfalls of Beaverbrook's breezy style: 'Britain will not be involved in a European war this year, or next year either.' Commercially, it did not seem to make much difference. In 1940 sales of the *Daily Express* hit 3 million.

Though an isolationist, Beaverbrook had always been a proponent of a strong rearmament programme. So it was not entirely surprising that Churchill should put him in charge of aircraft production when war did come. Beaverbrook galvanized output, driving up production before the Battle of Britain and fully living up to the nickname of 'Tornado' which the Duke of Windsor and Mrs Simpson had given him during the 1936 abdication crisis. In the process he made enemies, trampling over established reputations as he devoted all his energies to increasing the output of aircraft to defend Britain. (On his desk he had a slogan: 'Organization is the enemy of improvisation.') Given the nature of the man, it was perhaps not surprising that Churchill failed in an attempt to impose him as overall supremo of British production and that, amid growing enmity with Labour Party leaders, Beaverbrook left the war cabinet in 1942. His critics in the bureaucracy called him 'the Great Disorganizer'.

Out of government, Beaverbrook devoted much of his energy to campaigning for the quick opening of a second front by an allied invasion of continental Europe in order to relieve pressure on the Russians. He had made a successful trip to Moscow in 1941 and had a clear idea of the importance for the western allies of keeping the Soviet Union a strong ally. Michael Foot, who edited the *Evening Standard* before becoming a leading member of the Labour Party, believes that Beaverbrook's overall strategic grasp was better than Churchill's, particularly in his insistence on the prime importance of defeating Hitler in Europe with the help of a strong Soviet Union. In 1943 Beaverbrook was back in the government as Lord Privy Seal, but he was outside the war cabinet and owed his position essentially to his friendship with Churchill. Ernest Bevin, the Labour leader, said that with Beaverbrook Churchill was 'like a man who's married a whore; he knows she's a whore but he loves her just the same.'

In 1945 Beaverbrook's closeness to Churchill gave him a major hand in organizing the Conservative Party's campaign to sweep the war leader back to power. Never one for half measures, he went so far as to describe the Labour Party as 'the National Socialists', but his virulence rebounded and probably contributed to the Conservative defeat. His political career was at an end, though he was to live for another 19 years and enjoy a late but notable career as a historian. Newspapers remained his obsession.

The success of Beaverbrook's newspapers continued after the Second World War, despite the rise of the *Daily Mirror*, whose populist, left-wing appeal was lodged firmly in the working class. The two *Express* papers kept chasing those who saw themselves as rising to bourgeois success. Under the editorship of John Gordon, the canniest of many canny Scots in the Beaverbrook organization, the *Sunday Express* sold over 3 million copies each week, while Christiansen pushed the circulation of the *Daily Express* past 4 million six days a week.

In one of his most celebrated statements Beaverbrook told the 1947/9 Royal Commission on the press that he ran his newspapers for propaganda, not profit. What is less often quoted was his realistic addendum: 'No paper is any good at all for propaganda unless it has a thoroughly good financial position.'

The propaganda might be for the Empire, against the Socialists as he always called the Labour Party, for rearmament and isolation from Europe in the 1930s, for Churchill, for high wages, against British entry into the European Common Market, for any cause Beaverbrook was championing at the time and against anything he took a dislike to. The Northcliffe legacy of the self-appointed newspaper proprietor thundering out his views to millions of readers every day was stridently carried on. What effect it had on readers is unknown. One study of the political influence of newspapers indicated that it was fairly small. In many cases Beaverbrook was preaching to the converted, to readers who were likely to agree with what he said because they shared his outlook and prejudices. But many other readers were probably indifferent to the propaganda and bought the *Express* for its entertainment value without taking much notice of its politics. Figures for the period round Beaverbrook's death in 1964 showed that of 49 per cent of *Daily Express* readers who read another newspaper, the vast majority picked one which was pro-Labour.

Beaverbrook kept control of his newspapers by splitting the shares into voting and non-voting stock and retaining the majority of voting stock for himself. He did not have to worry too much about keeping a large number of public shareholders happy because the ownership structure of his company ensured that the majority of stockholders were non-voting and therefore powerless. As for himself, he had made enough money in

Canada not to need any income from his newspapers. He took fringe benefits, claiming trade benefits on goods bought through the *Evening Standard* and insisting on having the pick of review copies of books (which were sent out to the library of the University of New Brunswick). But he did not need to amass more money. He had quite enough to finance even his extravagant way of life.

Instead, Beaverbrook preferred to plough profits back into the newspapers, running them with high costs to produce the technical excellence he sought, rather than cutting back expenditure to maximize profits. This high-spending policy served another purpose – by paying lavish wages to journalists and print workers, Beaverbrook set pay levels which weaker newspapers found difficult to match. They faced the dilemma of trying to pay the same as Beaverbrook, which they could not afford, or running an inferior operation because they could not attract the best people. Although Beaverbrook's high costs were to prove a millstone after his death, they were an essential part of his approach to business. He always advocated high wages as an ingredient in economic success.

In 1954 Beaverbrook transferred his voting shares in the newspapers to the Beaverbrook Foundation, the trustees of which were drawn mainly from his family. 'I no longer control,' he said. 'I still dominate.' A Canadian Beaverbrook Foundation, worth $14 million, was established some years later to save his fortune from death duties in Canada.

Beaverbrook was particularly touchy about the allocation of credit for the success of the *Daily Express*. It had been a problem in Baxter's final days. In the late 1930s there had been trouble for Christiansen when *Time* magazine named him as the man who had pushed the circulation up by a million. Twenty years later a passage in a book by former *Daily Herald* editor Francis Williams, *Dangerous Estate*, caused a new explosion. Williams gave Christiansen almost as much credit as his boss for the success of the *Daily Express*. Beaverbrook was abroad when the book appeared but Christiansen had plenty of enemies in the organization and the passage was quickly brought to the owner's attention. Christiansen's health had not been good after his heart attack at La Capponcina and the combination of his poor health and Beaverbrook's angry reaction to Williams's book signalled the end of the one of the longest and most successful of Fleet Street editorships.

Beaverbrook's attitude to journalism led to celebrated comparisons between his approach and that of his fellow Canadian Roy Thomson, who followed him to Britain half a century later to buy *The Times*, the *Sunday Times* and a string of provincial newspapers. At a lunch with Thomson, Beaverbrook listened politely for a time while his host spoke about what most interested him in newspapers, the commercial and financial side of the operation. Halfway through the meal, the story goes, Beaverbrook could take no more. 'Now, Roy, let's talk about the interesting part of newspapers,' he said, and embarked on a lengthy dissertation on the news.

Conservative politician Edward Heath has another story, which he told at a dinner party given for Lord Thomson's 78th birthday. Twenty years before, he said, he had visited Beaverbrook at Cap d'Ail. The *Sunday Express* arrived and Beaverbrook went through it. He read the front page, the leading article, the gossip column and the sports pages and, when he had finished, expressed his satisfaction, saying: 'Now that's a good paper.' Ten years later Heath was with Thomson also in the South of France, when the *Sunday Times* arrived. Thomson ruffled quickly through the pages from the back, counting as he did so. When he had finished, he expressed his satisfaction, saying: 'Fifty-three columns of advertising. Now *that*'s a good paper.'

As he aged Beaverbrook's eccentricities became more pronounced, but he never lost his sharp wit. A young student who had the temerity to criticize his imperial policies as outdated was told: 'You are a very impudent young man. You will undoubtedly make an excellent journalist.'

Harold Keeble, the editor of the *Sunday Express*, ran a story headlined 'Eva Peron dying'. Beaverbrook telephoned him the next day with congratulations. After Keeble had expressed his appreciation, Beaverbrook said: 'Mr Keeble, you could say we're all dying from the moment we're born. What kind of time scale did you have in mind?' Keeble thought and said: 'Six months.' 'Very interesting,' Beaverbrook replied. 'I'll be watching.' In subsequent conversations Beaverbrook invariably mentioned that he noticed Eva Peron was still alive. Luckily for Keeble, she died five months after the *Sunday Express* story.

Working for Beaverbrook could be hair-raising but it was never boring. He was always driving himself and those who worked for him on to new things. He manipulated people who depended on him for the good material life which his newspapers could offer, in order to get the best of them for himself. Despite his eccentricities and his politics, many of the journalists who worked for him were, like Michael Foot and Tom Driberg, on the left of the political spectrum. The high wages were certainly an important factor, but so was the feeling of working for a proprietor who was passionately interested in the news and fascinated by young talent.

In 1961, after 34 years as a widower, Beaverbrook married again. His wife, Marcia Anastasia, known as Christofor, was the widow of an old Canadian friend, the industrialist Sir James Dunn. Beaverbrook died, aged 85, in Christofor's arms on 9 June 1964.

The newspaper empire he bequeathed to his son looked remarkably prosperous. Where other newspapers had flourished for 10 or 20 years and then gone into decline, the *Daily Express* had been a commercial success for more than 40 years. Despite an unsettled series of editorships after Christiansen's departure the newspaper still outdistanced all rivals, with the exception of the *Daily Mirror*, and was selling well over 4 million copies a day. The *Sunday Express* had the vast middle ground of Sunday readership to itself by the 1960s and was selling almost 4·5 million copies per issue. The *Evening Standard*, with a circulation of 750,000, did not make or lose much money but its position as one of the most intelligent and entertaining newspapers in the country made it a valued part of the Beaverbrook empire. In Glasgow the group's fourth newspaper, the *Evening Citizen*, provided a lively stable companion for the *Scottish Daily Express*.

The political message Beaverbrook had tried to deliver may not have had much success, but through his newspapers he had played a major role in shaping the ways in which people in Britain were informed and entertained in the 20th century. Churchill once referred to him as a magician and Ernest Bevin replied that the magician's chief stock-in-trade was illusion. So long as Beaverbrook was alive the illusion could be maintained. When he died, his successors had to show whether they had inherited the spells as well as the top hat and wand.

TWO

The Court of 'Hot Dog'

───────

SHORTLY BEFORE HIS death Lord Beaverbrook had been
asked by an interviewer what gave him most cause for pride.
He had replied: 'Well, I'm proud of my son. He's a fine
fellow. He's a nicer man than I was. A much, much nicer
man.'

John William Maxwell Aitken, known for most of his life as
'Young Max', was 54 years old when he took over the
Beaverbrook empire. He had hero-worshipped his father, but
that in itself did not always guarantee a smooth relationship.
His powers, from an early age, were acknowledged to be
physical rather than intellectual. At Cambridge he had excelled
at sport, gaining a soccer blue twice, playing cricket for the
Quidnuncs and golf with a handicap of one. He did not take a
degree. As a young child Max Aitken had been closest to his
mother, but she had died when he was seventeen. His mother
and father had been on terms of strictly limited intimacy.
Beaverbrook wrote later: 'My wife had a more lively interest
in me than I had in her.' And: 'I had not married under any
very compelling desire for marriage.' Max Aitken's mother had
a garden house built in the grounds of Cherkley to give her a
place to live away from his father.

Max's brother and sister, Peter and Janet, showed no
inclination to go into the family business, so he became the heir
apparent to the Beaverbrook newspaper empire.

Although newspapers were his destiny they did not appear to
be his passion. In his early twenties he was shuttled between a
variety of administrative jobs in the Glasgow and Manchester
offices of Beaverbrook Newspapers before coming to London,
where he promptly had a row with his father – Beaverbrook
told him to go out and earn his own living. 'Young Max' went

off to Los Angeles, where he worked for Lockheed as a pilot on problems of sound damping. The breach with his father soon healed enough for him to come back to England as general manager of the *Sunday Express*, but the *rapprochement* was not complete. The new job was sufficiently undemanding to leave him ample time for his favourite hobbies, of which his father did not entirely approve. Robert Bruce Lockhart, who worked on the *Evening Standard*'s diary page, recorded the following incident in his personal diary, on 10 June 1937: 'When I was having my talk with Max [Beaverbrook] at Cherkley on Monday about leaving Fleet Street, we were walking on grass terrace. Aeroplane came over dipped did tricks. It was young Max. Beaverbrook said: "Damn that boy," but there were tears of pride and sorrow in his eyes.'

Michael Foot, then making his way as a tyro journalist, saw 'Young Max' as a pleasant young man but with no particular interest in newspapers – 'His real interests were flying, women, boats and having a good time.' But the war in Europe abruptly terminated the amiable frivolity of his existence.

Max Aitken had an extraordinary war. He had joined the County of London Squadron of the Auxiliary Air Force in 1935 and went straight into the RAF, where his Lockheed experience, to use his own words, 'undoubtedly kept me alive'. In all he flew 161 operational missions, amounting to 2000 flying hours of which 400 were at night. He was in the midst of the fighting at the fall of France and throughout the Battle of Britain.

In the following year Max Aitken led the 'Czech' night fighter squadron, made up of British and Czechoslovak pilots with British and Canadian air crews, flying first Bristol Blenheims and then Bristol Beaufighters. A citation in 1942 described him as 'a brilliant pilot and a gallant leader', and added: 'This officer has set a most inspiring example.' In 1943 he led a fighter group in the Middle East whose main job was to protect allied shipping in the Mediterranean. In 1944 he commanded an anti-shipping strike air wing, based in Scotland, which flew night missions to sink German ships in the North Sea, using mainly torpedoes. While visiting an air squadron in the Western Desert he borrowed one of their fighters to join in an action over Crete and shot down two German troop-carrier planes. In all he was credited with having shot down 16 German planes.

Aitken resolutely refused offers of promotion so that he could keep flying and ended the war as a group captain commanding the largest Mosquito wing in Britain. His decorations included the DFC (Distinguished Flying Cross), the DSO (Distinguished Service Order) and the Czech War Cross. Among his proudest possessions were his wartime log books showing that he was in the air on the day the war began and still in the air on the day it ended.

After such a war, peace could only be an anti-climax, though Group Captain Aitken threw himself energetically into the task of getting himself elected to Parliament. Standing as a National Government (Conservative) candidate he won Holborn by 925 votes in a straight fight with Labour. But life in the House of Commons did not prove congenial. Like his father, 'Young Max' was bored with the minutiae of its procedures: unlike his father, he had no opportunity, or taste, for the backstairs role of political fixer. He made a few speeches pressing for a stronger air force and attracted some attention by being one of 12 MPs to vote against the Marshall Aid agreement. His division record, on his own admission, was 'appalling'.

Max Aitken did not stand for re-election in 1950, citing pressure of work at Beaverbrook Newspapers. In the same year he was divorced by his second wife Jane Lindsay, by whom he had had two daughters. (His first marriage, to Cynthia Monteith, which had ended in divorce during the war, had been childless.) On New Year's Day 1951 he married Violet de Trafford, daughter of leading racehorse owner Sir Humphrey de Trafford. The wedding took place in the Presbyterian Church at Montego Bay, Jamaica. Max Aitken's only son, Maxwell, was born a year later.

In 1955 Max Aitken became chairman of the board of directors of Beaverbrook Newspapers Ltd. The appointment was a good deal less portentous than it sounded. His father remained head of the Beaverbrook Foundation, which controlled the majority of the voting stock, while a long-serving Beaverbrook executive, Tom Blackburn, became executive chairman of the company. The two men effectively held the

reins of executive authority, and very little business of consequence was transacted through the board. Blackburn was
averse to delegating authority and kept the management of the
business under his personal control. Apart from a passionate
interest in strip cartoons he did not concern himself with the
journalistic content of the newspapers. 'The Beaver' still saw
himself as the fount of editorial inspiration. 'Young Max', now
in his mid-forties, had been given a position but no real power
in the family business.

Edward Pickering (now Sir Edward), who succeeded
Christiansen as editor of the *Daily Express*, believes that
Beaverbrook at this stage 'treated his son very badly'. He was
ready for responsibility and apparently eager to shoulder it but
the old man blocked him at every turn. The son's appointments
were ruthlessly frozen out by the father. One near-certain way
not to climb the Beaverbrook ladder in the late 1950s was to be
known as 'a Max man'. During the Suez crisis of 1956, when
Lord Beaverbrook was in the Bahamas, 'Young Max' had
impressed senior executives by the steadiness of his response,
but when Beaverbrook returned he proceeded to undermine his
son's newly acquired authority. Pickering, who was ready for a
natural hand-over of power from one generation to the next,
remembers 'a sense of let-down, individually and collectively'.

From then on 'Young Max' spent more time with his power
boats at Cowes, on the Isle of Wight, while the organization
chugged along its well-grooved lines. There were, none the less,
indications that the generally fair conditions that had benefited
all popular newspapers were coming to an end. In the late
1940s and the 1950s Britain's national newspapers had generally
enjoyed a boom. By 1957 sales of national morning newspapers
had risen by two-thirds over the 1937 figure and those of
Sunday newspapers had doubled. For much of that period
paper was rationed and newspaper sales were helped by a news-
hungry readership. After the end of newsprint rationing newspapers competed for readers by increasing the number of pages
per issue. At the same time the growth of television in the 1950s
and early 1960s affected reading patterns. The habit of buying
more than one morning newspaper declined, a tendency encouraged by the growing size and completeness of each newspaper. While the three quality dailies – *The Times, Guardian* and

Telegraph – benefited from the spread of higher education and affluence, the sales of the popular dailies begun to drop.

Most popular newspaper groups were as a result actively looking for new areas of expansion. Beaverbrook was an exception. Managerial initiative in this direction was frowned upon. 'Young Max' favoured an early entry into commercial television, which later, in the words of Lord Thomson, resembled 'a licence to print money', but Lord Beaverbrook opposed the move. 'Inaction', Pickering recalled, 'became identified with loyalty to Beaverbrook. Decline and Fall was sanctified. Prudence was all.'

In the later years of Lord Beaverbrook's life, when the main management philosophy was to freewheel, the *Evening Standard* needed new printing equipment. It had always been printed in a building a few hundred yards away from the two *Expresses*, on a different kind of press. New presses were ordered for the *Standard* building with no thought that the printing of all three newspapers might be combined in one building on compatible machinery. As a result, Beaverbrook Newspapers possessed two sets of expensive printing machinery within a few hundred yards of each other, neither of which could take over printing from the other in an emergency or to save costs.

Sir Max succeeded to his father's title and the chairmanship of the Beaverbrook Foundation on a high tide of goodwill. His immediate decision to renounce the barony – 'in my lifetime, there will be only one Lord Beaverbrook' – was seen both as a commendable obeisance to his father and as an assertion of his own independence. He had few enemies within the organization and, as an eminently clubbable man, many friends outside. In an interview with the *Sunday Times* a month after taking over Sir Max pledged himself to continue his father's policies – especially those of 'Empire'. 'We'd go haywire without them if we didn't. All our thinking is based on them.' He did not envisage any immediate editorial changes. He hoped that his own son, then aged 12 and at Cheam prep school, would come into the business some day. Sir Max saw his own inheritance as a fulfilling commitment. Other forms of business did not interest him. 'I wouldn't know how to make biscuits,' he said. 'But I do know about newspapers.'

In March 1966 Sir Max registered a signal achievement –

he drove his power boat, *Merry-Go-Round*, to a new world diesel water speed record of 60·21 mph on Southampton Water.

Soon after this the Economist Intelligence Unit (EIU) produced a study of the national newspaper industry which contained some harsh insights into Fleet Street in general and Beaverbrook Newspapers in particular. The report showed that half the national newspapers had a declining profit trend. Of 17 publications covered by the survey, only seven had increased revenue faster than costs between 1957 and 1965, though there were still good profits to be made by the successful. Four national dailies had made a total profit of £9·4 million, while the four others had lost £3·5 million, leaving an overall profit of £5·9 million. The total profit figure for the Sunday papers was £2·5 million. The report clearly detailed the way in which cost increases had particularly affected the five popular morning newspapers – the *Mirror*, the *Express*, the *Sun*, the *Mail* and the *Sketch* – and the two London evening papers – the *Evening Standard* and the *Evening News*. For this group costs had gone up by 72 per cent between 1957 and 1965 while profits had risen by well under half as much.

Among the issues highlighted by the report was the overmanning of the production departments in the national newspapers. Too many workers in Fleet Street were, by national standards, being paid too much for doing too little.

The intensely competitive nature of the national newspaper business had made it a profitable stalking ground for workers who knew that managements would prefer to give way rather than lose an edition. Complex sectionalized working arrangements meant that one small group of workers could bring the whole production of a newspaper to a halt. Lack of proper pension or welfare funds gave the unions a particular set of responsibilities, as did the high number of casual workers in some production branches. The managements of Fleet Street increased the standing of the unions and their chapels (workplace branches) still further by effectively delegating responsibility for hiring staff to them.

Within this framework it was not surprising that union chapels abrogated more and more power to themselves and that a myriad of practices known as 'old Spanish customs' grew up which had few, if any, equivalents elsewhere in British industry.

Double working, whereby a man on one newspaper would also sign on at another on a casual basis, was common, helped by the generous amounts of rest time built into working arrangements. An incidental problem was that the man might sign on for casual work under a false name, and then forget the pseudonym he had used when the time came to collect his money. There was no such danger with the money, appropriately known as 'fat', paid to compositors for work they had not done on advertisements set up outside the newspaper by advertising agencies. This material had originally been handled by the compositors. When the advertising agencies began to take over the work themselves, the compositors, paid at piece-work rates, saw that their income would fall and got an agreement from managements that they should be paid as if they had done the outside work. Such practices helped to produce a situation in which, the Economist Intelligence Unit reported, 'the general level of pay in the newspaper industry is out of proportion to the effort expended and the skill employed compared with most other industries'. The potential annual savings of £4,875,000 which, the report estimated, could be made by proper working arrangements was, it added, a cautious figure. Beaverbrook Newspapers could, it was estimated, save over £1 million by better and more efficient working methods. (The breakdown was: the *Daily Express*, £671,550; the *Sunday Express*, £210,250; the *Evening Standard*, £264,470.) One important factor preventing such savings was the ownership and management structure in the industry. In the report's view:

> When all allowances have been made for variations within the industry, its most striking feature, and possibly its greatest problem, is its dominance by a small number of highly individualistic proprietors with their own personal interests and philosophy of management . . . the attitude of some proprietors towards profits is not the same as that of the professional manager in industry. The professional manager looks upon profits as a yardstick of efficiency and success, but some newspaper proprietors often subordinate profitability to other considerations. . . . No one would suggest that profits should be the only criterion, but an inefficient industry is usually an unhealthy industry.

The report discreetly avoided naming names in its general criticism but the tradition established by Lord Beaverbrook, and so far left unchanged by his son, could not have been far from the researchers' minds. In a section devoted to Beaverbrook Newspapers the report commented: 'There is a much greater concentration of editorial and non-executive representation on the board than would normally be considered ideal.' Recalling the use of the newspapers to propagate Beaverbrook's ideas rather than to maximize profits, it said: 'There may therefore have been a tendency to neglect the foundations of efficient and continuing management.' Concentration of power at the top was possibly a reason why 'the general standard of middle to senior management with a few notable exceptions was not high'. This was reflected in the fact that 'communication within the company seemed to be poor, and at times senior management even up to General Manager level did not always appear to be clear on the policy adopted by the Company'. There was no formal system of budgets or profit planning, which made it 'difficult to see how costs could be controlled at all levels'.

At that time Beaverbrook Newspapers' costs were the highest in Fleet Street. Its profit/turnover ratio, at around 4 per cent, compared unfavourably with other newspaper groups such as Associated Newspapers (controlling the *Daily Mail* and the *Evening News*), the Thomson Group (*The Times* and the *Sunday Times*) and the International Publishing Corporation (the *Daily Mirror* and the *Sunday Mirror*), all of which were in the 9 to 11 per cent range.

In 1968, when Tom Blackburn finally retired as executive chairman, Sir Max moved to obviate some of the more severe problems highlighted in the EIU report. He himself took over the job of chairman of the company, abolishing his old post of chairman of the board. John Coote, a gregarious former Royal Navy captain and a favourite sailing companion of the proprietor, became joint managing director of the group with Sir Max. Coote had come into the company eight years earlier as 'a Max man' and had somehow managed to escape the full glare of Beaverbrook's hostility. Though new to Fleet Street he had earned respect in a succession of jobs, first as manager of the *Sunday Express*, then as Tom Blackburn's deputy and finally as general manager of the *Evening Standard*.

The board was strengthened by the recruitment of two young directors from outside the group, Brian Nicholson and Evelyn de Rothschild. Nicholson, then aged 38, had been first a journalist and later a brilliant advertising director of the *Sunday Times*. Rothschild, 37, had survived an erratic youth in which he failed to get a degree in Economics at Cambridge to become one of the most energetic partners in the historic merchant bank of N. M. Rothschild & Sons. On Rothschild's recommendation Sir Max also appointed a full-time finance director to the board: in February 1969 Michael Franks was recruited from Shell and promptly began to introduce financial planning at each level of the business. John Coote established a three-man study team, called the Forward Planning Group, to investigate the efficiency of the production (or 'factory'), side of the newspapers and to make recommendations.

The impression of a new liveliness at Beaverbrook Newspapers was further strengthened by the public activities of its chairman on the international scene. In the summer of 1968 Harold Wilson, the Labour prime minister, was casting round for a fresh initiative in his Rhodesian policy. It had been three years since the white settlers' regime, led by Ian Smith, had unilaterally declared its independence of Britain and the policy of economic sanctions against the illegal regime was not producing results. Wilson learned that one of the few Britishers trusted by the Rhodesian prime minister was Sir Max Aitken – they had met during the war in Alexandria when 'Young Max' was a group captain and Smith a pilot officer in the RAF.

Sir Max was summoned from Cowes by the Prime Minister and asked if he would undertake a mission to Rhodesia to pave the way for fresh talks. He agreed, provided he could take an experienced negotiator with him. Lord Goodman, the eminent London solicitor, became part of the team. In August, 1968, they left for Salisbury where Goodman's heart nearly failed in the rarefied air. Sir Max's presence probably saved Goodman's life. While they were waiting for the doctor, Goodman asked Sir Max to hold his hand. Their very close relationship dated from that time.

The mission itself was successful: Ian Smith greeted Sir Max warmly and agreed to meet Harold Wilson under certain conditions. Talks aboard HMS *Fearless*, off Gibraltar, in October 1968 were the result. Although the *Fearless* meeting proved abortive, Sir Max and Lord Goodman kept in communication with the Rhodesian premier and helped to develop other contacts between the two governments. In their messages they used code names: 'Old Mate' for Ian Smith; 'Friend' for Lord Goodman; 'Hot Dog' for Sir Max.

When Beaverbrook Newspapers turned its attention to its factory in 1969 it got a nasty shock. Of the 185 rotary printing presses used by the company in its three production centres – London, Glasgow and Manchester – 90 were more than 30 years old and 57 of those were over 40 years old.

Despite their age, the presses were being used well below their potential capacity because of a typical Fleet Street agreement between management and unions. Machines capable of running at 50,000 copies an hour were held back by the agreement to 38,000, to ensure that mechanical efficiency did not reduce working hours too greatly. But even this reduced figure of 38,000 was far above what was actually being achieved. For the *Daily Express* in London, the average printing press produced 17,200 copies an hour of a 16-page newspaper. Figures for the *Sunday Express* were even worse. At the *Evening Standard*, the sequence of short bursts of activity for each edition meant that the average printing press worked for only about two hours a day.

Because its work was a completely new development for Beaverbrook, the Forward Planning Group was careful about the way it presented its findings to Sir Max and John Coote. One of its members recalls that the report was watered down to make it palatable. It still presented the top management with inescapable facts about the neglect from which the business had suffered.

Highlighting the age of the machinery and the low level of productivity, the report warned that the *Evening Standard* might run into very serious problems within a few years as sales declined and competition increased from new local evening newspapers springing up on the edge of the London circulation area. But whatever the problems at the *Standard*, the urgent need was to cater first for the *Daily Express* and *Sunday Express*

– 'the breadwinners of the group' – to ensure that they could produce larger newspapers in the years ahead to maintain their competitive position. 'The matter could be very serious in the next few years,' it added.

To restore the situation, the Forward Planning Group presented a £17 million plan to:

- integrate the *Standard* into the *Express* building, possibly leading to the elimination of 206 jobs
- develop the *Standard* premises as lettable office space
- develop a site beside the black glass *Express* building in Fleet Street; this site, known as Racquet Court and already largely owned by Beaverbrook, would house the combined *Express/Standard* operation and also provide space to be let out
- replace old printing machinery with new equipment; the report estimated that 71 new printing units would be needed and that, after re-equipment, the newspapers could be printed with 157 presses instead of 185
- develop property in Glasgow and Manchester, where the northern and Scottish editions of the two *Expresses* were printed

The recommendations also offered a solution to the revenue problem. The Forward Planning Group estimated the cost of the new machinery at £5·5 million and the cost of property development at £11·2 million. It predicted reduced production costs with the new machinery and estimated that the property, when developed, would be worth just over £19 million, with an annual rent roll of £1·6 million. Overall, Beaverbrook Newspapers might be able to look forward to a level of profits which would enable it to feel confident about the future.

Meantime Coote set the company a new pre-tax profit target of £3·2 million a year, of which £640,000 was to go to shareholders and £320,000 into the bank, while the rest was earmarked for new equipment and building development. Reporting this ambitious proposal the trade journal, the *U.K. Press Gazette*, asked the basic question in a 1970 headline: 'Can Beaverbrook Newspapers survive?' Coote's answer was that there was a bright future ahead if the management acted resolutely. His resolution was relayed to staff in a pamphlet warning of falling profits and the need for manning cuts of up to 20 per cent in some departments.

The strength of the chairman's resolution was more problematic. On Sir Max's 60th birthday, in February 1970, Sam White, the veteran Paris correspondent of the *Evening Standard*, wrote a fulsome personal assessment of his proprietor, finding him 'an immensely likeable human being who craves affection'. White recalled a remark by Lew Grade, the showbiz entrepreneur: 'You fall for Sir Max like you fall for a girl.' The press proprietor's philosophy of life, according to White, approximated 'to the great Australian religion – pal-manship. Loyalty is the keynote of his character and friendships, like sacred vows, are for life.' On such a sentimental occasion, White did not dwell on the defects of these virtues, though these were becoming increasingly apparent.

The proprietor's easy-going nature rendered it difficult for him to make the hard decisions that were required. He had been commended for delegating authority in ways that his father would not have contemplated, but that did not alter the need for firm decision-making at the top. Whereas his father had often been disliked, sometimes hated, by his employees, they had never had any doubt about the tightness of his control. Sir Max spent more time in the office than his father had done for decades but this only accentuated the difference between the two proprietors.

Sir Max enjoyed excellent personal relations with his directors and senior executives but affability was no substitute for a sense of direction. By 1970 the need for decisive leadership was becoming apparent in three main areas – two financial and one journalistic. The fundamental problem was the company's narrow financial base. Apart from a modest 8 per cent stake in Lew Grade's Associated Television, at the end of the 1960s Beaverbrook Newspapers was still essentially a one-product firm. Many directors were aware of the need to acquire an alternative source of income to cushion the newspapers in the bad years but none was able to convince Sir Max that this was an urgent problem. The most common justification for this policy was his father's frequently quoted remark: 'If we divert our activities, we will undoubtedly damage our newspapers.' As an independently wealthy man it was a remark Beaverbrook could afford to make, but it had little relevance to the firm after his death and Sir Max Aitken depended on the company for his fortune in a way that his father never had.

The second financial problem was how to raise the money for the plant renewal programme and property development envisaged by the Forward Planning Group. Various proposals were made, among them a £5 million debenture at 10 per cent to be arranged by Evelyn de Rothschild's bank, but Sir Max turned them all down, saying: 'My father always said never mortgage the property.' When a director approached him to say that the company simply had not got the cash to finance its development, the chairmen replied amiably: 'You haven't been here long. We'll just have to sell more *Daily Expresses*.'

The *Daily Express* was the third problem, and perhaps the most serious. In 1966 Sir Max brought the unstable era of short-term editorships to a close by appointing Derek Marks, a leading political correspondent, as editor. But the new stability, symbolized by Marks's commanding physical bulk, did not hold the readers. Much as he was respected as a political journalist, Marks is not remembered by his colleagues at the *Daily Express* as a successful editor. He was a reporter rather than an editorial executive or technician. Talking to ministers was his forte, rather than planning a paper. In a newspaper that still lived in the Christiansen tradition of technique supreme, it was a serious disadvantage for an editor to have to call for help in designing a page on a major story. These technical shortcomings might have been of little importance if Marks had given the newspaper a new direction and lease of life, but he did not. Under him the *Daily Express* grew more stodgy, more political. This was not surprising in view of his professional background, but it was the opposite of what was needed at a time when other British popular newspapers were becoming more and more racy and visually exciting.

Marks could be relied upon to share his proprietor's concerns about the white Commonwealth and give vent to Sir Max's rare vendettas, such as the one against the Duke of Edinburgh, who had once incautiously called the *Daily Express* 'a bloody awful newspaper'. Unfortunately the Duke was not far off the mark. Its politics, still characterized or caricatured by the 'imperial crusader' on the front page, seemed increasingly out of touch with a country that had come to accept loss of empire as a fact of life. Marks also had two blind spots as a journalist – the interests of the young and the interests of women outside the home. In an era when both groups were increasing their economic stake and clamouring for attention, this was a serious handicap. There had been sweeping shifts in mass culture as Britain moved self-consciously through the 'swinging sixties'. However superficial many of these changes might turn out to be, a popular paper had to reflect and assess them if it was to succeed. The *Evening Standard* did it well; the *Daily Express* hardly tried. There was also evidence of hardening arteries in other directions.

From their earliest days, Beaverbrook's newspapers had stressed their appeal to youth. In the 1930s the youthfulness of the men who produced them had been a source of pride. An article produced at that time by one of Beaverbrook's writers, George Malcolm Thomson, went to extreme lengths to make the point:

> The revolution is in being. In Europe, the youth are giving Fascist salutes and hailing one Caesar or another. In Britain they are producing the *Express* and hailing themselves. These cubs are sharpening their claws on the world's news; taking on jobs which used only to be given to men full of years and timidity; sprawling all over the delicate mechanism of the commercial side of the paper and extracting brilliant results from it; pulling the beards of statesmen more than twice their age; questioning, exploring, innovating, achieving.

By the late 1960s the brilliant young cubs of the communications world were no longer looking to the *Daily Express* – the best of them were aiming at television and up-market publications like the *Sunday Times* and the *Observer*.

The *Express* editorial staff – still 30 per cent larger than that of any other popular newspaper – was overwhelmingly male and predominantly middle-aged. The arrogance that stemmed from a great past made its inheritors impatient with new methods that might guarantee the future. One story told in the corridors was that when a market researcher showed the editor a chart with a dramatic prediction of declining circulation he stalked out of the room, saying: 'I didn't come here to be insulted.' The circulation continued its dramatic decline.

It was a difficult time for the British popular press in general as it tried to come to grips with the challenge posed by television. The *Daily Express* shed more readers than most but all the popular papers suffered – between 1966 and 1971 their collective circulations fell by 12 per cent, from 13·5 million to 11·8 million. Marks alone cannot be blamed for the decline in the *Daily Express* in the late 1960s. Indeed it is difficult to blame him at all since he was so evidently not the right man for the job.

Sir Max's style of leadership inevitably maximized the potential for personality conflicts among his top advisers. The key conflict during the early 1970s was between John Coote, the joint managing director, and a tall, blond, handsome young man in a frantic hurry, Jocelyn Edward Greville Stevens. Stevens was once described by Russell Miller, a *Sunday Times* profile writer, as 'the archetypal hero of *True Romance* fiction: a fun-loving, good-looking, high-living, brilliant millionaire with everything money can buy and much that it can't'. John Coote came to think of him as a terrible pain.

According to Brian Nicholson, 'The greatest tragedy for Beaverbrook Newspapers was that Max put up his favourite against Coote. Without this, the history of the company would probably have been very different.' On the other hand, it would not necessarily have been more successful.

Born on St Valentine's Day 1932, Jocelyn Stevens was the grandson of the magazine and newspaper magnate Sir Edward Hulton and inherited £750,000 at the age of 13 days. He was educated at Eton and Cambridge. As a young man he attracted media attention as an escort of Princess Alexandra and a friend of Princess Margaret. His marriage in 1956 to Jane Sheffield, who later became one of Princess Margaret's ladies-in-waiting, was a major social event, graced by 12 bridesmaids and four pages. A few months later he bought himself an obscure magazine called *Queen* as a 25th birthday present at a cost of around £250,000. He appointed himself editor-in-chief, took on a few chums from Cambridge and sundry debs and turned it into one of the most talked-about magazines of the decade.

The basic Stevens formula was to mock the hands that turned his magazine's glossy pages. It was, he once said, directed at 'the fresh upper crust – crumbs held together by a lot of dough'. Titles, cars, debs, 'in' places were guyed in ways that subtly confirmed their glamour. In two years advertising revenue quadrupled, as much because of the bravura of its owner as anything. Circulation never rose above 60,000 but in the advertising world *Queen* was considered to have the cream of the up-market AB readership, young and high-spending.

The elevation of trivia made it a vehicle for all that Swinging London implied, but it also contained a fair amount of good serious journalism. Cases in point were a savage attack on Fleet Street gossip columns by Penelope Gilliat and a campaign for the reopening of the A6 murder case, for which Stevens considered James Hanratty had been wrongly executed. *Queen* sought out and obtained good writers and photographers as contributors.

The office atmosphere generated by Stevens was manic, verging on the hysterical. High-spirited operators were attracted by the possibility of lifting the telephone to callers and saying: 'This is the Queen speaking.' Visitors were often obliged to thread their way past debs crying on the stairs after a scene with the editor-in-chief. He once sacked a secretary over the office Tannoy system. One lady writer described working for Jocelyn as being 'like a wild love affair – tremendously exciting and stimulating, but always at the back of your mind was the feeling that it can't last for ever.'

There was a time when, having forced the resignation of a fashion editor, he helped her hurl the contents of her office into the street below. 'Until you've seen a four drawer filing cabinet hit the road after falling three floors, you haven't seen anything,' he said later. He had some legendary up-and-downers with Dennis Hackett, who worked as editor for a period. Some time after their acrimonious parting Hackett met his former employer at a fancy-dress ball in Claridge's, emerging from the hindquarters of a donkey costume. 'Hello, Jocelyn,' said Hackett, 'I've never seen you so well placed.'

Lord Beaverbrook was among those who watched Stevens rise with interest. He told a party of dinner guests: 'I hear that Jocelyn Stevens bites the carpet. Now that's no bad thing.' One evening after dinner at Cherkley, Beaverbrook offered Stevens a job. Stevens declined.

In the mid-1960s Stevens honed his maverick image by becoming one of the original backers of Radio Caroline, the first pirate radio station off Britain. By this stage he was attracting the attention of some very high-powered people in the business. Cecil King, the boss of the International Publishing Corporation, invited him to lunch, and said: 'Would you like a job here?' Stevens replied, 'Yes, yours.' Offered the job King had in mind, editorial director of IPC's 200 magazines, Stevens turned it down.

Sir Max Aitken found the Stevens brand of bumptiousness a good deal more beguiling. Stevens's first formal contact with Beaverbrook Newspapers was as a consultant on a retainer basis while he continued to run *Queen*. Sir Max was deeply impressed with the young man but advised him that further advancement would depend on his ability to calm down a little and stop wearing such bright shirts. In 1968 Stevens sold his magazine and assumed the livery of a Beaverbrook executive – dark blue suit, dark tie and pale-blue shirt – as the chairman's personal assistant. Stevens rapidly acquired a reputation as an administrative ideas man. One of his first tasks was to produce a study of production facilities which inspired the setting up of the Forward Planning Group. The FPG paid special tribute to the 'Stevens enquiry' in its introduction and described its effect as that of making 'people more able to accept new principles and new ideas'. On 1 January 1969, at the age of 36, he was appointed managing director of the *Evening Standard*. When Stevens asked for a brief, Sir Max's answer was 'Save it.'

Historians of Fleet Street detected a certain poetic justice in the appointment. The *Evening Standard* had once been part of the fiefdom of Stevens's grandfather, Sir Edward Hulton, before Lord Beaverbrook had separated him from the property in circumstances that were not wholly above reproach.

In 1923 Hulton was dying and was ready to sell his chain of newspapers, which included the Manchester *Daily Despatch*, the *Sporting Chronicle* and the *Daily Sketch* as well as the *Standard*. Negotiations with the Berry brothers (later Lords Camrose and Kemsley) were well advanced but were delayed when their lawyer fell ill. Lord Rothermere, the proprietor of the *Daily Mail*, was also interested, but Hulton would not sell to him.

Spotting an opportunity, Beaverbrook offered to buy the newspapers on Rothermere's behalf, taking the *Evening Standard* as his commission. Rothermere agreed. At that time Beaverbrook was considered to be Sir Edward's greatest friend and his Cherkley estate was close to Hulton's home at Downside, near Leatherhead. One afternoon Beaverbrook walked over to Downside, where the ailing Hulton was lying in a ground-floor bedroom, and ambled in through the French windows. The bedside negotiations ended with Hulton agreeing to sell for £5 million. Beaverbrook wrote out a cheque on a sheet of notepaper on which he had written 'Midland Bank Limited'.

When it learned of the transaction Hulton's family was horrified and tried to stop the deal going through, but it was too late. Lord Rothermere then proceeded to top up the operation with some elaborate stock manipulation and made a handsome profit by selling out most of the acquisition to the Berry brothers. The end result was that Sir Edward Hulton and his heirs received rather less than they would have got from the Berry brothers in the original deal, Lord Rothermere's companies made nearly £2 million and Beaverbrook got the *Standard* for nothing.

Jocelyn Stevens had been brought up to believe that Beaverbrook had in some way been responsible for depriving him of his birthright. It had been one of the main reasons why he felt he could not accept the offer of a job from Beaverbrook himself. In the early days of Granada Television's 'What the Papers Say' series Stevens had relished the opportunity of being able to appear and criticize Beaverbrook's *Daily Express*. An irreverent profile of Beaverbrook written by Stevens in *Queen* was headlined 'The Lord of the Lost Cause'.

Stevens's prickly relationship with 'The Beaver' was no impediment to a friendship with his heir which became unusually close. Sir Max derived a great deal of fun from having Stevens around. According to one old family friend, he seemed 'revitalized' in Jocelyn's company. A Beaverbrook director described them as having 'a father/son type relationship, though I don't know too many fathers who go to nightclubs with their sons.' At that time Sir Max's own son, Maxwell, was a schoolboy at Charterhouse.

Stevens was certainly a great socialite, though he did take

exception when the *Financial Times* alleged that he spent 300 nights of the year in nightclubs. He sued, but settled out of court for the amount of money he would have spent if it had been true.

The affection between Sir Max and his protégé was evidently mutual but of the two men Stevens had a far clearer view of his objectives. His ambition was so naked as to be almost engaging. John Coote complained to his chairman of being 'poor-mouthed' by Stevens even before he formally joined the company. Shortly after being appointed to the board of Beaverbrook Newspapers in June 1971 Stevens told a fellow-director: 'I'm out to get Coote and put myself in a position where Max needs me more than I need him.' *Private Eye* matched up the fierceness of his smile with the fierceness of his ambition and dubbed him Jocelyn 'Piranha Teeth' Stevens, the kind of character it loved to lampoon.

The saving grace of Stevens's ambition was that it was linked to a solid dedication to hard work. At the *Evening Standard* it produced results. During his spell as managing director the circulation decline slowed and advertising improved dramatically. After a long record of lean years, profitability improved to £1·2 million in 1971/2. Stevens also introduced a style of man management that echoed the days of his illustrious grandfather, who owned a string of racehorses as well as newspapers. Whenever trouble threatened in his newspaper business Sir Edward Hulton made a point of going round the plant dispensing tips for the 2.30 to key troublemakers, who were also invariably racing fanatics. According to legend, his selections always won and helped ensure a happy workforce. Stevens was not a racing man but he was a wonderful exponent of the cavalier style. Negotiations with him were high on drama and table-thumping, though they often ended up conforming to the old Fleet Street management adage: 'If the men put their hand out, put silver in it.'

He was, none the less, sometimes capable of persuading employees to do things which they had never contemplated before. One such incident was when Stevens arranged the advance printing of over 500,000 copies of the *Standard* announcing with colour pictures the successful landing of the first man on the moon the day *before* the event took place. When

Sir Max heard of this he warned Stevens that he had broken one of the cardinal rules of journalism and that if the moon landing went wrong he would have to dismiss him. The following day the *Standard* sold over a million copies.

Another stunt which also resulted in a million sale came after a strike in Fleet Street. An agreement was reached with the unions shortly after midnight. By means of an elaborately organized communications network the *Standard* workforce was summoned and started printing at 05.43 in the morning, producing the only newspaper on sale in London that day. Proprietors of other newspapers, infuriated by what they regarded as a breach of an understanding between them, summoned a hasty meeting of the Newspaper Publishers' Association Council. Sir Max Aitken was invited to explain how it had been done and how much the workers had been paid. Sir Max revealed that Stevens's reward to each man who had worked that night had been a necktie decorated with the image of an *Evening Standard* van and the numerals 0543.

In July 1972 Stevens went to Sir Max and told him that the *Standard* was on a secure financial footing and his inclination was to go back to magazines. Sir Max promptly promoted him to the board's five-man executive committee.

'Ambassador from Shoe Lane to the Court of St Max' was how Stevens gaily explained the appointment. 'It's a sign of how autonomous each group had become within Beaverbrook that the *Evening Standard* should need an ambassador.' He was now almost eyeball-to-eyeball with John Coote.

In November 1972 Stevens moved up another notch, leaving the *Standard* to take over as managing director of the *Daily Express*. The *Standard* unions gave him a memorable farewell dinner at the Café Royal during which he was presented with an antique blunderbuss, engraved with a list of the paper's achievements during his time as managing director. One union man, referring to his new job, said: 'If you hadn't been appointed, Guv, we would have elected you.' Huge quantities of alcohol and emotion flowed. Stevens thought it was perhaps the nicest thing that had ever happened to him: 'Everyone blubbed; it was agonizingly marvellous.'

For a time it seemed as if Coote might ride out the challenge of the younger man. While Stevens had been buried in the day-to-day affairs of the *Standard* Coote had strengthened his corporate position. In June 1971 he had been appointed vice-chairman of the group, while an industry-wide advertising boom had rouged the company's pale complexion. In July 1972 Beaverbrook declared a record pre-tax profit of £3,348,011, for which Coote naturally got the lion's share of the credit. The figures gave a spurious impression of vitality, masking the group's underlying problems.

At the *Daily Express* Derek Marks had finally given way as editor to Ian McColl, a Scot who had enjoyed a successful career in Glasgow as an editor in the barnstorming Beaverbrook mould. One of McColl's more engaging characteristics was to call for 'chips and six forks' when edition time was pressing; he would then share his favourite food with his co-workers, who might or might not find it so irresistible. It made for a matey office but the circulation continued to fall, reaching 3·3 million in 1972, a drop of a million copies in a decade.

Part of the blame for the paper's continued decline was apportioned internally to a voluntary redundancy scheme introduced by John Coote, which had inspired some of the more valued journalists to pick up their money and go to fresh jobs elsewhere. A more realistic reason was the success of the *Sun*, which was cutting a swathe through the down-market readership of the other popular newspapers under its new proprietor, Australian Rupert Murdoch.

Jocelyn Stevens breezed into the *Daily Express* job dispensing optimism. At a meeting with staff representatives in January 1973 he announced what he had in store. The meeting was scheduled to last one hour but went on for three as the new managing director warmed to the glow of future prospects. He reported board approval for £7 million to be made available for re-equipment which would make the *Daily Express* one of the most modern newspapers in the world. There would be more colour pages. He was aiming for a 64-page newspaper, compared to the 32 pages which had been the maximum envisaged up to then. Apart from a passing swipe at Coote's voluntary redundancy scheme, it was a general morale-building exercise. Stevens was generously applauded, though there were cynics present. The union leader who wrote up the account of

Stevens's remarks concluded his draft with an observation of his own: 'I felt the applause from the meeting for Mr Stevens was for having entertained rather than reassured us about the future. His frankness and enthusiasm are to be applauded and we can only hope that for all our sakes his judgement will be found to be accurate. Certainly more accurate than it was in anticipating the duration of the meeting. . . .'

The cynicism became more pronounced a few months later when Stevens launched his editorial 'new look' for the paper. The operation, known as 'DX 80', was designed to turn the *Daily Express* into a smart, modern and successful paper by the end of the decade. It was to change direction once again. Under Derek Marks it had aimed up-market, to compete with the *Daily Telegraph*, if it had aimed anywhere. McColl had taken it down again in an unsuccessful attempt to check the inroads from the *Sun*. Now DX 80 was to try to push the paper up-market again, aiming at a younger, more intelligent and more affluent readership. Some of the journalists who were to write and edit the paper were incredulous about the possibility of another switch in direction. At a presentation in a West End restaurant, they were shown a film of the kind of paper they were now meant to produce. Some of them pelted the screen with bread rolls and sugar lumps.

Commercially 1973 proved an exceptionally lean year for Beaverbrook Newspapers. Newsprint prices soared and the group began trading at a significant loss overall. Only the *Sunday Express*, under the experienced editorship of John Junor, was keeping the company alive though its predictable formula as a right-wing family newspaper seemed to be in gradual decline. One young journalist, who fancied himself as a writer, moved on from the *Sunday Express* after a frustrating two years. Junor took the parting of the ways philosophically: 'Your stuff', he told the young man, 'was either brilliant, or very poor, but what I need, laddie, is mediocrity – consistent mediocrity.'

In the summer of 1973 Lloyd's Bank called in Sir Max and John Coote to warn them that the company had reached the limit of its credit. In October the management produced a 10-page internal document entitled 'Daily Express – The Facts'. It showed up the seriousness of the position in a series of charts and graphs: The *Daily Express* had gone into a trading loss of £1 million in 1972/3 and the loss for 1973/4 was forecast at £4·8 million. Revenue was rising, but much more slowly than costs. The £1·9 million additional earnings forecast for 1973/4 were dwarfed by the anticipated increase in costs of £5·7 million. According to the pamphlet, the loss per issue of the *Daily Express* was sometimes as high as £18,000.

Connoisseurs of the Coote/Stevens power struggle were intrigued to see what the outcome would be. Should Coote, who had taken the credit for the preceding year's record profit figure, carry the can for the overall losses? Or should Stevens, who had direct responsibility for the *Daily Express*, the main loss-maker, bear the brunt of the blame?

The head that rolled was Coote's.

On 23 January 1974 the *Daily Express* ran a short story that began as follows:

> Mr. John Coote, vice-chairman, becomes deputy chairman and managing director of properties, newsprint and subsidiary companies.
>
> Mr. Jocelyn Stevens is appointed deputy chairman of Beaverbrook Newspapers and managing director responsible for the group's newspapers.

The story diplomatically put Coote's name first, but the fact that Sir Max had 'dropped the pilot' scarcely needed underlining. Coote had been stripped of real authority and 14 months later he quietly left Beaverbrook Newspapers.

Although Coote had many friends in the organization there was a general sense of relief that the central power struggle seemed to be over. Now that the main issue of personalities was resolved the long-promised regeneration of the company might occur.

THREE

Fleet Street's El Cordobes

ONE OF Jocelyn Stevens's favourite analogies is to compare labour relations in the newspaper industry with a bullfight, the unions being the bull. As managing director of Beaverbrook Newspapers his personal bullring became a spacious office on the third floor of the *Express* building. In the corner, overlooking Fleet Street, there was a large lectern on which the various editions of each newspaper could be displayed. His taste in furniture ran to modern chrome with black upholstery. From the bookshelves a bust of Sir Edward Hulton impassively contemplated his grandson's first move. It was suitably dramatic.

Stevens recalls that when he looked at the overall figures for the group in February 1974 he had a disagreeable surprise. He told Sir Max that disaster lay ahead. There was no hope of increasing revenue quickly in the proportions that were needed, while sales of the *Daily Express* were falling at an even faster rate than before.

A major reduction in costs clearly had to be made. From the nature of the business, nothing could be done about the most worrying expense of all. Newsprint had soared in price from £69 a tonne in 1970 to £154 a tonne. By 1974 the group's annual bill for its basic raw material was running at £21 million – a rise of £8·8 million over the previous year.

The rise was caused mainly by the jump in the cost of oil, a major element in the production and transport of paper, and by the weakness of sterling, which sent up the price in Britain of newsprint imported from Canada and Scandinavia. It followed a long period of stability in newsprint prices. Even after the huge jump in 1974, paper still represented a smaller proportion of total newspaper production costs than it had in 1960, but that did not make it any easier for a firm like Beaverbrook to handle the price rise.

On top of that, the government's Price Commission pegged newspaper prices and controlled advertising rates, thus hitting Beaverbrook's revenue at a time when it could least afford it. Sir Max talked to the government and warned that rising costs could force all his newspapers out of business.

Within 14 days of taking over Stevens submitted a confidential summary of the company position which reached an inevitable conclusion: in view of the shortage of cash and the losses that were piling up, Beaverbrook could not survive for more than another six months unless it closed its Scottish operation in Glasgow. Quick surgery was needed to save the whole group from ruin. A last effort to persuade their bankers to lend more money had failed. The scenario for the closure was worked out, in conditions of great secrecy, by a small management team in Jocelyn Stevens's office.

Glasgow had always occupied a very special position in Beaverbrook Newspapers, based partly on Lord Beaverbrook's Scottish ancestry and partly on the kind of newspapers it produced. Sir Max Aitken had begun his newspaper apprenticeship in Glasgow. Beaverbrook himself had christened the *Scottish Daily Express* 'a Big Idea' when it was launched in 1928. With a mixture of personal commitment and hyperbole, he called it 'the greatest landmark in the history of journalism as far as I am concerned', stressing its 'characteristics and doctrines, which are essentially Scottish – Independence, Self-reliance, Reverence and Patriotism'. For many years the Scottish *Daily Express* and *Sunday Express* were lively, popular publications. They sold more copies than any other newspaper in Scotland by concentrating on Scottish interests and providing coverage of big local stories which competitors could not hope to match. 'When a big story broke, the other Scottish papers might send along a couple of reporters and a photographer,' one former staff man recalled. 'The *Express* sent a dozen.'

The *Scottish Daily Express* thrived editorially on this traditional, high-spending journalism, though the costs meant that the Scottish operation never made money. Then in the late 1960s circulation started to fall. From 650,000 in 1969, sales were down to 550,000 in 1974. Jocelyn Stevens's DX 80 campaign to take the *Daily Express* up-market had not suited the Scottish market and a revival of the rival *Daily Record*, following a £6 million investment in new printing plant by its *Daily Mirror* owners, added to Beaverbrook's troubles. Still, the *Scottish Daily Express* was going into 44 per cent of Scottish homes in 1974 – a considerably better percentage than its sister paper achieved in England.

Glasgow also presented Beaverbrook with a growing problem as it had the distinction of being the only city in Britain outside London with two evening newspapers. This distinction was becoming an expensive one for Beaverbrook. The rival *Evening Times*, owned by the SUITS holding company, was outselling the *Evening Citizen* by 181,000 copies a day to 166,000. There were also problems on the advertising side: Glasgow did not produce enough revenue to support two evening newspapers, and one major source of advertising – the department stores – was largely in the hands of the big drapers, the House of Fraser, which was owned by SUITS.

One key reason for secrecy on the closure operation was the need to maintain a notional value for the title of the *Evening Citizen*. In February 1974 Sir Max and Stevens sold it to Sir Hugh Fraser at Harrods before any of the unions, or Sir Hugh, had a clue what was going on. Without the £2·75 million SUITS paid for the *Evening Citizen*, Beaverbrook would not have had enough cash to meet the redundancy bill.

On 19 March, Jocelyn Stevens flew to Scotland to take the Glasgow bull by the horns. The *Evening Citizen* was to close. Printing of the *Scottish Daily Express* and the *Scottish Sunday Express* would be moved to Beaverbrook's plant in Manchester. Of the 1,942 Beaverbrook employees in Glasgow, some 1,800 would be made redundant.

Stevens and, to a lesser extent, Sir Hugh Fraser had a bruising time. On his way to a meeting with Scottish union leaders Stevens was showered with soot by irate print workers. At a press conference, Sir Hugh was asked pointedly why he had paid so much for a newspaper which was about to close. Stevens manfully grabbed the microphone and took the heat – 'The reason he paid so much was because he didn't know it was going to close, because I didn't tell him.'

The closure was a bitter, sullen affair, culminating in a row over a statement inserted on the *Scottish Daily Express*'s front page by a workers' action committee calling on Beaverbrook to keep faith with its workers and to support a proposed new morning newspaper. The editor ordered the statement to be taken out; the action committee refused. There was a scuffle. The management halted production and Beaverbrook's final print run in Glasgow totalled 3000 copies.

The Glasgow saga was to continue in a different form until November 1975, as former Beaverbrook employees, with government financial aid, attempted to run a new newspaper on a co-operative basis. Their experiment with the *Scottish Daily News* failed for a number of reasons, some of which had little to do with the co-operative nature of the project. If it did nothing else, the *Scottish Daily News* provided at least one revealing spotlight on a major factor behind Beaverbrook's failure in Scotland and its problems in London. The *Scottish Daily Express* had employed 1459 people; the *Scottish Daily News* co-operative ran with 500.

In an interview with Russell Miller of the *Sunday Times* shortly after the Glasgow closure Stevens said:

> When I first came here there was a strong tendency to look back at the great days of Christiansen and bewail that what had happened wouldn't have happened in his time.
>
> I don't really care about history too much and so, not having those sentiments, I found it gave me no pain to cut great swathes through this organization. I hated shutting the Glasgow office and getting rid of 1800 people, but I was completely cold about it because I knew that otherwise we would not survive.
>
> If I have a reputation for being a cold-blooded sacker, it is justified in a way simply because I believe that people who are not fully employed or are past their best should go if the rest are going to survive. If one hesitates about making some move one just has to remind oneself of that: it is for the greater good. There is no room for charity today.
>
> You have to be strong to survive in Fleet Street. It's the open boat syndrome, isn't it? The fewer people in the boat the longer the water will last out. When it looked as if we would go over the side, that meant better shares for those left

. so they tried to push us. Everyone who had quite good reason to dislike or despise the Daily Express rubbed their hands; it was the most fascinating wave of hate and a lot of people got a lot of pleasure out of seeing an erstwhile hero with head bowed.

In fact the Glasgow closure . . . has provided the most immense savings. It has given us breathing space which will get us into the future.

'We would have needed three Glasgows to become viable,' Jocelyn Stevens said much later. Dramatic as it had been, the closure in Scotland provided no more than a respite for Beaverbrook as the firm moved towards declaring its first annual loss since Lord Beaverbrook built up his newspaper after the First World War. In late March 1974 new increases in the price of newsprint and government budget measures added some £1,750,000 to the company's annual costs. 'We are', Stevens complained, 'the flotsam on the rising tide of increasing prices.'

The strength of that tide was shown clearly in the accounts for the financial year ending in July 1974. Operating costs had risen from £49 million in 1969/70 to £75 million in 1973/4. Inflation had undermined the traditional recipes for newspaper success by adding an uncontrollable boost to already overblown costs. Beaverbrook's non-voting shares, which had stood at 125p the previous year, were down to 25p. Sir Max Aitken was not exaggerating when, in announcing a million pound loss for 1973/4, he said that it was the most traumatic time he had known in the newspaper business.

Insufficient though they might be in the longer term, the savings from the Glasgow closure helped to alleviate the trauma in the next year. As a result Sir Max was able to announce a pre-tax profit of £3·2 million for the 12 months ending in June 1975. It was still nowhere near enough to cover the bills for the new plant previously ordered on the recommendation of the Forward Planning Group. In late 1975 Beaverbrook extended its borrowings to £14 million. The group could not afford another lean year without the risk of going bust.

Cecil King, the boss of IPC, once wrote: 'No more difficult task exists in journalism than to conduct a newspaper wisely once it is in full decline. There is enormous pressure to try formula after formula and to give none of them a long enough test. Each experiment is abandoned as inevitably it fails to win instantaneous success. And in the general failure of the paper it is difficult to distinguish the good from the bad. Everything in the paper is suspect; so is every executive, every writer.'

Cecil King was writing about the old *Daily Herald*. Jocelyn Stevens was to find that the words applied even more forcefully to the *Daily Express*, where he instituted another round of editorial musical chairs.

Ian McColl went back to supervise what remained of Beaverbrook's interests in Scotland in 1974, to be succeeded by an unexpected choice, Alastair Burnet from *The Economist*. The economic and political weekly seemed light years removed from the *Daily Express* tradition. In fact the choice was not as eccentric as it may have seemed in view of Jocelyn Stevens's hankering to take the *Daily Express* up-market. Under Burnet, *The Economist* had evolved a skilful technique of handling complex stories for the intelligent layman. He was also a familiar figure on television and may have appeared the right man to carry through a late flowering of the DX 80 project.

Burnet's influence, while apparent from time to time, did not permeate the paper as a whole. Like other editors before him, he had to deal with an entrenched conservatism, a set pattern of news judgements dictated by 'the back bench' – a corps of senior sub-editors and lay-out men who could keep the paper much as they liked whoever was editor, particularly if the editor was not able to dominate them in technical terms. Whatever directives the editor of a daily newspaper issues, his power is very limited unless he can actually execute them himself. Burnet had another problem, reflected in a remark which a senior colleague of his remembers: 'Burnet said that on *The Economist* he had 22 journalists, all cleverer than him. At the *Daily Express*, with hundreds, he was the cleverest.' It was not a self-image that encouraged the highest forms of loyalty by the staff. The circulation ducked below 3 million.

Burnet left early in 1976 to be replaced by Roy Wright. The hope was that the new editor might turn out to be 'another Arthur Christiansen' – a shirt-sleeved production man whose single-minded ambition was to produce a lively, attractive newspaper. Wright certainly looked the part. Born in Lancashire, he had failed to get into grammar school and started work the day before his 15th birthday on a local newspaper in St Helens. After moving from the provinces to Fleet Street he became features editor of the *Daily Express*, then deputy editor of the *Standard*, and now he was moving into the top journalistic job Beaverbrook had to offer. His tough approach won him the nickname of 'Jaws' after the shark in a popular film of the time.

Wright declared himself an apostle of the radical Right and promised to go after women readers, young readers and the group he defined as 'the newly affluent upper working class who are rapidly taking on the concerns and aspirations of the middle class'.

Everybody agreed that Wright should be given time to prove himself, but time was becoming a premium commodity at Beaverbrook Newspapers. The febrile atmosphere at the top of the group was such that even the most minor incident could be inflated by being given a Doomsday-like significance. The day on which the annual *Evening Standard* drama awards were presented in February 1976 was a case in point.

The early editions of the *Standard* had not appeared that day because of a labour dispute. While Stevens and most of the other directors were at the presentation ceremony at the Savoy Hotel, Tony Dyer, the deputy managing director and expert on labour relations who had chaired the Forward Planning Group, stayed behind to talk with the personnel manager and the chapels involved. Just as Stevens returned from the lunch in mid-afternoon the strikers went back to work and the late editions of the *Standard* began to appear. As Dyer tells the story, Stevens stormed into his office and accused him of having given way to the union demands to get production resumed. Dyer said he had not given anything away. The personnel manager was called in. Stevens repeated his allegation. The personnel manager and Dyer again denied it. Dyer then swept everything off his desk and said he could put up with no more from Stevens and was resigning. The next day he went to see Sir Max Aitken and said either he or Stevens had to leave. Sir Max said he had overheard the previous day's scene and agreed that the situation was impossible. He spoke to Stevens. Dyer stayed.

That same morning the *Daily Telegraph* carried a report on the *Standard* stoppage in which Stevens was quoted as saying that he rated the paper's chances of survival as 100 to 1 against. He was also quoted as saying: 'The fact is that these people are destroying their jobs knowingly and intentionally. I don't give much for the survival of the *Evening Standard*. I think it is an absolutely dead duck.' One director remembers Sir Max saying after the 'dead duck' outburst: 'I'll never forgive Jocelyn for that.' But he apparently did.

The next annual accounts showed that the boost given by the Glasgow closure had not been sustained. Costs had shot up again, increasing slightly faster than revenue, and the profit was down to £434,000. On top of that Sir Max forecast a loss for the second half of 1976, caused mainly by a new spurt in newsprint prices. Such profit levels were far short of what Beaverbrook needed to finance its business. Most of the new printing plant recommended in 1969 by the Forward Planning Group had been bought and had to be paid for. Property development, while not as far-reaching as originally planned, had gone ahead in the Racquet Court site beside the *Express* building in Fleet Street. The new building was to be called Aitken House.

By this stage the financial direction of the company was in the hands of Peter Hetherington, an accountant with limited experience in newspapers. Hetherington had been brought in by Sir Max after the departure of the previous financial director, Michael Franks, who had pleaded in vain for a proper plan to finance the company's development. Hetherington's initial contact with Beaverbrook had been when he gave tax advice to one of the *Express*'s most famous stars, the cartoonist Carl Giles. Then, in the summer of 1973, Sir Max had asked him to provide financial expertise for the company on what was expected to be a half-a-day-a-week basis, but Hetherington, a partner in the leading accountancy firm of Rawlinson and Hunter, soon found that the job was considerably bigger than that. Before long, he was on the board as finance director.

Beaverbrook Newspapers had a number of small loss-making or marginal activities with which Franks, and Hetherington after him, wished to dispense. Among these was a travel company called Cunard Crusader World Travel, which had been formed by Beaverbrook and the Cunard shipping line, recently bought by Trafalgar House Investments. The idea had been that Cunard would supply the ships and Beaverbrook the promotion and they would share the profits. Unfortunately the tour business began to run into difficulties and Cunard Crusader World Travel became a leading candidate for liquidation. That operation was carried out very amicably between Hetherington and Trafalgar's managing director, Victor Matthews, and Beaverbrook bowed out of the travel business.

This was not Victor Matthews's first contact with Beaverbrook Newspapers. He had at one time worked for the construction firm of Trollope and Colls, which was later taken over by Trafalgar House and had been Beaverbrook's builders for decades. It was said that one Trollope and Colls employee had spent the whole of his working life in the *Express* building in Fleet Street. During the Second World War Lord Beaverbrook had pushed the claims of Trollope and Colls to build a special safe building for Churchill. With that background it was natural to turn to Matthews for advice on the planned property development in Fleet Street.

After Trollope and Colls had played its part in the building of Aitken House Victor Matthews let it be known that he would be interested in joining in the development of the *Evening Standard* premises in Shoe Lane, behind Fleet Street, following the planned integration of the *Express* and *Standard* operations. In 1976 Matthews's involvement with Beaverbrook began to go beyond that of the helpful builder. At a 'Saints and Sinners' charity lunch in June Jocelyn Stevens outlined to him the problems Beaverbrook was facing and Matthews said Stevens should contact him if there was anything he could do. Trafalgar's chairman, Nigel Broackes, had previously said something similar to Peter Hetherington.

That winter Stevens and Hetherington took Matthews up on his offer. With the authorization of Sir Max Aitken, they met Matthews at Trafalgar House's head office in Berkeley Street off Piccadilly, a few hundred yards from another once-failing institution, the Ritz Hotel, which Trafalgar had bought and was busy reviving. Stevens and Hetherington took the relevant annual accounts with them. The meeting might be the beginning of some form of negotiations and Matthews remained poker-faced as he examined the Beaverbrook figures. At the end of the meeting, Matthews told them to send him a proposal. They did not.

Had they done so a long story might have been rendered exceptionally short. There were two main reasons why there was no follow-up on the Matthews contact. One was a mis-judgement on Stevens's part – he did not think Matthews was *seriously* interested. The second was that he and Hetherington had already embarked, in conditions of maximum security, on the project of reaching an accommodation with the hereditary enemy, the Associated Newspapers group, headed by the *Daily Mail* and the *Evening News*.

The decision to re-open negotiations with Vere Harmsworth, chairman of Associated, was made after Sir Max Aitken's first stroke in November 1976. The original initiative had been a joint one involving Stevens and Lord Goodman, who had become a close personal friend of Sir Max as well as his legal adviser since their mission to Rhodesia. Both men were deeply concerned by the chairman's state of health and its effect on the company. Behind their conversations was the unspoken feeling that, even if he recovered, Sir Max would not be able to play his full role as executive chairman. Hetherington undertook the task of drawing up draft papers for a possible deal with Associated, going away for several days and working on them 'with a block of ice'. Sir Max had wanted to go on as before, but he was persuaded that they had to look at other alternatives in what Hetherington recalls as 'a fairly rough and hard meeting', with Stevens and himself at Sir Max's flat in Marsham Court.

On the face of it a deal linking the Aitken and Harmsworth families appeared as unlikely as a Montague and Capulet marriage. Publicly they had almost always been at loggerheads. Michael Davie later caught the essence of that rivalry in an article for the *Observer*: 'For longer than anyone still in the news-paper business can remember, the two dinosaurs, the Mail and the Express groups, have been slogging it out in the mud. Forests have been levelled, aeroplanes needlessly hired, expense accounts fudged and marriages smashed in pursuit of victory.'

The name of Harmsworth was in itself almost synonymous with the creation of the popular press. Before Beaverbrook arrived in Britain the press world had been revolutionized by

Vere Harmsworth's great-uncle Alfred, who became the first and only Viscount Northcliffe.

Alongside the heavy journals of record and opinion which had previously made up the British newspaper world, Alfred Harmsworth launched a new kind of paper based on entertainment and mass circulation. Like most successful newspaper innovators, Harmsworth's editorial success was based on his own interests and character. His initial breakthrough had been with magazines filled with items of miscellaneous information which he himself found fascinating. His first weekly, *Answers*, instructed its readers on such questions as 'What the Queen Eats', 'How to Cure Freckles', 'How Madmen Write' and 'Strange Things Found in Tunnels'. Serials and competitions, as well as the snippets of information, pulled in the readers and gave Alfred Harmsworth and his six brothers a publishing empire. The development of mass education in the last decades of the 19th century provided them with their market and before long the Harmsworths were ready to apply their editorial flair and commercial acumen to daily newspapers. In 1894, when their magazines were selling more than a million copies a week, they bought the London *Evening News* for £25,000.

The lessons learned at *Answers* were applied to the daily press. Newspapers were to be made attractive and reading them was to be a pleasure rather than a duty. Alfred Harmsworth reduced the length of stories, introduced new type, started a women's page, ran competitions and even reproduced some old faithfuls from *Answers* such as 'Burials Alive' and 'Secrets of the Dissecting Room'.

Successful as it was, the *Evening News* was a dress rehearsal for the Harmsworths' entry into the morning market with the launch of the *Daily Mail* in 1896. The new paper applied all the lessons the Harmsworths had learned on a new and larger scale. For its time the *Mail* was strikingly easy to read, bright and attractive. It appealed to women as well as men. It was heavily promoted. It contained a mass of information packed in short items. It boasted on its front page of being both 'A Penny Newspaper for One Halfpenny' and 'The Busy Man's Daily Journal'. 'Explain, simplify, clarify' was Harmsworth's instruction to his staff. A new breed of journalist, the sub-editor, was given authority to cut copy according to its news interest, rather than letting it be printed at the length chosen by the original writer. From the start the *Mail* was a success. Alfred Harmsworth had anticipated a sale of 100,000. By the end of the century the circulation had reached 750,000. As Alfred commented: 'We've struck a goldmine.'

The Harmsworths faltered briefly with their third newspaper, the *Daily Mirror*, which they started in 1903. Inspired by the success of the women's page of the *Daily Mail*, the *Daily Mirror* was aimed at a market of genteel ladies and staffed, according to its publicity, by 'cultivated, able and experienced women'. It was a flop and the *Mirror* lost £100,000 before it was turned into 'An Illustrated Paper for Men and Women'. In that form it prospered, gaining readers steadily and reaching 1,200,000 by 1914.

As well as setting the editorial and financial patterns for the British popular press, the Harmsworths also established a number of precedents for the future. Northcliffe developed his newspapers as organs for mass-campaigns dictated by their proprietor, in a way that anticipated Lord Beaverbrook. Some of his campaigns, notably the *Mail*'s patriotic drum-beating during the Boer War and Northcliffe's sustained anti-German drive before the First World War, set a new standard for the use of popular newspapers as a medium for political persuasion. The thunderings of the Northcliffe press, particularly over the alleged shortage of shells on the western front in 1915, helped to propel Lloyd George towards Downing Street and to topple Asquith's 'old gang'. But Northcliffe's vision of himself as a man of destiny who could run the country in tandem with Lloyd George remained a figment of his increasingly disordered mind.

Other campaigns, unpolitical but pursued no less energetically, tried to persuade everybody to eat wholemeal bread or to wear a newly designed 'Daily Mail Sandringham Hat'. Whatever their seriousness, the campaigns were dictated by Northcliffe. They gave the newspapers in which they appeared an added focus while creating an impression of importance and dynamism. But their central character, like the titbits in *Answers*, derived from one man, and it came to be accepted as a natural part of newspaper life that an individual proprietor should be able to pass on his judgements and prejudices to millions of people every day.

In tandem with his campaigning, Northcliffe established the model for the press baron as an eccentric despot running his newspapers on flair and intuition. Some of the quirks were amusing. He put a mock telephone on his desk and kept a bell push underneath which, when pressed, made a noise like the telephone ringing. To impress visitors, Northcliffe would press the bell push, grab the telephone receiver and pretend that he was being asked for advice by the Prime Minister. In his later years the eccentricities became more sinister and the despotism more pronounced. His fascination with Napoleon grew until it came close to wishful identification. Employees, from editors to clerks, were regularly humiliated. The *Mail's* literary editor was ordered to read out to the paper's editorial conference a message from Northcliffe accusing him of 'gross neglect and carelessness'. Another member of the staff was ordered to kneel in front of his employer, who then turned to a watching editor and said: 'There you are, I can make them do anything I like.'

He finally went off his head. Northcliffe attributed his poor health at the end of his life to having been fed poisoned ice cream by German agents in Brussels. Returning from a final visit to France, he tried to push a porter into the sea and drank 13 bottles of Perrier water on the train from Dover to London. He bombarded his staff with ludicrous messages. He ordered one journalist to stop walking down Fleet Street in a tall hat. Another was instructed to give his grey suit to a poor man. The staff of *The Times*, which Northcliffe had acquired to the horror of the British Establishment, suffered agonies. He ordered that the editor's telephone should be cut off. Fearing that Northcliffe might carry out his threat to sack everybody at *The Times*, the manager put a guard on his bedroom door. Inside, Northcliffe lay with an unloaded revolver under his pillow, placed there because it seemed to give him a sense of security. The precautions had been necessary – he attacked a male nurse with a poker. After the torment, he died peacefully on 14 August 1922.

Northcliffe had already sensed that leadership in the popular newspaper field was about to pass out of his family, despite the continued ascendancy of the *Daily Mail* over the *Daily Express*.

In one of his more lucid moments he had remarked that people who underrated Beaverbrook were fools: 'He is a younger man – far younger than I am. He is an ambitious man and a clever man.'

While Alfred supervised the editorial upheaval his younger brother, Harold, had dealt with the commercial side of the newspapers, particularly advertising. Harold Harmsworth, later the first Lord Rothermere, was a businessman whose appreciation of newspapers lay more in the balance sheet than in their editorial content. His commercial ability was an indispensable element in the success of the Northcliffe empire and the foundation of the British popular press.

Lord Rothermere, who inherited control of most of his brother's earthly kingdom, never caused Beaverbrook any great concern. Indeed while their newspapers were fighting the great circulation battle the two press lords often made common cause on commercial matters. The dubious method by which Lord Rothermere had acquired the Hulton empire, with Beaverbrook's assistance, had been an early case in point. In later years they were linked through a series of cross-shareholdings by which Rothermere's Daily Mail Trust held 49 per cent of London Express Newspapers while Beaverbrook held 80,000 shares in the Daily Mail Trust.

The co-operation seems to have been initiated by Rothermere and gratefully accepted by Beaverbrook as a means of gaining capital for his growing newspapers from the established empire centred round the *Daily Mail*. Rothermere's motives are not clear. There is no indication that he ever thought of gaining control of the *Daily Express*, except for one despairing bid after Beaverbrook had made it into a runaway success. More probably he thought that his holding was a good investment and would enable him to maintain a mutually beneficial association with the newcomer to Fleet Street. As it turned out, Rothermere made a serious misjudgement despite his reputation for financial acumen. The co-operation produced mutual advantages, enabling the two press lords to co-ordinate some of their commercial policies, but the real benefits soon began to run mainly one way – towards Beaverbrook.

The Harmsworths had been pioneers in floating shares in their newspaper company to the general public. Their organization was a publicly quoted company whose shares were bought and sold on the stock exchange as investments like any others. This meant that many investors bought them for their dividends or in the hope of capital growth without having any particular interest in the newspapers as such. To keep favour with the stock market, Rothermere followed a conventional policy of maximizing profits and paying out good dividends to his shareholders, among them Beaverbrook.

Beaverbrook, on the other hand, had a free-spending attitude to newspapers and a parsimonious one towards shareholders. The net result was that Rothermere got little in the way of income from his 49 per cent share of London Express Newspapers, while the generous dividends and soaring share price of the Daily Mail Trust helped to build up Beaverbrook's rival newspapers. Despite this, the Beaverbrook/Rothermere arrangement lasted until 1932/3, by which time the *Daily Express* had forged far ahead of the *Mail*.

Rothermere, like Beaverbrook, was eager for political power and influence but was less successful in its pursuit. At various times in the 1930s he supported Sir Oswald Mosley's Blackshirt Movement, was an admirer of Hitler and Mussolini and backed the reactionary regime in Hungary to the extent of toying with a proposal that he should become King of Hungary. He detested Tory prime minister Stanley Baldwin and for a while dived into the Empire Crusade with as much enthusiasm as Beaverbrook.

The front page of the *Daily Mail* was plastered with news of the campaign in its early days and the personal attacks on Baldwin by the Rothermere press helped to goad him into a celebrated counter-attack. In a by-election at St George's, Westminster, where the United Empire Party made its final stand, Baldwin rounded on the *Express* and *Mail* and their owners. They were not, he said, newspapers in the ordinary sense of the word but

... engines of propaganda for the constantly changing policies, desires, personal wishes, personal likes and personal dislikes of two men. What are their methods? Their methods are direct falsehood, misrepresentation, half-truths, the alteration of the speaker's meaning by putting sentences apart from the context, suppression, and editorial criticism of speeches which are not reported in the paper. . . . What the proprietorship of these papers is aiming at is power, but power without responsibility – the prerogative of the harlot throughout the ages.

At one stage the two newspaper dynasties apparently hoped for a marriage alliance. A friend of both families recalls a French Riviera holiday in the late 1930s when a succession of young Harmsworth ladies were almost paraded for inspection by the dashing 'Young Max' Aitken. The scheme never got much beyond a twinkle in their lordships' eyes. At that time 'Young Max's' attention was almost totally riveted on a young lady whose evening appearances were illuminated by a tiara of multi-coloured lights. Its secret was a small battery located behind her left ear. The electricity worked and the tiara lady, Miss Cynthia Monteith, eventually became the first Mrs Max Aitken.

Lord Rothermere's son and successor, Esmond, was no match for Lord Beaverbrook in the national newspaper field, though he kept a firm grip on the business. Through the controlling family shareholding in the Daily Mail and General Trust, which in turn controlled Associated Newspapers, the newspapers were, as they had always been, the personal fief of the senior member of the Harmsworth family. Board meetings under Esmond Rothermere were generally a forum for directors to agree to what he wanted. On occasion, the other directors would not even see the agenda until they arrived in the boardroom.

The *Sunday Dispatch*, one of the main rivals of Beaverbrook's *Sunday Express*, enjoyed some success for a while by purveying a regular series of mildly salacious fiction to titillate its readers. This useful formula collapsed after Randolph Churchill, Sir Winston's son and a close friend of Beaverbrook's, launched a public attack on its proprietor. The main offending text was *Forever Amber*. According to Randolph Churchill, Rothermere desired 'not only what his father was accused of by the late Lord Baldwin – "power without responsibility, the prerogative of the harlot throughout the ages" – but the cash that comes from the sale of pornography without the shame attaching to this squalid form of life'. Rothermere, aghast at his new nickname of 'Pornographer Royal', promptly cleaned up the paper. The circulation fell away and in 1961, when the *Sunday Dispatch* was losing £600,000 a year, he folded it, selling the title to the *Sunday Express*, which now had the vast middle readership market to itself.

As usual there was no reticence in the Beaverbrook camp about what the closure of the *Dispatch* meant and a front-page statement in the *Sunday Express* trumpeted:

> Consider the strange position now existing in the field of Sunday journalism.
>
> At one extreme are the ponderous, pompous small-circulation 'heavy' papers.
>
> At the other end are those papers which have built up large sales by sensationalism and salaciousness. IN THE IMMENSE CHASM BETWEEN STANDS THE SUNDAY EXPRESS – AND ONLY THE SUNDAY EXPRESS.

As a daily newspaperman Rothermere's touch was equally infirm. The tabloid *Daily Sketch*, acquired from Kemsley Newspapers in 1953, failed to establish any consistent identity and was a constant drain on the company's resources. The *Daily Mail* managed to pick up readers – reaching 2·6 million – after its take-over of the *News Chronicle* in 1961 but failed to hang on to them. The shifts in direction and changes of editorship at the *Mail* became a Fleet Street joke. Some of the editors, such as William Hardcastle and Michael Randall, were exceptionally able but none was given long enough to establish real authority.

One story reflects the way Fleet Street saw the position of the *Mail* editor under the second Lord Rothermere. It was said that an editor was sent on a three-month round-the-world cruise by his proprietor. Realizing that his replacement would be found in his absence, the editor had a relaxed and pleasant time. However, as his ship was approaching its berth at Southampton he could not help being touched by the sight of Lord Rothermere apparently waiting to receive him on the quayside. The editor waved from the ship's rail and heard the proprietor's voice wafting up to him through cupped hands: 'Go round again.'

As a press lord, Esmond Rothermere could indulge his interest in Wild West cartoon strips, which he saw in proof form before they appeared in his newspapers. He also maintained contact with the *Daily Mail* through a regular late-afternoon telephone call. At a few minutes before 5 pm it became a routine for the *Mail* editor to switch on the red 'no entry' light outside his door as he prepared for Rothermere's call. Like all routines, the call sometimes went wrong. On one occasion the editor was away and the switchboard put Rothermere through to the *Mail* news desk. The journalist who picked up the call had been doing the weather report and forecast. When Rothermere asked what was going on, the journalist told him about the meteorological conditions. Rothermere seemed quite happy to talk about that rather than politics or the next day's leading article and the conversation moved gently round the country as the journalist and his employer discussed the weather prospects region by region.

Rothermere did, however, strengthen the base of his business in a way that some Beaverbrook managers found enviable. His major contribution to the Harmsworth empire was the construction of a chain of provincial newspapers stretching through Hull, Grimsby, Derby, Stoke, Gloucester, Cheltenham and Swansea. These newspapers were to become one of the financial backbones of Associated Newspapers, though they were light years away from the hectic glamour of Fleet Street. He also diversified the group outside newspapers, buying into Canadian pulp, London taxis and eventually North Sea oil. His other main contribution to the future of the group was to hand over authority to his son, Vere, early enough for him to enjoy its exercise.

Vere Harmsworth's apprenticeship, like Sir Max Aitken's, had combined privilege with a series of mundane positions in the various departments of his father's business. He started work for the family firm at a logging camp in Canada. In 1957 he married Beverly Brooks, a young actress who had appeared in a film of the Douglas Bader story, *Reach for the Sky*, and been featured as one of the top ten beauties of the year in an *Evening Standard* series. His father settled a £2 million trust fund on him in the same year.

In 1963, aged 38, he became vice-chairman of Associated Newspapers. A large, amiable man, it was some time before he made any kind of mark, though this was more a consequence of his father's autocratic style than a deficiency on his part. Even so, he acquired the unfortunate nickname 'Mere', which stuck longer than seemed just. In 1971 his father abruptly resigned, handing over the chairmanship to his son. Vere Harmsworth was just 45 and eager to prove himself.

The hand-over of authority of Associated almost exactly coincided with the culmination of a series of highly secret talks between the *Mail* and *Express* groups. Their origin was a series of lunch engagements between M. J. 'Duke' Hussey, the managing director of Associated, and John Coote, then Beaverbrook's managing director. The two men had a tradition of regular business and pleasure lunches dating back to the mid-1960s, when Hussey managed the *Evening News* and Coote the *Evening Standard*. The custom was that the one whose paper was doing less well would add to his costs by paying for the lunch. As they rose through their respective organizations their plans for the future grew more ambitious.

By 1970 Hussey had two struggling dailies on his hands and a London evening which, though still profitable, was in decline. From a peak sale of 1·5 million the *Evening News* had slipped below 1 million copies a day. Coote, as we have seen, was confronted with the awesome task of finding finance for the proposals of his Forward Planning Group, and ensuring that the new machinery was used at an efficient level. The FPG had in fact already envisaged some form of co-operation with Associated by suggesting that the *Standard* and the *News* stop competing on Saturdays and produce a joint evening instead. The idea arose to prevent any clash between the *Standard* and *Sunday Express* schedules when their production facilities were integrated. Coote and Hussey thought they could go much further and create Britain's most profitable press group ever.

The economics were relatively simple. In place of a loss-making *Daily Mail* and a faltering *Daily Express*, Beaverbrook and Associated would run a joint national morning newspaper which would have the whole of the market to itself between the tabloid, down-market *Mirror* and *Sun* and the up-market quality dailies. A simple addition of the *Express* and *Mail* circulations would have produced a figure of 5·5 million daily sales. Clearly such a figure would not be achieved, because some readers took both the *Express* and the *Mail*, but there seemed good reason to hope for a daily circulation of 4·5 million. With the *Mirror* threatened by the reinvigorated *Sun*, a merged

Express/Mail might become the country's biggest-selling news-paper. Equally important, it would be a magnet for advertisers, offering unmatched access to millions of affluent consumers. With the new plant planned by Beaverbrook its size would go up to 32 or even 40 pages, providing even more scope for advertising.

In the London evening newspaper field a similar agreement would turn a declining competitive market into a profitable monopoly. There would be problems with trade unions in cutting the very expensive distribution costs, but a monopoly evening paper with resolute management would have a good chance of bringing about a reduction that two competing newspapers could never hope to achieve. All in all, John Coote believed that a single evening paper could rack up profits of £7 million a year. Apart from the profits, the proposed merger had two other big attractions for Beaverbrook. One was that the Coote/Hussey plan excluded the profitable *Sunday Express*. The other was that the merged papers could be printed on the new plant recommended by the Forward Planning Group, thus ensuring that the expensive machinery operated at full capacity and that the investment would be quickly recouped. For Associated the profitability of the deal was increased by the prospect of developing the vacated premises after production had moved into Beaverbrook's new plant. With a property boom in full spate, the attractions of developing Associated's sprawling properties between Fleet Street and the River Thames were considerable.

Like all good secret negotiations, the talks had their code-words. 'Quags', after Quaglino's restaurant, stood for a deal covering only the evening newspapers. 'Cavendish', after a hotel of the same name, denoted a morning and evening paper agree-ment. Detailed studies of the options were made by working parties within the two groups – Michael Mander headed the one at Associated, Tony Dyer headed that at Beaverbrook. Coote and Hussey favoured the full Cavendish deal and so, it appeared for a while, did their masters. One evening in January 1971 the leading figures from Beaverbrook and Associated gathered in Warwick House, Rothermere's London home beside St James's Palace. The site of the meeting carried with it a memory of Lord Beaverbrook – he had lived for years in the adjoining mansion, Stornoway House. Rothermere, a tall, elegant old man, presided. His son sat behind him. On the Beaverbrook side Sir Max Aitken and Coote were accompanied by Lord Goodman.

Under the Coote/Hussey deal Beaverbrook and Associated would have remained independent companies but the titles of the *Mail*, *News*, *Daily Express* and *Standard* and their goodwill would have passed to a new joint operating company. Beaverbrook would have kept the *Sunday Express* and the *Glasgow Evening Citizen*. Chairmanship of the joint operating company would have alternated between the chairmen of the two groups.

The Warwick House meeting went well, except for the lighting. In the middle of the discussion there was a sudden power cut. The participants sat in darkness until a footman brought in candelabra and Esmond Rothermere gave his verbal agreement by candlelight. He was going on a safari for six to eight weeks, he said. The detailed papers should be ready for signature when he returned.

Next day, before leaving for Africa, Rothermere called a board meeting of Associated Newspapers. His message to the directors was short and simple – he was going to retire as chairman of the company. One of the directors present recalls Rothermere's words as having been: 'I'm going to resign as chairman of the company. Some will no doubt say I should have done so before. Others will no doubt say I have done so too soon.' As he spoke, he looked at his son and successor.

The Beaverbrook/Associated deal foundered before it ever became public – in the end neither Sir Max nor Vere Harmsworth could bring himself to sign.

Within Beaverbrook Newspapers the arch critic of the proposed deal was Jocelyn Stevens. He knew nothing of the negotiations and had reacted violently when he heard of them. In his own words: 'I threw myself at Sir Max and implored him not to go through with it.' Sir Max was won over to the go-it-alone philosophy, against the advice of his managing director. It was Stevens's first, and perhaps most significant, victory over Coote.

Within Associated the reason for backing off appears to have been a deliberate, though unspoken, declaration of independence by Vere Harmsworth. After spending so many years learning the business he liked the idea of untrammelled proprietorship and thought he could make a success of it without any co-operation with the *Express* and *Standard*. Beyond that, he was said to relish the idea of head-on competition with Beaverbrook. According to one rumour he had marked a target date in his diary for the closure of the *Daily Express*. The brief prospect of co-operation had given way to an intensification of the hereditary battle.

Six weeks after he had become chairman of Associated Newspapers Vere Harmsworth took the step his father had long avoided and closed the *Daily Sketch*. He also announced that the *Daily Mail* would be remodelled as a tabloid newspaper. To some people it appeared that, far from dying, the *Sketch* was in fact taking over the *Mail*.

The new *Mail* editor was to be David English, one of the brightest stars on the *Daily Express* before Rothermere and Hussey recruited him to edit the *Sketch*. A profile printed in the *Mail* on 10 March 1971, under the headline 'Here's our new man at the top', lauded English for his experience as a foreign correspondent, his editorship of the *Sketch* and his 'young, middle-class family', which was said to reflect the typical *Daily Mail* reader. With English from the *Sketch* came his number two, Louis Kirby. Department heads, reporters and columnists moved over with their editorial bosses. The *Mail* switched from its traditional broadsheet size to the tabloid form of the *Sketch*. It was a bitter time for many old hands on the newspaper which was supposed to be the heart of the Harmsworth empire. Bernard Levin, once a distinguished columnist on the *Daily Mail*, wrote a vitriolic analysis of the event in *The Times* which earned the newspaper a writ for libel. (Levin and *The Times* apologized and acknowledged that their charges against Harmsworth were unjustified.) A *Mail* foreign correspondent, told his services would not be required on the new paper, went out into his garden to a tree that had been given to him by the Harmsworths and solemnly peed on its roots.

Harmsworth, to what later emerged as his credit, resolutely stuck to the team he had selected. It was not an easy game to play at first. The *Mail's* circulation continued to decline in its first years as a tabloid, though the fall was measured in tens of thousands and never came close to the steep slide in *Daily Express* sales which was taking place at the same time. By the end of 1976 the trend at the *Mail* was positive, with circulation above 1·8 million for the first time since the 1971 change. Under English the *Mail* had emerged as a newspaper with a strong character of its own, up-beat, punchy, slick, militantly conservative and appealing strongly to women. It catered for the resentments of the economically pressed middle classes and the aspirations of the ambitious young who had once been the target readership of the *Daily Express*. Whatever cavils there might be about the *Mail's* political treatment of news there was little doubt that David English, with the strong backing of his proprietor, had achieved an effective formula for a mid-market paper.

Vere Harmsworth also accentuated the policy of building up the company's interests outside Fleet Street begun by his father and grandfather. First it had been provincial newspapers and newsprint, then commercial television. By 1976 Associated Newspapers owned some 50 subsidiary companies outside the newspaper business, ranging from North Sea oil to pizza restaurants, from taxicabs to mirror manufacturers. Responsibility for building up this side of the business was primarily in the hands of Harmsworth's managing director, Ronald 'Mick' Shields, who had earlier pioneered the commercial application of opinion polls. Associated's provincial chain, run mainly by its subsidiary, Northcliffe Newspapers Group, contained over 20 local newspapers, representing about 9 per cent of provincial morning sales and 16 per cent of evening sales. Associated could be reckoned to be the biggest publisher of evening newspapers in the country, with a specially strong position in the Hull, Grimsby and Lincolnshire area. With the growth of monopoly circulation areas the provincial press had become increasingly profitable.

There are commentators who believe that a newspaper should be allowed to die if it cannot pay its way on its own. The press, according to this line of argument, should not go looking for handouts from oil companies or non-newspaper interests. On the other hand senior managers in Fleet Street will point to the cyclical nature of the national newspaper business, with sudden swings in advertising revenue and sharp rises in newsprint costs, and draw the conclusion that big newspapers need some form of outside backing as insurance for the bad years. The insurance which Associated had built up was shown clearly in its balance sheet. While the newspapers made £3·8 million profits from a turnover of £83 million in 1975/6, the non-press subsidiaries made £2 million profits from a £20 million turnover. In contrast, Beaverbrook Newspapers at that time still derived over 99 per cent of its revenue from newspapers.

Harmsworth had made a better fist of his newspaper inheritance than Sir Max Aitken, but there was one notorious black spot on his record. The *Evening News*, whose profits had once masked the losses of the group's dailies, was losing money at an unnerving rate. By 1976 its circulation was down to 564,000 and it was losing about £4 million a year. The *Observer*'s Michael Davie later uncharitably observed: 'The *Evening News* should be in *The Guinness Book of Records* as the most disastrous newspaper of all time.'

It was this fact, above all others, that had made Harmsworth receptive to the initial approaches from Jocelyn Stevens and Lord Goodman at the end of 1976. What they had in mind was something between the 'Quags' and 'Cavendish' proposals that Coote had canvassed six years earlier. It offered the mutual advantage of stopping the losses of both groups in the London evening newspaper field, while preserving some continuing, though lesser, role in the business for the Aitken family.

The key difference between 1970 and 1976 was the relative strengths of the two groups. In 1970 Beaverbrook could reasonably consider itself on a par with Associated; in 1976 there was no disguising its position as a petitioner.

Contacts between Beaverbrook and Associated had gone on fitfully after the failure of the Coote/Hussey plan. In 1974 Sir Max Aitken had let it be known that he was willing to swallow part of his pride and allow Vere Harmsworth to be chairman of a joint subsidiary company. But nothing came of that. Nor did talks at the end of 1975 on joint printing get anywhere though they led Beaverbrook to speed up the transfer of *Evening Standard* production to the *Express* building in Fleet Street as a defensive measure. Other contacts in the 1970s concerned the distribution costs of the two London evenings. The *Evening Standard* had taken steps to reduce its costs by axeing its Saturday edition and withdrawing from outlying circulation areas which were expensive to reach, but these cut-backs were only minor remedies. By 1976 the cost of getting each edition of the *Standard* to street sellers and newsagents throughout the London area was running at £3.5 million a year – 18 per cent of the paper's total costs. The figure for the *News*, with a wider circulation area and a Saturday edition, must have been appreciably higher.

Although talks on distribution brought Beaverbrook and Associated executives together several times nothing came of them. On one occasion the circulation director of the *Evening News* borrowed his aunt's bungalow in Southend for a secure meeting with his counterpart from the *Standard*. As the *News* man told the story, he arrived with sheafs of documentation for the talks. The *Standard* man produced an envelope with some figures written on the back of it. At that, the *News* man gave up. However much that story may have been exaggerated in the telling, there were some people at the *Evening News* who believed it illustrated the fact that there was no point in subordinate executives talking about specific matters. Better, they believed, to wait for the moment when Vere Harmsworth and Sir Max Aitken would get together to talk about an overall deal.

With Sir Max's health so uncertain in the latter part of 1976 there was little prospect of his being able to take any active part in negotiating the group's future. There was, however, a third generation of newspaper Aitkens occupying a high executive position and ready to play a part in charting the family destiny.

Outside Beaverbrook Newspapers Maxwell Aitken, still only 25, was almost an unknown quantity. A slender, pale-faced young man he gave a diffident impression of his abilities. A congenital deformation of his left hand naturally rendered him less well equipped for the robust sporting activities that delighted his father, but he had chosen the tough world of newspapers at an early age.

Maxwell Aitken had been shielded from publicity throughout his upbringing and during his newspaper apprenticeship. His only real impact on the public prints until the age of 23 had been the news of his wedding in July 1974 to Susie More O'Ferrall, whose father headed the Anglo-Irish Bloodstock Agency. The *Daily Express* report of the occasion noted that Susie wore 'a Zandra Rhodes dress of organza and lace, and a diamond tiara borrowed from Lady Margaret Fortescue, daughter of the 5th Earl Fortescue'. The groom wore a blue velvet suit, explaining: 'I hate morning dress.' After the reception, where a ragtime band played in a marquee in the grounds of the More O'Ferrall home in Rudgwick, Sussex, the couple were flown by helicopter on the first leg of their honeymoon.

A more illuminating glimpse of Maxwell Aitken's character was provided later that year in a *Sunday Times* series about the sons of established figures under the headline 'Heirs to a Name'. At that time he was assistant general manager of the *Evening Standard*. He told the interviewer, Susan Raven:

I was a trainee at Rothschilds between Charterhouse and Pembroke, Cambridge – but Cambridge felt very provincial and I couldn't wait to get back to London. So I only stayed a year and then jumped straight into newspapers. I wasn't sure when I started, I don't think it was in my blood, but it certainly gets under the skin.

I started here as a management trainee and went round every department for a year. It was bloody, but I found it fascinating.

I did three months on the editorial floor, but I don't claim to be a journalist at all.

The challenge to me has always been on the management side. Yes, any executive in my position at my age would certainly want the top job – it's certainly my ambition. I love the industry. My father doesn't interfere. I'm left on my own to get on with it.

Grandfather was a frightening figure, one held him in awe. I do remember him, but I was only 12 when he died. We were always taken down and sort of presented to him. No, I never saw myself following in his footsteps, at that age I wanted to be a policeman or a train driver. I suppose one's first hero in life is one's father – that was the situation with me, and that was probably the situation with him.

One saw more of one's mama, but a dressing down from one's papa was certainly more memorable. Manners were drummed into one. Any slip was sat upon. Really one had a nanny since the year dot, a marvellous nanny. I think strict is the word for our upbringing. One wasn't showered with everything one wanted. One was always conscious money didn't grow on trees.

I was brought up with horses, but I'm not very interested myself. I was very lucky, I used to be taken ski-ing almost every year. I enjoy boating, not sailing so much, I don't like getting wet.

Susie and me – our views on sailing aren't far apart. I've got my own boat on the Hamble. But I've always been most interested in cars, they're really my No. 1 love. I've got a Mini-Moke which I had when I was 17; it's just been completely restored.

I went to Cheam and Charterhouse. I regard that as one of the best things my parents ever did for me, sending me to Charterhouse. When I got to University I noticed the Old Etonians were less able to mix – I think that Eton can be a disadvantage.

No, I shan't go into politics. I think one is well aware of the achievements of the people in one's family, but I've never thought one should try and exceed them. Lately, there's been a lot of anti-family talk. I believe not just in my family but in the family as a unit.

In January 1977 Beaverbrook Newspapers announced a series of boardroom promotions. Jocelyn Stevens became chief executive and joint deputy chairman. Peter Hetherington was promoted to joint deputy chairman. Two other senior executives – Michael Murphy, general manager of the *Daily Express*, and Paul Sergeant, Hetherington's deputy – joined the board. All this was formally recorded in the trade press.

What was not announced was the fact that the board had nominated a three-man negotiating team to explore a deal with Associated Newspapers. The three men were Stevens, Hetherington and Maxwell Aitken, also newly elevated to the board. It amounted to formal recognition of the fact that the economics of the moment and the uncertainties of the future were pushing the great hereditary enemies of Fleet Street to think of co-operation rather than rivalry.

Yet there was an element of schizophrenia about the whole operation. Even enthusiasts for a deal with Associated were sometimes gripped by the feeling that such an accommodation was unthinkable. It was therefore not entirely illogical that the board should have been simultaneously plotting a major change in the *Daily Express* designed to trounce the *Daily Mail* at its own game. It was one last throw which had to be made, if only so that nobody would accuse Beaverbrook Newspapers of not having tried everything in the struggle to preserve its independence.

FOUR

Enter the Grocer

THE IDEA OF a tabloid *Daily Express* was not entirely new. Back in 1971, when the *Daily Mail* adopted the form, an internal study group spent three months before deciding against doing the same thing at the *Express*. At that time the paper was still being aimed up-market and the traditional broadsheet was believed to be the most appropriate format in which to hunt for *Daily Telegraph* readers. The tabloid size, it was then felt, belonged more appropriately to sensation-hungry newspapers like the *Mirror* and the *Sun* at the bottom end of the market.

By 1976 the *Daily Mail* had shown convincingly how a mid-market mass-circulation paper could use the smaller page to great effect. The tabloid form – producing a page which measured 15 inches by 12 inches instead of the broadsheet's 24 by 15 – was held to have a number of advantages. Editorially, it allowed greater projection of stories and photographs. The restricted size of the page, and the tendency to use only one or two items on the front page, made it possible to achieve greater visual impact. The increased thickness of a tabloid could give readers the impression they were getting better value for money and the smaller pages were easier to handle. More pages also made it easier to split a newspaper up into a series of sections, each occupying its own page or pages. Advertising revenue could, in theory, be boosted since more full-page or large-scale display advertisements could be sold in a tabloid without any cut in rates charges – on the principle that a page is a page, whether it is tabloid or broadsheet size.

In the summer of 1976 Beaverbrook Newspapers set up another internal study group to examine the tabloid question. The decisive moment came some months later, once again under pressure from the group's economic position. Management projections showed that the selling price of the *Daily Express* would have to go up once again in an attempt to raise more revenue. It had almost doubled since 1974 and there was a danger that the rise from 7p to 9p planned for early 1977 might have an adverse effect on sales. The danger was particularly strong because the thin, broadsheet *Express* would be at a disadvantage compared to the plumper tabloids. Stevens's deputy managing director, Tony Dyer, said he thought a tabloid format might be one way of inducing readers to keep on buying a more expensive *Express*. Roy Wright, the new editor, said he could do it editorially. Stevens spoke to a few other senior executives and then told Sir Max Aitken that he wanted to change the *Daily Express* into a tabloid. According to one participant, the final decision took less than an hour.

Before the launch the *Daily Express* team was unexpectedly strengthened by a change of editor at the *Evening Standard*. After 17 years in the editor's chair – a longer term than any other serving editor of a Fleet Street daily – Charles Wintour finally insisted that the time had come to hand over to a younger man. The successor he had groomed for the role, Simon Jenkins, aged 33, took over after the Christmas holiday. Wintour, still an active 59, was free to move to the *Express* building, where he became managing director of the *Daily Express* with special responsibility for the tabloid launch, scheduled for 24 January 1977.

Charles Vere Wintour was an editor's editor. Tall and austere in appearance he looked, and sometimes acted, more like an academic than a journalist. He was the son of a major-general and had been educated at Oundle and Peterhouse, Cambridge, where he took a first-class honours degree in English and History. Like Sir Max Aitken he had a distinguished war record, but of a very different kind: Wintour had served with the Royal Norfolk Regiment before his gift for organization was eventually deployed on the HQ staff of chief of staff to the Supreme Allied Commander. His decorations included the French Croix de Guerre and the American Bronze Star.

An introduction to Lord Beaverbrook had secured him a job on the *Evening Standard* on leaving the army. His rise was rapid: he became political editor in 1952 and then worked through a series of senior executive positions on all three Beaverbrook newspapers before being appointed editor of the *Standard* in 1958.

Some found his abruptness of manner and his resolute habit of saying precisely what he thought disconcerting. The story is told of an interview he had with an opinionated young man applying for a post on the *Standard*. Among the job-hunter's credentials was a first novel, which had been sent to Wintour in advance. 'I suppose', said Wintour at the interview, 'that like most first novels the central character is largely based on the author's own personality.' The applicant modestly acknowledged that this was so. 'A remarkably unattractive character, I thought,' said the editor. His short way with cant and humbug was no respecter of persons. He was once invited to appear on a television programme in which Woodrow Wyatt, then a Labour MP, interviewed leading press figures. Most of the editors who appeared stoically endured Wyatt's overbearing manner. Wintour was a notable exception. 'That is a very silly remark,' he said of one observation by Wyatt, and at another point: 'You are misrepresenting what I say and you are doing so deliberately.'

Wintour's frostiness on such occasions earned him the nickname 'Chilly Charlie', but there was no mistaking the warmth of his dedication to his newspaper. Above all he was a brilliant spotter of talent, and having discovered it, he respected its development. Under his editorship the *Standard* achieved and maintained a reputation for good writing, liveliness and wide cultural sympathies. With journalists of quality like Anne Sharpley, Angus McGill, Sam White and Jeremy Campbell, its standards were often higher than most of the national press. On major issues it was consistently liberal, though its main concern was with the quality of life in the metropolis. Wintour always made it clear that he did not want to edit the *Daily Express*, preferring to run a small but, to his mind, more creative enterprise. In 1967 he was a leading candidate for the editorship of *The Times* and the *Sunday Times*, but lost to William Rees-Mogg and Harold Evans when the Thomson board decided to make their appointments from within the group.

Jocelyn Stevens once described Wintour as 'the best editor in Fleet Street' and many outside Beaverbrook Newspapers shared this view. It was unquestionably true that under him the *Evening Standard* consistently displayed more intellectual vitality than the other two major titles in the Beaverbrook Group. This was not a fact that all Expressmen found palatable. Some resented what was deemed to be the general uppityness of the *Standard* staff and part of the feeling rubbed off on Wintour. Shortly after he took up his new quarters in the black glass building, an editorial corridor was graced with the graffiti: 'Now is the Wintour of our discontent.'

Though the management and senior editorial staff were convinced of the need to go tabloid, the rank and file were not so easily persuaded. To many it seemed like another desperate gimmick, and one that destroyed an essential difference between the *Express* and the other popular newspapers. While the dissidents were being talked round by their new managing director a development of major consequence for the future of the whole group occurred at the Boat Show in Olympia.

A traditional feature of the Beaverbrook-sponsored show is the editors' luncheon. Each editor in turn gives a lunch to which a variety of distinguished guests are invited to make the acquaintance of the Beaverbrook top brass. On 11 January the host was John Junor of the *Sunday Express*. Sir Max was too unwell to attend but Maxwell Aitken was there, as was Jocelyn Stevens. The guest of honour was the Conservative leader Mrs Margaret Thatcher, but the guest who made the greatest impact was a tall, fast-talking businessman with a restless manner. Sir James Goldsmith had chosen this occasion to reveal that he had recently invested over £1·5 million in Beaverbrook Newspapers, acquiring 35 per cent of the company's non-voting stock – far and away the largest single shareholding. Given his reputation as a genius at take-overs the news was little short of electrifying.

Sir James Goldsmith was a man who had grown accustomed to getting his way, though at that time his credentials as a friend of the British press seemed decidedly suspect. For the past year he had been involved in a no-holds-barred series of legal battles with the satirical magazine *Private Eye* which were threatening to put that publication out of business. At one point the quest for evidence by Goldsmith's hired investigators had led to their rummaging through the magazine's overflowing dustbins.

The legal marathon had begun after the magazine published an article headed 'All's Well that Ends Elwes' in its issue of 12 December 1975. The piece referred to the recent suicide of the painter Dominick Elwes, a close friend of Lord Lucan, who was wanted for questioning by the police in connection with the murder of his children's nanny, Sandra Rivett. Reference was also made to 'the circle of gamblers and boneheads with whom Lord Lucan associated'. The story named Goldsmith as 'the richest and most powerful member of this group'. The key allegation was that he helped obstruct the course of justice during police inquiries into Sandra Rivett's murder. Subsequent articles dealt with Goldsmith's business interests, questioning in particular his fitness for the task of leading a rescue operation on the financial conglomerate Slater Walker Securities after its original chairman Jim Slater – a close friend of his – had resigned.

An avalanche of writs descended on *Private Eye* – at one stage there were 93 outstanding actions against the magazine, its publishers and distributors. The principal one against the editor, Richard Ingrams, was an action for criminal libel over the Lucan allegation – the first brought against a newspaper for 53 years. Conviction could earn Ingrams a jail sentence of up to two years. Although the magazine forfeited much sympathy when it emerged that it had not got its facts straight, there was a general concern among journalists about the implications of Goldsmith's chosen remedies. Many thought criminal libel a crude and outmoded action, while his initiative in issuing writs against distributors was considered a threat to any publication of a controversial nature.

In January 1977 these legal issues were still unresolved, but the *blitzkrieg* method of attack demonstrated the obsessional capacity of the man who had just bought his way into Beaverbrook Newspapers. At 43 Sir James Goldsmith had come a long way at great speed and was still gathering momentum.

No great hopes could have been entertained for him as a young man. The son of a French Roman Catholic mother and an English Jewish father, who had once been the Tory MP for Stowmarket, he had seemed bent on frittering a rich cosmopolitan inheritance. His father, Major Frank Goldsmith, had been content with life as an English country gentleman until the

First World War, during which he served in the Gallipoli campaign. He had settled in France after the war and as 'Monsieur le Major' became a leading figure in Hôtels Réunis, which owned over 40 hotels, among them the Carlton in Cannes. James Goldsmith was born in Paris but educated in England. His schoolboy career at Eton was undistinguished, though it ended with an unconventional flourish. He left, aged 16, after turning £7 into £8000 on a three-horse accumulator at Lewes races.

Four years later Goldsmith met and fell in love with 18-year-old Isabella Patino, heiress to the £75 million Bolivian tin empire, but his reputation as a playboy and gambler was deemed one of the main arguments against him as a suitor. The other was his Jewish background, which gave rise to a famous exchange between Goldsmith and his intended's father – Señor Patino: 'In my family we are not in the habit of marrying outside the Catholic faith'; Goldsmith: 'In my family we are not in the habit of marrying descendants of Red Indians.'

The young couple's elopement and marriage, celebrated on the *Daily Mirror*'s front page as 'The romance that thrilled Britain', had a tragic sequel. Isabella died in childbirth and Goldsmith had to fight his parents-in-law in the Paris courts for the right to bring up his daughter, Isabel.

Although Goldsmith could claim to be related to several European banking families – the Rothschilds, the Belgian Lamberts and the German Oppenheims – his own career as a businessman got off to an erratic start. His first venture, a cut-price drugs company based in Paris, had to be sold when he ran out of cash. A bold entry on the British business scene in the mid-1960s encountered trouble when his main company, Cavenham Foods, had its accounts for 1966/7 qualified by the auditors, an unusual occurrence that aroused City suspicion of his wheeler-dealer methods. Goldsmith survived this treacly episode, with the help of his cousin, Baron Alexis de Gunzberg, by injecting £500,000 of his own and his friends' resources into the company as a public act of faith.

By 1970 Cavenham's recovery was complete and Goldsmith moved into the big league in the following year with a spectacular take-over of Bovril, fighting off an establishment counter-bid from Rowntree in the process. In 1972 the acquisition of Allied

Supplies retail chain, consisting of Home and Colonial, Maypole and Lipton stores, earned him the title of 'Britain's Number One Grocer'. In the United States Goldsmith obtained a majority shareholding in the Grand Union supermarket chain. The European operation, through his main company in Paris, Générale Occidentale, also proceeded apace.

By 1976 Cavenham could claim to be, after Unilever and Nestlé, the third largest food company in Europe – in six years its turnover had increased from £33 million a year to a prodigious £1800 million. The products that flowed from its cornucopia included Bovril, Marmite, Procea, Slimcea, Palm Toffee, Ambrosia rice, Jaffa juice and *foies-gras de Strasbourg*.

Though he was a devout and sometimes vociferous apostle of free enterprise and high profits Goldsmith's connections spanned a wide political spectrum. In London he had been taken up by the Labour establishment, earning the golden opinions of Harold Wilson and his political secretary Lady Falkender. Goldsmith's knighthood had been conferred in Wilson's resignation honours list and would, but for a premature disclosure of his controversial preferment, probably have been a barony. In Paris his eminence was symbolized by a directorship of the French Banque Rothschild and part-ownership of the Eiffel Tower.

Goldsmith's family life compared favourably with Alec Guinness's arrangement in the film *Captain's Paradise*. Weekends were spent mainly in Paris, where his second wife, Ginette, the daughter of a métro official, and their two teenage children lived on the Left Bank in a palatial house once occupied by Cole Porter. Weekdays were spent primarily in London, where Goldsmith lived with the sister of the Marquis of Londonderry, Lady Annabel Birley, and his two young children by her in a beautiful house on the edge of Richmond Park. Lady Annabel was the estranged wife of another old Etonian, Mark Birley, whose Berkeley Square nightclub, Annabel's, had become a mecca for well-heeled swinging Londoners.

Goldsmith's appetite for success remained undiminished but it had begun to express itself in different forms. The main difference was an eagerness to take part in what he termed 'the national debate'. Though regarded as a man of the Right, he was not a conventional Tory. He gave money to Friends of the

Earth in support of their campaign against fast-breeder nuclear reactors and shared many of the views of his brother Teddy, whose magazine the *Ecologist* had pioneered the ecological debate in Britain through its analysis 'Blueprint for Survival'. As far as conventional politics were concerned he did not have a high regard for Mrs Thatcher, nor did he have the inclination to serve time on the back-benches of the House of Commons. It was logical that he should want to own a powerful newspaper. The Beaverbrook A shares seemed the beginning of a way in.

The parcel of shares which Goldsmith had acquired with such dramatic suddenness had an intriguing history, starting with a series of purchases by the Australian publisher Rupert Murdoch, back in the early 1970s. The tradition of cross-shareholdings between newspaper proprietors, dating back to Beaverbrook and Rothermere, was by no means dead and in strictly economic terms Murdoch considered the shares 'a good punt'. Eventually he built up a 20 per cent block of the A stock at prices of around 80p a share. In 1973 he sold them at a handsome profit – at 125p a share – to Sir Max Rayne, the property magnate.

The reasons for Rayne's acquisition, at such an inflated price, were soon made manifest at Beaverbrook boardroom level: Lord Goodman, who acted for Sir Max Rayne as well as for Sir Max Aitken, had apparently seen a method of enhancing both their futures.

The Goodman scheme, as it emerged in 1973, provided for a division of Beaverbrook into two companies by issuing one share in a new property company for every existing share in the newspaper company. The idea was that Sir Max Aitken should swop his shares in the property company for Sir Max Rayne's shares in the newspaper company, thus gaining absolute control of the newspaper company even if the A shares were to be enfranchised.

Sir Max Aitken would continue to run the newspapers, while Sir Max Rayne would own and manage the properties Beaverbrook possessed in London, Glasgow, Manchester and Bristol. It was argued that the price of Beaverbrook shares was based on the trading results of the newspapers and did not take account of the full value of the group's property assets. A take-over bidder might therefore be able to buy control of the company through the stock market at less than its real value, and would then be free to close down the newspapers and develop the property to its full value. A secondary argument was that newspapers and property did not really belong together in the same company and that both would operate more efficiently if a split took place.

The proposal was not universally welcomed by the directors of Beaverbrook. Some felt that it pointed the company in exactly the wrong direction – at a time of rising costs and declining revenue, the newspapers would need all the financial support they could get from the properties owned by the group. To some it looked like a plan to deprive the newspapers of any benefit from the land and buildings which had been paid for out of their past profits.

There were also doubts about the defensive argument put forward as a guard against a below-value take-over. Two of the leading take-over specialists of the time, Jim Slater and John Bentley, had made approaches to Beaverbrook, but neither had followed through with bids. Above all the opponents of the scheme feared that the end result would be to speed up the decline of the newspapers and to turn Beaverbrook into a property concern. They were further discomforted by a remark from one of Goodman's aides when the scheme was unfolded. If the newspapers closed down, he said, 'then we'd be able to develop Fleet Street'.

Opposition to the plan came to a head at a dinner given by Evelyn de Rothschild attended by Stevens, Wintour and Nicholson. Michael Franks, then the Beaverbrook finance director, was also against it but Sir Max Aitken remained clearly in favour. At one point Goodman was asked to the Beaverbrook boardroom to give a formal exposition of the plan. During the meeting he was roughly questioned, particularly by Stevens and Junor. That afternoon Stevens was telephoned by his chairman. 'Traitor', said Sir Max and then hung up. The plan was never implemented, partly because of the internal opposition and partly because it would have publicly exposed the weakness of the newspaper operation.

Sir Max Rayne became deputy chairman of Beaverbrook Properties, but this was a subsidiary of the newspaper company and not the independent property concern Goodman had en-visaged. By 1976 Rayne was ready to sever the link with Beaverbrook. He had seen the Aitken House development go up in Fleet Street but Beaverbrook was in no position to under-take any further property development. Aitken House was proving difficult to let as the property market sagged and the one major success on the property front, the Bristol develop-ment known as Tollgate House, was about to be sold for £6 million. There seemed no reason why Rayne should not dispose of his shares, which by now amounted to 32 per cent of the non-voting stock.

Beaverbrook Newspapers did not have the money to buy them but Rupert Murdoch was happy enough to try another punt, buying the stock back from Rayne at 33p a share – a quarter of the price Rayne had paid four years earlier.

In the autumn of 1976 Murdoch and Goldsmith found them-selves in the motley crowd of bidders vying for the chance to restore the fortunes of Britain's oldest Sunday paper, the *Observer*, whose circulation, after swinging around 800,000 in the early 1970s, had fallen away to 670,000, half the figure for the *Sunday Times* and just below the other quality Sunday, the *Sunday Telegraph*. The paper's plight had been rendered more desperate when *The Times* moved out of the building in Printing House Square it had shared with the *Observer*. This left the Sunday newspaper with a printing plant which it used only one day a week.

When the Astor family, which owned the paper, decided to give up the unequal struggle, the Observer Trust, under the chairmanship of the ubiquitous Lord Goodman, cast its net wide for alternatives. The exercise provided some rollicking copy for rival newspapers and amply demonstrated one of Fleet Street's central problems.

When newspaper proprietors and national trade-union leaders tell employees that their high wages and restrictive practices are putting their jobs in jeopardy, a common response is to pooh-pooh the possibility of newspapers closing down by pointing to the queue of bidders which forms whenever a paper is for sale. In the case of the *Observer* the bidders who followed Murdoch included an oil heiress, a consortium of Saudi Arabians, a Hong Kong newspaper owner whose fortune was based on patent medicines, Vere Harmsworth, and Sir James Goldsmith.

Goldsmith's plan for the *Observer* was ingenious, offering a lifeline to Beaverbrook Newspapers as well as a springboard for his own ambitions. His intelligence on Beaverbrook's problems in the production and property fields was informal but impeccable. Jocelyn Stevens had been a contemporary at Eton and they had remained on 'Jocelyn' and 'Jimmy' terms ever since; Sir Max Rayne was what he described as 'a *de facto* brother-in-law' – Lady Annabel Birley was the sister of Rayne's wife. Goldsmith's solution was that he should take over the *Observer*, guaranteeing it the necessary financial backing. He would then close down the uneconomic plant in Printing House Square and move production to Beaverbrook's new presses in Fleet Street. Under arrangements which he drafted with Jocelyn Stevens and Beaverbrook's finance director, Peter Hetherington, a Goldsmith-owned *Observer* would have moved its editorial staff into the largely empty Aitken House. The savings for the *Observer* were estimated at £500,000 a year and Beaverbrook's benefits would also be considerable. Some of the *Sunday Express* printing would have to be moved to Manchester to make room for the *Observer*, but that was not likely to cause major problems. A deal with Goldsmith would enable Beaverbrook to use its expensive new printing equipment closer to full capacity and would bring in rent income from Aitken House.

Like other well-laid schemes, Goldsmith's foundered when the American oil company Atlantic Richfield (ARCO) bought the *Observer* for a symbolic £1 and gave pledges to preserve editorial independence and put the necessary money into the company. Shortly after ARCO's triumph Goldsmith and Murdoch met for a drink in New York. At that time both men were considering major expansion in the United States, but conversation turned naturally to the British press. As there was no point in licking wounds from the *Observer* episode they looked to the future. Murdoch needed capital for a major venture he was planning in New York; Goldsmith needed a hand-hold for another assault on the commanding heights of the British press. The Beaverbrook A shares solved both their problems.

When he got back to England Goldsmith met Murdoch's managing director in London and agreed that Cavenham would buy the share block which Murdoch had recently purchased back from Rayne. He paid a total of £1,566,264 for 4,400,000 Beaverbrook shares, giving him 32 per cent of the A shares.

Because of Beaverbrook's ownership structure, this large stake gave Goldsmith no formal power in the company's affairs. Control and authority still lay with the voting shares, held predominantly by the Beaverbrook Foundation and the Aitken family. But Goldsmith thought that the A shares were still a good buy. He had learned about the bad state of Beaverbrook in the autumn of 1976 when making his unsuccessful attempt to take over the *Observer*. If the company went on declining it might well be forced to try to raise capital by issuing new shares. Under current stock exchange practice these would be voting shares and Goldsmith, as a large shareholder already, would be able to take a substantial number. He would then have a voice in the running of Beaverbrook. Alternatively, if the Aitken family decided to sell the company he would be well placed either to buy control or to make a profit by selling out to a take-over bidder. If, on the other hand, Beaverbrook recovered, he would also profit as the share price went up. Goldsmith felt he could not lose.

However, he took a little time to tell Beaverbrook about his new interest in their affairs. In the interval he built up his holding from 32 per cent to 35 per cent, by discreet buying in the market. After making the news public at the Boat Show lunch, Goldsmith wrote to Sir Max Aitken saying that he hoped Cavenham would prove a useful shareholder. He thought that he might join the board and play a useful and significant role as a director. 'My intention was to act gradually,' he said later. 'My real interest was to become involved.' He also thought it would 'be amusing' to own a national newspaper.

Sir Max Aitken, as it turned out, was not in the least amused. The reasons for the strength of Sir Max's reaction against Goldsmith are still not entirely clear, though it appears to have had more to do with personal antipathy rather than any worries over the implications of Goldsmith's litigation against *Private Eye*. Another factor may well have been the attitude of Lord Goodman, whose opinion Sir Max cherished above all others at that time. Although Goodman had once acted for

Goldsmith in ironing out legal problems connected with Slater Walker Securities' activities in Singapore, their relations subsequently became strained for reasons that Goldsmith found unclear, though he thought it might be connected with 'a matter of court intrigue' in Harold Wilson's entourage.

During the *Observer* take-over struggle Goodman had been quoted by the *Daily Mail* as saying that Goldsmith would not get the paper under any circumstances. When Goldsmith later tackled him on this statement, Goodman indicated that he had been misrepresented. None the less Goldsmith formed the impression that Goodman was 'a passive enemy' throughout the *Observer* battle. As the Beaverbrook battle developed, his impression was that the enmity became 'active'.

Although Jocelyn Stevens had initially been excited by the possibilities of Goldsmith's intervention, he was obliged to change his tune within a few days of the Boat Show luncheon. Icy proprietorial references to him as 'Goldsmith's friend' had made him realize that it would be unwise to explore the Cavenham option any further. Before leaving for Cap d'Ail on 16 January Sir Max made it clear that whatever methods were required to save the company, the one saviour he did not wish to hear about was Sir James Goldsmith. The Beaverbrook board, meeting in their chairman's absence on 20 January, dutifully resolved to repel any advances by Cavenham Foods and the negotiating team of Stevens, Hetherington and Maxwell Aitken undertook to make this clear to Goldsmith himself.

Next day Sir Max had his serious stroke in Cap d'Ail. The necessity of fighting off what was seen as the Goldsmith threat became more pressing. As Stevens organized the private flight for Lady Violet that was to bring Sir Max back to London, Maxwell Aitken came up with a suggestion designed to assist the anti-Goldsmith campaign. Through a polo-playing cousin he knew of a man who could give advice on how to repel unwelcome business intruders. He was David Karr, an American businessman who mainly operated from Paris.

Karr had developed an expertise which was highly specialized. He had started as a journalist on the *Washington Post* and wrote a book called *Fight for Control* that made him an expert on take-over struggles. Side-stepping from the public prints into private enterprise, he made a profitable living advising clients involved in such battles. By the time Beaverbrook Newspapers turned to him, his advice had been sought in over 30 take-over situations. In Britain his clients included Charles Forte and Bernard Delfont. His Paris office was on Avenue Kléber, next to the French international conference centre where the formal Vietnam peace talks were held. Stevens was given the impression that there was no better man to fight off Goldsmith, whose operation was also centred on Paris. 'My understanding', Stevens recalled, 'was that Karr knew more about Goldsmith than Goldsmith did himself.'

On 23 January, as Lady Vi Aitken flew from Nice to London with Sir Max on board, Stevens, Maxwell Aitken and Peter Hetherington were on their way to Paris. They dined with Karr that evening at the Plaza Athénée hotel and unfolded the dilemma of Beaverbrook Newspapers.

Karr's account of the encounter was that the three Beaverbrook directors were 'scared of Goldsmith', seeing an unwelcome takeover attempt as a distinct possibility. His suggestion was to press ahead with the Associated deal as fast as possible – an option that was already more than half formed in his hearers' minds.

Stevens, Aitken and Hetherington were evidently impressed with the adviser they had acquired, though his identity was kept secret from other directors for some time. In references to him Stevens, deploying his flair for the dramatic, called him 'the Jackal'. The reference was drawn from Frederick Forsyth's novel of the same name about an assassination attempt on the life of the French president. In this instance the presumed victim was not General de Gaulle but Sir James Goldsmith, commercially speaking of course.

Stevens and his companions hurried back to London on the night of 23 January to see the first tabloid *Daily Express* being produced. It was impressive, but less than dazzling. Roy Wright had laid out an attractive newspaper of which the centrepiece was a high-cost serialization of a book about the last days of Howard Hughes, the American millionaire recluse. In an attempt to wean more Sunday readers to the new *Daily Express*, the first episode of the Hughes revelations began in the *Sunday Express*.

The effect was slightly marred by the appearance in a Glasgow Sunday newspaper of a series of stories about Hughes which contained highlights of the material for which the *Daily Express* had paid $100,000. An attempt to stop the *Glasgow Sunday Mail* publication failed and the whole affair became more embarrassing when it emerged that one of the stories appearing in Scotland had been sold to the Glasgow paper for £50 by the London Express News and Features Service, a Beaverbrook syndication operation.

The episode was not allowed to dim the jollity of the launch breakfast held on the following day at the Inn on the Park hotel, a one-time residence of Howard Hughes, overlooking Hyde Park. Lady Violet Aitken was in attendance, deputizing for her husband, who was lying in King's College Hospital. Over 400 guests assembled to sip a specially concocted champagne cocktail called 'Sparkling Success' and to hear that the first tabloid *Daily Express* had been a technical triumph. The run of 3·6 million copies had been trouble-free and had actually finished 44 minutes ahead of schedule. They were also able to appreciate some knockabout fun with the opposition.

Forewarned of an Associated plan to distribute specially printed copies of the *Daily Mail* at the launch party, Beaverbrook had blocked the approach road to the hotel with delivery vans and crowded the pavement with vendors selling the first edition of the *Evening Standard*. The *Mail*, anticipating such a defensive move, had booked rooms inside the hotel, to which bundles of the special edition had been sent disguised as luggage. Fearing that the Beaverbrook men might recognize them, the *Mail*'s promotion staff sent in women from the circulation and research departments, as undercover agents. They went to the rooms booked by the *Mail*, opened the cases which had been sent in and distributed 250 copies of the mock edition of the *Mail* to the *Express* guests. Its message was clear enough: a huge headline reading 'SUPREMACY' with a graph below showing the *Express* and *Mail* circulation trends. 'Express down: younger readers vanishing fast,' proclaimed the caption under the chart.

That evening the Beaverbrook stop-Goldsmith movement reached a climactic phase. The setting was an elegant flat owned by Hambro's Bank at 2 Wilton Terrace in Belgravia.

The occasion was a dinner given by Charles Hambro, the chairman of the bank and Goldsmith's banker. The guests were Stevens, Hetherington and Maxwell Aitken from Beaverbrook, Hambro's director Peter Hill Wood, and Sir James Goldsmith. What should have been an agreeable evening combining business with pleasure turned into a very different affair. 'It was', said Goldsmith later, 'as though everybody had taken LSD.'

Stevens began by informing Goldsmith that the Beaverbrook board regarded his shareholding as hostile. Goldsmith remembers Stevens saying that if he thought *Private Eye* had tried to attack him, he should wait and see the power of the Beaverbrook press if it decided to go after him. That, Stevens added, was what would happen unless Goldsmith sold his shares. Goldsmith's response was that he would bid for full control of the company at the first sign of any Beaverbrook campaign against him. He instructed his bankers, in the person of his host, accordingly.

Stevens was naturally under considerable suspicion at Beaverbrook. He was an old friend of the man his company regarded as prime enemy and the need to demonstrate that personal feelings had not clouded his business loyalties no doubt fuelled his performance at the Hambro dinner. In any event the performance partially served its purpose. Goldsmith went off on holiday and disappeared from the Beaverbrook scene for three months, though he kept the A shares as a reminder of his capacity to come back. As Goldsmith was resolved not to push any further into the Beaverbrook operation without the tacit blessing of Sir Max Aitken, there seemed no likelihood that this eventuality would arise. But stranger things had happened.

Whether Stevens could have delivered on his threat to harry Goldsmith in the Beaverbrook press was highly questionable, though the *Daily Express* had just acquired the services of Bruce Page, a brilliant journalist who had developed the investigative techniques of the Insight column on the *Sunday Times*. Page, a socialist who later became editor of the *New Statesman*, was no fan of Goldsmith's and had actually negotiated a contract with Beaverbrook Newspapers which gave him the right to terminate his services if Sir James took over. He was, none the less, somewhat taken aback when Stevens suggested that he might like to start his term as associate editor of the *Daily Express* with an exposé of the boss of Cavenham Foods. Page politely declined the invitation on the grounds that he did not see his role as that of 'a management hit-man'.

As the Goldsmith threat receded, so did the prospect of any startling breakthrough by the tabloid *Daily Express*. The promotion which launched it had cost half a million pounds. The initial return for that expenditure was a circulation boost of 400,000 copies a day. Charles Wintour immediately expressed his satisfaction at having attracted new readers without having lost many of the old, traditional *Express* buyers. But once the initial enthusiasm had worn off sales slipped. By February they were down to around 2·65 million, an increase of only 70,000 over the figure at the end of 1976.

The *Daily Mail* had counter-attacked with journalistic *élan*: against tough competition from all the tabloids editor David English had secured the personal diary of the Tyler family, who had been held captive by rebels in Ethiopia. The *Express* apparently lost in the bidding because of Mrs Tyler's aversion to the headline on its story about her first shopping expedition after achieving freedom: 'Happiness is a new bra.' The *Mail* followed up this success with another coup, landing Mrs Gill Moran's account of her horrific experiences at the hands of the escaped prisoner William Hughes, who had kidnapped her after murdering her family. In a confident interview with the advertising trade weekly *Campaign* English said he thought the circulation of the *Mail* would overtake the *Express* in 1978. When that happened, he predicted, Beaverbrook Newspapers would have three choices – to close the *Daily Express*, to get new money by being taken over, or to be absorbed by Associated.

FIVE

Getting A. Goodman

THE NEWS FROM Sir Max Aitken's bedside in King's College Hospital was not encouraging. His life was not in any immediate danger but the advised medical regimen was complete rest for a minimum of six weeks. During this time he was, on doctor's orders, to be protected from any upsetting information of a personal or business nature. As the affairs of Beaverbrook Newspapers were a fount of such information, the chairman was effectively cut off from management of the company at the most critical stage in its history. 'I was in an appalling position,' Jocelyn Stevens recalled. 'As deputy chairman the one person I was bound to keep straight with was my own chairman. Yet there I was unable to communicate with him.'

There was no way the company could wait for the chairman's recovery before steps were taken to secure its future. Fortunately the way ahead seemed clear enough. With young Maxwell Aitken on the negotiating team, effectively acting as a trustee of his father's interests, Stevens felt he had the authority to pursue what seemed the best course of action. Subsequently there was to be considerable doubt about whether Sir Max and his son viewed the crisis in the same terms, but there was no such confusion in February 1977. The negotiating team saw an early accommodation with Associated Newspapers as the way out of the immediate cash crisis and, incidentally, the best way of combating Goldsmith.

In pursuing this objective they had an active and powerful ally in Lord Goodman, whose skill in such matters had assumed legendary proportions. Although he had recently reduced his legal workload to become Master of University College, Oxford, the capacity which had, at different times, enabled him to represent the leaders of all three major political parties remained intact. His ability was essentially that of a go-between, so well developed that it called to mind Edmund Burke's famous reflection on the subject: 'The world is governed by go-betweens. These go-betweens influence the persons with whom they carry on intercourse by stating their own sense to each of them as the sense of the other; and thus they reciprocally master both sides.'

Goodman was more admired by those who ran newspapers than those who wrote them, but it is difficult to think of anyone more suited to the task that Beaverbrook Newspapers had in hand. He was well versed in both the general and the particular problem under discussion. He had been chairman of the Newspaper Publishers' Association, the top Fleet Street management body, from 1970 to 1975, and had worked closely with Vere Harmsworth and the print union leaders. Goodman's connections in government, which might feel obliged to take an interest in the deal under the terms of its monopolies legislation, were without equal. A popular Whitehall phrase ran: 'If you want to get a good man for the job, get A. Goodman.' Above all he was convinced of the merits of a deal between Associated and Beaverbrook as a way of easing the burden of responsibility on his friend Sir Max Aitken. He was also an advocate of speed in negotiation as a matter of technique as well as necessity. 'When I go in to negotiate,' he once said, 'I always go for a quick solution. If you hang around too long you just become part of the furniture and nothing happens.'

The two sides formally came together in the Master's Lodge at University College on 3 February 1977. Goodman's negotiating skill was normally deployed in the Little Essex Street offices of Goodman Derrick & Co., or in his Portland Place flat, south of Regent's Park, but Oxford seemed a more suitable venue for this particular meeting. It provided a peaceful and reflective atmosphere and, more especially, it promised discretion. The Beaverbrook trio, Stevens, Hetherington and Maxwell Aitken, had driven themselves from London, leaving their chauffeurs behind for security reasons and to have an opportunity to talk freely during the journey. Jobs were bound to disappear and in such circumstances the Beaverbrook management – as in the case of the Glasgow closure – felt that secrecy was vital. Vere Harmsworth arrived with his managing director, Mick Shields.

There was a natural disparity in negotiating strengths. In 1977, for the first time since the 1920s, Associated could go into negotiations with Beaverbrook as the more successful and dynamic of the two groups. With its oil, its far-flung non-newspaper interests, its monopoly provincial press chain and the revived *Daily Mail*, Associated was moving up, whereas Beaverbrook, with 99 per cent of its income dependent on three declining newspapers, was pointed steadily downwards. The Associated Group's latest half-year earnings, before tax, had shown healthy growth at £6·1 million compared to a £1·5 million loss at Beaverbrook. One possible strategy for Associated in 1977 might have been to sit back and wait until Beaverbrook declined even further, but Goldsmith's intervention presented a strong motive for prompt action.

One of Goldsmith's reasons for buying into Beaverbrook had clearly been the possibility that if the company declined even further he would be well placed to gain control. Against Beaverbrook alone Associated might look strong, but its £126 million turnover and £12 million profits for 1976–7 looked a good deal less impressive when measured against the £1800 million turnover and £38 million profits of Goldsmith's Cavenham Foods company. The relative scale of a Fleet Street newspaper business and Europe's third largest food concern was shown by the fact that Goldsmith estimated Cavenham's total investment in Beaverbrook as equivalent to its takings in three hours of a normal trading day.

Discussions in the Master's Lodge of University College centred on the question of creating a monopoly London evening newspaper out of the *News* and the *Standard*. It was the logical first meeting-point for the two groups. Any thought which Beaverbrook might have had of closing down the *Daily Express* and shedding its growing losses was scuppered by the fact that the *Sunday Express* needed the printing facilities in Manchester used mainly by the *Daily Express* for its northern editions. If the *Daily Express* were closed, the *Sunday Express* would not be able to print effectively and Beaverbrook's one profit-maker would be crippled.

A merger of the two London evening newspapers offered the prospect of substantial profits in place of major losses. While both existing evening papers were in financial trouble, the *News* was considerably worse off than the *Standard*. Losses at the *Standard* had totalled £1·3 million in the seven months up to January 1977, but it then began to break even and expected to make a profit in the spring and summer. The exact losses of the *Evening News* were hard to define as they were closely affected by the allocation of common costs shared with the *Mail*, but Associated did not deny estimates of annual losses running between £4 and £5 million at the beginning of 1977.

Both papers had had to deal with the same problems of declining population in inner London, changing commuter reading habits, competition from radio and television and the growth of local evening papers. They also bore the financial cross of production and distribution costs on the scale of a national newspaper while being essentially local newspapers in character and circulation area. The *News* still outsold the *Standard* – by 536,000 to 418,000 – but the *Standard* enjoyed a richer audience, which made it more attractive to advertisers. The difference between the *Standard* and *News*, and their readers, was so distinct that London street sellers were said to be able to tell at a glance which of the two an approaching buyer would ask for.

If the *Standard* belonged to the more prosperous reaches of commuter land and to those who could afford to live in the choicer parts of the inner city, the *Evening News* had initially been, in the words of one of its managers, 'the Cockney paper'. It had gloried for years in having the largest evening newspaper circulation in the world. It distributed at great expense in south and east coast resorts, where its predominantly working-class readership went on holiday. It was a proletarian newspaper *par excellence* and it suffered heavily when its readers turned to television or simply got out of the habit of taking a paper in the evening as well as the morning. Its editorial character became increasingly chaotic in the late 1960s and early 1970s. It was, according to one senior executive, 'a shambles of a paper' when Louis Kirby moved over from the *Daily Mail* as editor in 1974. Under Kirby it turned from a broadsheet into a tabloid, but sales went on falling. At the start of 1977 its editorial character was as unclear as the *Evening Standard*'s was precise. Kirby was anxious to improve it, to take it up-market and to outdo the

Standard, but the *News* remained weighed down by its past without having found a way ahead.

Before they could get down to working out how these very very different newspapers could be merged, and their long history of intense competition be buried, the Associated and Beaverbrook negotiators had to settle three basic issues. One was who would own a merged London evening newspaper. The second question was who would print it. The third was whether the *Standard* or the *News* would dominate the editorial character of a merged newspaper.

At the Oxford meeting the first two questions became balanced in a tit-for-tat pattern. Beaverbrook could have control of the monopoly evening paper if Associated could print it. Alternatively, Associated might run the merged paper with printing done on plant owned jointly by Beaverbrook and Associated. The third, and ultimately most important, question was not gone into for the moment.

While the first alternative would have given Beaverbrook the profits of a monopoly evening paper and the possibility of perpetuating the *Evening Standard* in another form, it would have been disastrous from the production point of view. Printing of the new evening paper by Associated would have meant that Beaverbrook's expensive presses would have been used even less than they were already and the amalgamation of printing of the *Express* and *Standard* on the new plant in Fleet Street would have to be undone.

The second alternative was more attractive for both sides. It would enable Beaverbrook to use its presses fully. Through the establishment of a joint printing company Associated would take a 50 per cent stake in Beaverbrook's plant. Beaverbrook would also get an infusion of much-needed capital in return for giving Associated control of the new evening newspaper.

For Vere Harmsworth and Mick Shields such an arrangement presented a number of major benefits. Associated would have a monopoly London evening newspaper which could hardly fail to make money if properly run, in place of the loss-making *Evening News.* That was attractive enough in itself. But an equally strong motive was that it would free property which Associated owned between the river Thames and Fleet Street. After the *News* printing plant had been moved away, the site could be developed to add valuable rent income to the company's non-press revenue.

In the background were the deeper implications that would flow from such a deal. The cash injection would provide Beaverbrook with a breathing space, but there was no certainty that it would last very long. That would depend largely on the fate of the two remaining Beaverbrook newspapers and the omens were not particularly bright. The attempts to revive the *Daily Express* had all been unsuccessful and in February 1977 it was becoming clear that the tabloid relaunch had not hit the jackpot. The *Sunday Express*, while still profitable, was losing sales steadily. Its readers were getting steadily older. They were, said one Beaverbrook executive, 'like an army marching over a precipice – readers dying off each year and not being replaced'. Associated, after its failure to buy the *Observer* the previous autumn, might start a Sunday version of the *Daily Mail* at any point, posing a major threat to a newspaper which had remained virtually unchanged in the luxury of a market monopoly position for 15 years.

If trends within the two groups continued as they were, the stage could be set before too many years had passed for a further step – the merger of the *Daily Mail* and *Daily Express*, with Associated Newspapers clearly the dominant partner and Vere Harmsworth raised to Northcliffean stature in Fleet Street.

Although they were aware of the longer-term dangers, Jocelyn Stevens and his colleagues had to concentrate on short-term survival. Before motoring back from Oxford to London Stevens and Shields agreed to work out details of possible sales, advertising revenue and profits of the proposed monopoly London evening paper.

Next day Stevens reported the substance of the talks to Charles Wintour, the director most likely to be personally affected by the proposed deal. Although he had moved in January from the editorship of the *Standard* to be managing director of the *Daily Express*, he was still chairman of the *Standard*. All his fundamental loyalties were with the paper he had edited for 17 years and his feelings about the *Standard* were matched by a contempt for the *Evening News*, both editorially and commercially. His immediate reaction to Stevens's news of the Oxford meeting was to say that he was perturbed about the *Standard*. As far as he was concerned, the new paper would have to be a continuation of the *Standard*, even if it was owned by Associated.

Years earlier Wintour had been upbraided by his proprietor in terms that had a contemporary relevance. The occasion was a leader in the *Standard* supporting unification of the Anglican and Methodist churches. Lord Beaverbrook took exception to it and his note of reproof to Wintour read:

> Next we'll have a leader saying that there should be an amalgamation between the *Evening Standard* and the *Evening News*.
> What will be the result of that?
> The circulation of one or the other will disappear. . . .

Wintour put his thoughts in writing in a letter to his chief executive dated 7 February. If the new paper could be the *Standard*, either *in toto* or in essence, then he thought a major victory would have been won. 'If AN [Associated Newspapers] insist that it should be the *Evening News*, what happens then?'

Wintour crystallized the question that had been deliberately left unanswered, and unasked, at the Oxford meeting. The spirit there had been to maximize the common interests and, in Stevens's phrase, 'the industrial logic' of a union. In such a context the issue of journalistic quality could only be embarrassing. Wintour's question remained unanswered for what turned out to be a perilously long time.

In the interim a number of developments occurred that tended to confirm the view of those who considered that the management of Beaverbrook Newspapers was falling apart. As sales of the new *Daily Express* fell away the souped-up optimism that had attended the launch turned to a familiar sinking feeling. On the editorial side the *Daily Mirror* stole the limelight among the tabloids with its serialization of the memoirs of Harold Wilson's former aide Joe Haines, cleverly held back for publication until the first impact of the *Express's* switch to tabloid had passed.

Brian Nicholson, the group's joint deputy managing director, who had been put in charge of the new paper's promotion campaign, felt strongly that more money should be made available for a second campaign. Peter Hetherington opposed any further expenditure. With a loss of £1·5 million forecast for the year, Hetherington won the boardroom argument. Nicholson was offered a major increase in salary to join the *Observer* as joint managing director and accepted with alacrity, though the terms of his departure from Beaverbrook Newspapers had still to be decided. Stevens sent round to the *Observer* a handwritten letter threatening legal action if the paper made a premature disclosure of Nicholson's move.

News of Nicholson's impending departure almost coincided with the information that Tony Dyer, the other joint deputy managing director, was also opting out. After a second heart attack in the previous year Dyer decided on early retirement from the affairs of Beaverbrook Newspapers – before the summer. Two other important managers, Brian Lawrence, the works director, and David Kirkby, general manager of the *Daily Express*, also decided to leave, Lawrence for the *Financial Times* and Kirkby for the London weekly *Time Out*. Within the group it began to seem as if Stevens would not be able to hold an effective management team together.

There was no doubt that some aspects of his style contributed to the general demoralization. All newspapers tend to operate in a hothouse atmosphere, but at Beaverbrook this was pushed to extremes by the long hours and the almost improvisatory way in which the business was often run. Stevens alone was not responsible for this. It was a method of working that could be traced back to Lord Beaverbrook and the way he dealt with his staff. But even if he did not create the atmosphere single-handed, it was one in which Stevens thrived and which his presence accentuated. His rages and transports of joy became an integral part of the way Beaverbrook Newspapers operated. At one time Tony Dyer kept open on his office shelf a page from the *Sunday Times* colour magazine with an article saying that the man most likely to be paranoid was tall, fair-haired and blue-eyed. He had waited for tall, fair-haired, blue-eyed Jocelyn Stevens to notice it, but he never did and the magazine got yellow with age before Dyer removed it.

Stevens was surrounded by stories which, like those about Lord Beaverbrook, were somehow no less true for being apocryphal. The image and the man joined, each feeding off the other. A former Beaverbrook executive recalls telling Stevens that he was a great team player in a team of one. Yet Stevens had operated in the same intensely personal way throughout his career, first at *Queen*, then on the *Standard* and *Daily Express*. The final upward move, to chief executive, had not changed him. It just meant that he worked on a wider canvas.

As a rule Stevens got on better with journalists than he did with managers. Journalists recognized that he had two of the qualities most valuable in a newspaperman – flair and energy – and were more prepared to gloss over his deficiencies. His two most consistent allies at the top of the organization had always been Charles Wintour and Brian Nicholson, who had originally trained as a journalist. On the *Standard* the ebullient Stevens and withdrawn Wintour had complemented each other and carried their complicity into joking exchanges which, one *Standard* journalist recalls, would make them giggle together like school-boys. When the subject of Stevens's erratic behaviour came up on one occasion, Nicholson remarked: 'Jocelyn may be a shit, but he's a likeable shit.'

Managers with day-to-day responsibility for keeping the complex human and mechanical machinery of a modern newspaper going were less easily persuaded of his virtues. The consensus of opinion was that he could be very good when his chairman was resolute – as at the time of the Glasgow closure – but when Sir Max was absent or inclined to let things drift he could be the reverse. His flair for the dramatic, so useful in dealings with journalists and the unions, was often at odds with the more dispassionate requirements of management. As the Beaverbrook crisis deepened so did Stevens's tendency to overreact.

On 10 March the *Daily Mail* published a short item, headlined 'Two top executives to quit Express', with the first public mention of the impending departure of Nicholson and Dyer. It was a fairly innocuous story but Stevens chose to see it as a monstrous example of 'dog-eat-dog' at a delicate stage of negotiations between the two newspaper groups. When the negotiators met in Oxford the following day he was loud in his demands for an apology, threatening legal action if none was forthcoming. Solicitors were consulted and honour was satisfied when the *Mail* subsequently published an apology for not making it sufficiently clear that Dyer's departure was reluctant and on medical advice. It was not, however, a good omen for the prospects of co-operation between the two groups.

A more significant flare-up came three days later, on 14 March, when Stevens went to Manchester for a consultative meeting with chapel leaders there. The meeting was meant to be a confidential session in which both management and men could speak their minds without fear of being reported. When leaders of the printing chapels criticized the editorial content of the *Daily Express*, Stevens said he was not going to argue with them and allowed his frustration to boil over. One of the journalists present logged his remarks, which were soon circulating in Fleet Street's black glass building in a document headed 'Things You Ought to Know'.

It quoted Stevens as having said that the *Daily Express* was dull and not worth its price of 8p. The *Mail* was a better buy. 'I am an angry man. I am unsure whether it is worth going on,' Stevens had said. 'Our internal battles are inexcusable. I can't get the London chapel to understand our crisis. There are too many people making too much money. There is excessive greed.' According to the pamphlet, he had added: 'I am desperate and bitter, but I am not giving up. We may be entering the final chapter of the company. I want that recorded.'

Publication of Stevens's remarks inevitably angered journalists on the *Daily Express* and further undermined morale. It also annoyed the Aitken family and contributed to a feeling among some people at the top of Beaverbrook that their chief executive was running out of control. Hetherington said later: 'Once Sir Max's influence was removed by illness, the reins were off and Jocelyn ran wild.' *Private Eye*'s mocking description of the black glass building as 'Château Despair' did not seem so very far off the mark.

Through it all, the secret negotiations with Associated continued and by the third week in March they had assumed a comprehensive character. The shape of the deal which emerged was basically the same as that originally outlined at Oxford, but with more far-reaching implications. It fell into two parts: Part One provided for Associated to buy the *Evening Standard*, valued at £7·5 million, and for Associated and Beaverbrook to divide the estimated £4·3 million redundancy bill resulting from a merger of the two evening papers.

Part Two had a code name – 'The Black Glass Printing Company'. It envisaged the establishment of a joint company which would buy Beaverbrook's properties and printing plant in Fleet Street. This new company, to be called Fleet Street Printers, would print the *Daily Express*, *Daily Mail*, *Sunday Express* and the merged evening paper. Associated would buy a 50 per cent share in the company, in the process assuming responsibility for half the £8 million loan made to Beaverbrook by the Finance Corporation for Industry.

The agreement would give Associated the profits of a monopoly London evening paper and the benefits of joint, modern printing machinery, while Beaverbrook would be able to keep its presses busy, cut costs through shared overheads and concentrate all its efforts on using the cash inflow, estimated at £10 million, to make the *Daily Express* profitable. Another attraction for Beaverbrook was Associated's promise not to start a competitor to the *Sunday Express* for three and a half years. On the property side, the editorial staffs of the merged evening paper and the *Daily Mail* would move into Beaverbrook's office development in Aitken House, which was still largely empty. But Associated's property gains from the development of its three prime sites behind Fleet Street, with a capital value estimated at up to £100 million, would overshadow any income Beaverbrook might gain.

The physical proximity of the newspapers – produced on the same presses and with their editorial staffs in adjoining buildings – would mark the final coming together of the hereditary opponents. Not surprisingly one of Jocelyn Stevens's files of working papers was marked 'Romeo and Juliet'. If the Montagues and Capulets of Fleet Street were to get as close as envisaged under the Black Glass Printing Company, there would be little to hold them back from the ultimate union, of the *Daily Express* and the *Daily Mail*.

Seen in the light of commercial and industrial logic, the case seemed overwhelming. At Associated there was increasing confidence that the Harmsworths were about to establish themselves as the dominant force in the middle of the national newspaper market and to rediscover the goldmine which

Northcliffe had tapped when he founded the *Daily Mail* 80 years earlier.

At Beaverbrook, the sick chairman had finally been told about the negotiations. When Stevens and Hetherington made the revelation Sir Max Aitken asked why a deal had to be made with Associated. His joint deputy chairmen told him that things were very bad. A deal was necessary if Beaverbrook was to survive in some form. They also, Stevens recalls, mentioned the possible threat from Goldsmith. They left with the feeling that Sir Max was not opposed to what they were doing. That was a relief for Stevens. He had become steadily more enamoured of the agreement which was emerging from the talks with Associated. 'I was', he said later, 'in the position of an architect who falls in love with the design of his own building – perhaps without enough regard for what was to go on inside.'

Charles Wintour, in contrast, was becoming increasingly unhappy about the architecture of the whole deal. On 18 March he expressed his concern in a letter to Sir Max Aitken's solicitor:

Dear Lord Goodman,

Jocelyn Stevens has kindly kept me informed about the general progress of negotiations with Associated Newspapers. Obviously the proposals under discussion would represent an immense coup for Beaverbrook Newspapers.

But as you can imagine the point that concerns me is the identity of the surviving evening newspaper. If it is to be the *Evening Standard*, then there are no problems. The present editor and editorial staff can perfectly well maintain the character and quality and integrity of the paper under different ownership and management.

If however the survivor under the scheme were to be the *Evening News*, then a great injustice is contemplated and an act which is clearly contrary to the public interest. For the *Evening Standard* is close to breaking even now while the *Evening News* by all accounts is making desperate losses. Above all the *Evening Standard* does attempt to play some serious role in the life of the community and the *Evening News* does not.

If therefore the deal involved closure of the *Evening Standard*, I would clearly have to oppose it and I would do so on the gronds that another buyer might be found, and that the *Evening Standard* need not stop publication. Whether this would lead to delays in securing Department of Trade approval for the arrangement under the Monopolies legislation, I don't know, but it is a possibility.

I am sending a copy of this letter to Jocelyn Stevens who is already aware of my view and understands my reasons.

The letter was delivered to Goodman by Stevens at the next negotiating session on 21 March. On the following day Wintour and Stevens had a late-morning conference with Goodman at his office in Little Essex Street. News of Sir Max's condition was still discouraging – after being allowed home he had had a relapse and been forced to return to hospital. Once again they had to guess at his desires in the matter. Goodman wanted to know what might be considered the heart of the *Evening Standard*. Wintour thought it might be the editor and 12 executives, though the editor, Simon Jenkins, might wish to nominate 50 per cent of the staff.

The talks between the three men ranged over various possibilities, including an arrangement under which Beaverbrook would keep the *Standard* and sell the *Daily Express* to Associated, with both companies taking an interest in each other's newspapers. It was not an idea which appealed to Vere Harmsworth when Goodman put it to him. Harmsworth wanted to acquire the *Standard* and create a monopoly evening paper in London. New permutations could be worked out almost endlessly as a theoretical exercise, but any deal with Associated would clearly come down to one basic first step – ceding the *Standard*.

Tuesday, 22 March was also the day on which Simon Jenkins first learned that his newspaper was threatened by a prospective deal with Associated Newspapers. Charles Wintour told him. As he was so young, still only 33 and fresh to the job, it might have been thought that Jenkins would easily fall in with whatever was decided by his superiors in the company. He was, however, a man of independent judgement.

The son of a clergyman, Jenkins had been educated at Mill Hill and St John's College, Oxford, where he took a degree in politics, philosophy and economics. He had done postgraduate research in Sussex and London before making a relatively late entry into journalism. He worked briefly on *Country Life* and was news editor of the *Times Educational Supplement* before moving to the *Evening Standard* where his gravitas at an early age on the leader page staff of the *Standard* had attracted the benign attention of Charles Wintour.

Within four years Jenkins had risen to the post of features editor and established himself as a writer about London's architectural heritage and the threats posed to it by modern development. This interest was developed in two books, *A City at Risk* and *Landlords to London*, the second of which had some uncomplimentary things to say about Beaverbrook's favoured property developer, Sir Max Rayne. Jenkins's journalistic range widened when he went to edit the *Sunday Times* Insight section for a year, but he was back at the *Evening Standard* by 1975, as deputy editor. A crisp, composed young man, his outstanding passion was the city served by his newspaper: 'One of the things I regret about my life', he told an interviewer, 'is that I was born in Birmingham.'

Wintour and Jenkins jointly decided that their best course of action would be to seek alternatives to the framework imposed by the Associated deal. In simple turns this meant finding another potential proprietor for the *Evening Standard*. As Wintour had told Goodman, the emergence of another bidder would at least mean that the Associated deal had to be referred to the Monopolies Commission. Although their efforts did not have the full authority of the Beaverbrook board behind them, they were not wholly clandestine – Stevens was told of their intentions and gave a qualified blessing. At the very least they would help to keep the Associated negotiators under pressure. There was also emotional appeal to the enterprise. The brave little *Standard* looked a more suitable case for sympathy than the complacent *Sunday Express* and the ungainly *Daily Express*. Stevens's metaphor for the initiative was: 'Laying our tender goat upon the altar while concealing the fat old sow and the huge mangy camel.'

Wintour's first call was on Lord Barnetson, a former editor who had risen to the chairmanship of the prosperous United Newspapers provincial chain. United Newspapers had no interest in buying the *Standard*, but Barnetson had become chairman of the *Observer* after the Atlantic Richfield take-over the previous year and Wintour wondered whether the philanthropic oil men of Los Angeles might be interested. Barnetson estimated that £5 million would be needed to put the *Standard* right. He thought Atlantic Richfield would not want any more problems on top of those it had bought with the *Observer*, but he agreed to check. On 25 March, Barnetson telephoned Wintour to say that the decision was, as he had forecast, negative.

During their initial talk Barnetson had asked about some other possible saviours for the *Standard*, notably Rupert Murdoch and Goldsmith. Wintour noted later that he and Barnetson had agreed that Murdoch was busy with his recent acquisitions in New York and that 'Goldsmith was unacceptable'. Both were to come into the Beaverbrook picture at a later date, but in late March Wintour looked elsewhere for help.

He went to see Gordon Brunton, managing director of the Thomson Organisation in Britain. Brunton was friendly and complimentary about the *Standard*. He agreed that *The Times*, owned by the Thomson family, and the *Standard* were compatible editorially. His main concern, however, was not to buy new papers, but to get labour-saving computer technology installed at *The Times* and *Sunday Times*. The message was made all the clearer when Jenkins saw Sir Denis Hamilton, chairman of Times Newspapers. Hamilton knew that his managerial team was already at full stretch. He was concerned about the 'grey faces' round him and was not going to add the *Standard*'s worries to the existing ones. 'I hope I was a good listener,' Hamilton says about his conversation with Jenkins. 'But I just kept a sphinx face.'

Wintour's contacts with the S. Pearson conglomerate, owners of the *Financial Times* and the Westminster Press provincial chain, produced more expressions of sympathy but, once again, no concrete promise of support.

It was a bad time to be peddling problems round Fleet Street. Most managements were obsessed with the complexities presented by the new technology, to the exclusion of most other concerns. For them the future lay in introducing computer-based techniques, not in acquiring a struggling London evening paper. Earlier in the year the Joint Standing Committee of the Newspaper Publishers Association (NPA) and union general secretaries had produced a report, 'Programme for Action', laying down guidelines for the phased introduction of the new technology. To nobody's great surprise, these forward-looking proposals were rejected by Fleet Street chapels, with the exception of the journalists. A concerted solution to Fleet Street's manning problems looked as remote as ever and management enthusiasm for joint initiatives naturally declined. The Mirror Group pursued its own private route to modernization as the *Financial Times* had been doing. The NPA was weakened by distrust and disputes which led the Mirror Group and Murdoch's News International to threaten to leave. Most newspaper groups were experiencing a marked increase in unofficial disruption, which in many cases could be traced to the impending threat to jobs posed by the new technology. Disputes in Fleet Street, most of them unofficial, resulted in the loss of 45 million copies of national newspapers in the six months of the autumn and winter of 1976/7. The mood of the period was aptly symbolized by Mark Boxer with his cartoon in *The Times* of a reporter barking down a telephone to his office: 'Hold the front page – if there is one. . . .' In such an atmosphere the problems of the *Standard* might excite sympathy but not the will to deal with them.

By the end of March the Wintour-Jenkins quest for alternative possibilities seemed to be going nowhere. Jenkins suggested two new courses of action that did not involve established Fleet Street managements – an attempt to get Goldsmith to give a clear statement of his attitude towards the *Evening Standard* on the question of editorial independence, and a sounding-out approach to Nigel Broackes, the chairman of Trafalgar House. Wintour gave him the go-ahead on both. Neither he nor Jenkins was aware that Stevens and Hetherington had discussed the Beaverbrook position with Victor Matthews at Trafalgar some months earlier. Life at Beaverbrook Newspapers was starting to go round in circles.

SIX

A Spring Holiday

EVERYONE AGREED THAT Jocelyn Stevens needed and deserved a holiday. He had worked frantically hard on the talks with Associated in an attempt to supply Vere Harmsworth's gargantuan appetite for detail and by the fourth week in March the negotiations seemed on the brink of completion.

Secrecy on the whole operation had been well preserved. An intelligent article in the 4 March issue of the advertising weekly *Campaign* on the problems of the London evening paper market had charmed Beaverbrook's security-conscious board of directors. The writer suggested that Associated and Beaverbrook might sensibly pool distribution and marketing costs in this field. 'And', ran his peroration, 'as the two publishers work more closely together perhaps an even more radical solution will occur to them: a *single* London evening, jointly owned.' On 25 March *Campaign* ran a news item quoting Stevens as confirming that talks were going on about possible co-operation between the *News* and *Standard*. The report also said that the discussions were confined to cost-saving measures such as joint distribution and specifically excluded the merger of the two evening papers.

There was also better news of Sir Max Aitken's condition. He was out of hospital and fit enough to undertake a tough daily course of physiotherapy at his Westminster flat in Marsham Court. Vere Harmsworth was going off to Canada for a fortnight and there seemed no good reason why Stevens should not enjoy some rest and relaxation on his own account.

He left London on 25 March for a ski-ing holiday at Sir Max's chalet in the Austrian resort of St Anton. As a parting thrust, Stevens told Associated that he was going to see Rupert Murdoch. He did not in fact do so, but the suggestion was designed to prevent Vere Harmsworth from becoming too confident. As it turned out, Jocelyn Stevens was the one who should have been guarding against over-confidence.

The heir to the Aitken inheritance thought it was time to look for a new arrangement at the top of Beaverbrook Newspapers.

On the day after Stevens's departure Maxwell Aitken paid a Saturday visit to his father at Cowes and formed the impression that Sir Max was prepared to see changes in the leadership of the company. On his return from the coast, Maxwell Aitken contacted Peter Hetherington, Beaverbrook's most senior executive after Stevens. 'He telephoned me in the country to say that he must see me most urgently that day,' Hetherington recalled. 'I was in bed with 'flu and since he pressed for a meeting I agreed to see him on the Sunday afternoon. He came from Cherkley to my home near Haslemere and told me of his visit to his father, and that it was the family's wish that Jocelyn Stevens should be removed.' Although he is emphatic that the impetus for the move against Stevens came from the Aitkens, it was a development that Hetherington welcomed. He felt relieved that somebody else had said what he had been thinking. 'It took the lid off the simmering saucepan,' he recalled.

It was now time to bring a newspaper professional to join the accountant and the family heir.

Tony Dyer was the automatic choice. He had started his working life as a circulation representative and had risen to be personal assistant to Tom Blackburn, going on to manage the *Sunday Express* and then the *Daily Express*, with a seat on the Beaverbrook board. He was the solid, competent professional who could deal with the nuts and bolts of newspaper production and sales. He was respected by union leaders and Fleet Street colleagues outside Beaverbrook. Inside the firm he was regarded as the essential counterweight to Stevens. Apart from his experience, Dyer was of major value to the move against Stevens precisely because he was known as a 'straight man', an honest and dependable figure who would act only from the best of motives.

Dyer's formal resignation from the company, mainly on health grounds, was due to take place on 1 June, but he still took an active interest in its affairs. Shortly after submitting his resignation he had a tête-à-tête lunch with Hetherington to discuss his departure. Hetherington asked Dyer what he thought should be done to strengthen Beaverbrook. Speaking with the freedom of a man about to leave, Dyer said he thought that a strong management group should be created to take over the actual running of the organization and that Stevens should be moved away from immediate operational involvement. His basic concern was to stem the outflow of managers who could not stand the nervous strain or the physical exhaustion that came from working with Stevens.

At Hetherington's request, Dyer agreed to see the chairman and state his views. The meeting took place at Marsham Court at 10.15 am on 31 March. The next day Dyer, Hetherington and Maxwell Aitken saw each other in the morning. In the afternoon they met Sir Max again. By the evening of Friday, 1 April the coup against Jocelyn Stevens was firmly launched.

Those involved in the move to get rid of Stevens all say that it was not connected directly with the Associated talks. Rather it was the outcome of dissatisfaction with the way Stevens was running the company and the desire to put a different structure and different men in his place. But the Associated negotiations were bound to play a part in any thinking about the future of Beaverbrook Newspapers. Maxwell Aitken was concerned that they were not going at their proper speed. Peter Hetherington was not completely happy with the shape they were taking. He felt that the combined draft which he had drawn up with Stevens at the end of 1976 was not being properly implemented. 'There was a wonderful deal there, but it was watered down,' he said later. He also felt that more could have been made of the interest expressed by Victor Matthews of Trafalgar House.

Over the next few days there were other significant comings and goings at Marsham Court. Lord Goodman visited Sir Max, as did Evelyn de Rothschild. Given his condition it was hard to make a specific reading of the chairman's intentions, but he did give the impression of favouring change. Roy Wright, who was a director of Beaverbrook as well as editor of the *Daily Express*, was also among the visitors. The chairman was particularly incensed by Stevens's reported remarks to the Manchester unions that the *Mail* was to be preferred to the *Express*. 'This was too much,' he told Wright and Rothschild. Sir Max gave the impression that he had steeled himself to get rid of Stevens and put Hetherington in his place.

What was envisaged after Stevens had gone was a new structure with Hetherington as chairman, or as deputy chairman effectively exercising a chairman's authority. Dyer would become managing director, or alternatively joint managing director with Maxwell Aitken. As the discussions ranged from getting rid of Stevens to the structure which would subsequently be put in place, there was no mistaking Maxwell Aitken's eagerness for action. Dyer recalls that during the discussions Sir Max had a fall. Dyer and Hetherington suggested that, as he now seemed even more unlikely to be able to continue as chairman, somebody should take his place, and that the anti-Stevens move should be postponed until it was seen how things worked out under a new chairman. According to Dyer, Maxwell Aitken was strongly averse to any change of plan, saying: 'This is bigger than my father's health or than anyone's health.'

No attempt was made to draw Charles Wintour into the enterprise. Stevens's other main boardroom ally, Brian Nicholson, still working out his notice before joining the *Observer*, also escaped the shot and shell. He took off for a spring holiday motoring with his sons through northern France to drink champagne in Rheims.

Jocelyn Stevens felt uneasy as he flew back from Austria to London on the morning of Tuesday, 5 April. He had been struck by the unusual, embarrassed tones of voice which he had detected during his telephone talks about company business from St Anton with Hetherington and Dyer. He had also received a phone call from Sir Max. The chairman had told him not to hurry back. On his last night at the ski resort Stevens had dined with the banker Charles Hambro, who had asked him if he was going back to work. 'It could be for the last time,' he replied. Later Hambro assumed that Stevens had known what was about to happen. But Stevens says he had no specific cause for anxiety as he stepped off the plane at Heathrow, just a gut feeling.

His driver was waiting for him at the airport with a message:

Mr Hetherington would like Mr Stevens to call at the Mayfair office of his accountancy firm in Green Street. 'He has something important to tell you,' the chauffeur added. Stevens thought the invitation strange and wondered why Hetherington wanted to meet him in Mayfair rather than at the *Express* building. Perhaps, he concluded, there had been a development in the Associated talks and a meeting had been arranged away from Fleet Street for security reasons.

When Stevens arrived Hetherington told him the Beaverbrook board had decided he was overworked and that it would be in his best interests to leave the company. There was no need for him to return to Fleet Street – his personal effects would be sent on to him at home. Maxwell Aitken and Dyer were waiting downstairs to back Hetherington. They came up and confirmed what Hetherington had said. It was suggested that Stevens's stressful style of decision-making was responsible for seven vacancies on the management side of the company. He was also reproved for spending too much time with 'less weighty' directors such as Charles Wintour and Brian Nicholson. Wintour was criticized for sending 'hundreds' of critical memos to Roy Wright about the conduct of the *Daily Express*. (When told of the charge later Wintour said: 'It was only about twenty.')

Stevens refused to accept the notice of dismissal. His next move was to go straight to the *Express* building in Fleet Street. After he had left Hetherington telephoned Sir Max Aitken to tell him that Stevens had refused to accept his dismissal. From the conversation he got the clear impression that Sir Max would see Stevens the next day and sack him. The coup had misfired at the first attempt, but it seemed only to have been suspended for 24 hours.

Once back in Fleet Street Stevens was reassured by the fact that the commissionaires in the front hall didn't try to stop him going up to his office. He reasoned that if there had been a firm decision that he should go, they would have been told not to let him in. He telephoned Charles Wintour to find out whether the board had met in his absence. Wintour, hearing about the coup attempt for the first time, told him there had been no meeting. Stevens then confirmed a meeting with Sir Max arranged for the next morning. After that, he went to the Mansion House for dinner.

The host at the Mansion House was the Lord Mayor of London, Sir Robin Gillett, on behalf of his firm, the insurance company Wigham Poland. It was a city tradition that the Lord Mayor gave a dinner for his own company during his term of office. Since Cavenham Foods had a controlling interest in Wigham Poland, Sir James Goldsmith was naturally among the guests. The prospect of seeing Goldsmith had been one of the factors bringing Stevens back from St Anton. But the guests at the Mansion House also included people from whom Stevens was anxious to keep news of what had happened that afternoon, among them Vere Harmsworth and Arnold Goodman.

There was no possibility of any real exchange of intimacies with Goldsmith at the dinner, but Stevens managed to convey the essence of the situation. Goldsmith had heard rumours that a move against Stevens was being planned at Beaverbrook, but he said he was 'utterly amazed' when told of the day's events. Although it was only 10 weeks since their last explosive encounter in Charles Hambro's flat, the two men easily reverted to the 'Jimmy' and 'Jocelyn' terms that had previously characterized their relationship. They might fall out when their interests clashed, but basically they understood one another.

They were also aware that their interests might shortly coincide. 'My loyalties', Stevens said later, 'were shattered at that point.' At the suggestion of Jacob Rothschild, Evelyn's cousin, they decided to go on to a party which might afford greater privacy for their discussion.

Hamayoun Mazandi, the socialite wife of a Persian diplomat, who had acquired a certain notoriety in the London cab trade by her habit of hiring taxis to guide her chauffeur-driven Rolls-Royce around town, was giving one of her lavish parties at her home in Chester Square. Once inside the Mazandis' residence Goldsmith and Stevens holed up in an unoccupied room that contained the guests' coats to discuss the affairs of Beaverbrook Newspapers into the small hours.

There was much ground to be covered. Since their last meeting in January Goldsmith had demonstrated the seriousness of his intentions as a publisher by buying into the group headed by *L'Express*, France's leading news magazine. His 45 per cent shareholding, which had reportedly cost £3·64 million, was enough to give him effective control over *L'Express*, and make him the successor to the maverick politician–publisher Jean-Jacques Servan-Schreiber. *Le Nouvel Economiste* had hailed the change: 'Après J.-J. Voici Jimmy.' Despite his enlarged responsibilities Goldsmith's appetite for Beaverbrook had not diminished. If anything it had sharpened. The incentive now was not only to acquire a national newspaper but also to take revenge on another. Goldsmith did not like the *Daily Mail* and was particularly averse to its celebrated gossip columnist, Nigel Dempster. Goldsmith described himself as 'a very reliable life-long enemy' of Dempster and anything that prevented the expansion of the *Daily Mail*'s interests could, in his view, only be a force for good. His instinct, as well as his business interest, was opposed to a Beaverbrook–Associated deal.

As far as Stevens's current situation was concerned Goldsmith pledged his support but still felt unable to do anything along the lines of a rescue operation for the company without some positive signal from Sir Max Aitken himself.

Next morning, Wednesday, 6 April, Stevens went to see his chairman at Marsham Court. According to Stevens it was a tense encounter: 'I was in a cold-blooded rage.' His anger was not directed at Sir Max, although the chairman had clearly allowed the move against him to develop, but against Hetherington. 'I couldn't wait to get my hands round Hetherington's throat.'

Sir Max started by telling Stevens: 'They've been at me every day. They've been trying to get rid of you.'

Stevens immediately felt relieved. The tense Sir Max had used and the word 'they' told him that his chairman was distancing himself from his opponents.

He asked what Sir Max thought.

Sir Max, according to Stevens, replied: 'Well, I'll tell you what they have been saying – you're working too hard, driving them too hard, causing heart attacks. Hetherington says the Associated negotiations could be better handled.'

'What do you want?' Stevens asked.

'I want you to stay,' Sir Max replied.

Stevens told Sir Max that if he was to stay, Hetherington and Dyer would have to go. For his son, Maxwell, a special arrangement should be made. Stevens proposed, and Sir Max endorsed, an accelerated promotion to the rank of joint managing director of the whole group, making him Stevens's immediate deputy.

The Aitken heir would go everywhere with his chief executive. In this way Stevens hoped to ensure that there was no possibility of a manoeuvre behind his back. Equally, his new status would give young Maxwell a ringside seat in the battles that lay ahead. Stevens gaily described the job of his deputy as a punishment, 'the worst in Fleet Street'. But there were compensations: Maxwell Aitken's salary rose from £8,200 to £22,500 a year.

Stevens's first move after his restoration was to send for Hetherington and tell him his time was up. His next engagement was to accept a cheque from the National Coal Board pension fund for the sale of Beaverbrook's successful property development at Tollgate House in Bristol. During a celebratory lunch that followed in the *Express* building Stevens, Hetherington, Maxwell Aitken and Dyer, the Beaverbrook directors present, had to behave as though nothing unusual was going on. It was a particularly tense meal for Dyer because he had no idea of what had happened between Stevens and Sir Max. He found it ominous that Maxwell Aitken deliberately avoided his eye throughout the lunch.

After the meal it rapidly became clear that Stevens's authority had been restored. As soon as he realized that the coup had failed, Hetherington left a resignation letter with Sir Max's secretary and sent a similar telegram to Stevens's home address. At 5.15 pm Stevens and Maxwell Aitken met Vere Harmsworth and his team under Goodman's chairmanship as planned. As the Beaverbrook pair arrived, somebody asked the whereabouts of their third negotiator, Hetherington. 'He's gone to see his mother,' replied Stevens.

On Thursday, 7 April Stevens further cemented his position by taking Maxwell to see his father. 'In case there is any doubt,' he remembers telling the Aitken heir, 'I want you to hear from your father what he thinks of this dirty little plot.' As the two men prepared to leave the *Express* building, Stevens lingered for a brief private word with Charles Wintour. Stevens said: 'The Aitkens are nearing the end of the road.'

After he had taken Maxwell to see his father Stevens had a final appointment – the annual dinner-dance of Beaverbrook's production overseers. It was another occasion on which appearances had to be maintained. As Stevens recalled: 'All executives appeared smiling.'

For Tony Dyer, the loyal, life-long Beaverbrook servant, the rewards of what had appeared to be his final duty to the Aitkens were bitter. When Dyer saw Maxwell Aitken a few days after the failure of the coup, the chairman's son seemed content to be working directly for the man he had been trying to get rid of a few days earlier. According to Dyer, Aitken said his new post was better than the one he would have had if the coup had worked. 'Don't worry,' he told Dyer. 'We always look after people.' Under the circumstances, Dyer found little comfort in the reassurance. On 9 April Dyer wrote a long letter to Stevens with copies to Sir Max, Maxwell Aitken and Hetherington. The contents reflected the bitterness of his feelings:

Dear Jocelyn,

On Maundy Thursday morning you said to me 'The plotters are defeated and now they must go. You must revert to the arrangement for leaving on 1st June. I cannot trust you behind my back.'

I completely refute the implications and totally reserve my position.

The Chairman, his son, the Joint Deputy Chairman Peter Hetherington (who I regret to learn has resigned), Mrs. Westover [Sir Max's secretary], Directors and executives can testify to statements and actions which do not support the assertion.

If your claim is that I have at times been critical – and to your face – that I accept.

However I am now more concerned about the effect of your Thursday statement on my position, emoluments, pension and my future.

Exactly seven days beforehand the Chairman asked me to explain my position. I told him that I had been advised to give up my present role and its attendant stresses. I had to say that the same function under a person other than yourself would not be too onerous for my health. I was considering the change with great reluctance. I had maintained a slightly different 'Public Front' for the sake of the company image and out of respect for you.

He asked me if I would be prepared to continue working under you in different circumstances or to take up a position as Managing Director of the Newspapers and in conjunction with Maxwell Aitken, run the group while responsible to a Deputy Chairman.

I asked for forty-eight hours to consider the situation – was given twenty-four and met the Chairman again at Marsham Court.

I accepted that I would carry out either function for a period of up to five years when there would be a joint review of performance and health. I was thanked.

These offers, and my acceptance, were made known to some other Directors and members of the Foundation – not by me. It was also known that I had, during the past few days, stressed concern for the maintenance of the company's image, for the Chairman's health and indeed for your own health and well-being. At one stage I even advocated (together with Peter Hetherington) that for some of these reasons nothing should be changed.

Since my acceptance of this proposal I have heard nothing from the Chairman. I can only conclude that he has changed his mind.

I have moreover had it suggested that some of the functions it had previously been proposed should become my responsibility in a consultative capacity, will now be carried out by another.

In all these confusing and unreasonable circumstances I feel that I am entitled, on my return, to a written statement clearly setting out my future options and relationships with the company. If my duties are to change or be terminated, I wish to have a statement to this effect, setting out the reasons and any terms proposed.

My letter should be addressed to the Chairman but I have to assume you are acting on his behalf. At no other time during my twenty-four years with the company would I have considered such action should be necessary and I greatly regret it should be so now. I write with a feeling of some resentment and the knowledge that I have been 'used'.

Anything I have done has been through concern for the company, the Aitken family and many colleagues. I have nothing to be ashamed of and nothing I regret. I hope this remains unchanged.

Dyer stayed with the company for the rest of year but lost his position and authority. In the final analysis, however valid the motives of the participants, the coup did not deserve to succeed because it was so ineptly organized. The lack of a motion passed by the board, or a piece of paper signed by Sir Max, to formalize Stevens's dismissal was a major failure on the part of those who wanted to get rid of him. The omission was all the more striking because of the way in which the directors of the International Publishing Corporation had ousted the much more dominating figure of Cecil King a few years earlier by holding a secret board meeting and presenting their chairman with a *fait accompli*.

The other serious miscalculation was to underestimate the strength of the connection between Sir Max and Jocelyn Stevens, which ultimately proved stronger than that between Sir Max and his own son. Exasperation with Stevens was part of the price Sir Max paid for being exhilarated by him at other times. It did not necessarily mean that he wanted to get rid of him.

The urbane Brian Nicholson, who breezed back from his French holiday after the carnage was over, later gave the most elegant interpretation of Sir Max's role in the coup: 'He did not want Jocelyn to go. He just wanted to have a go at Jocelyn.'

At the end of the first week in April the number of people who wanted to have a go at Jocelyn Stevens was vastly increased by the first public mention of the Associated talks. On 6 April *The Times* carried a well-informed story on its front page mentioning merger talks between Beaverbrook and Associated with the closure of one evening paper as a possible outcome. The story underrated the progress that had been made when it said that experts were producing plans and that executives of the two groups were not yet involved. It was still enough to set off intense speculation in Fleet Street and chill the staffs of the two evening papers.

SEVEN

A Naked Lunch

Consultation procedures abounded on both London evening papers. The men, through their union representatives, could easily meet the management to embroider a wide variety of fringe benefits including holiday pay, expense allowances, days in lieu and the minutiae of staff canteen menus. The one thing they had not discussed in the early months of 1977 was whether there would be any fringe left to benefit from by the end of the spring.

For the vast majority of employees *The Times*'s scoop of 6 April gave them their first real inkling that their actual livelihoods might be at stake. That was the tradition in such matters. When closures were pending the Fleet Street management style had often been to act now, consult later. It did not make the immediate reality any easier to bear.

The story in *The Times* was written by Sheila Black, an able newspaperperson who had made her way in a man's world long before Women's Lib was invented. She had learned her trade on the *Financial Times* and had come to be on first-name terms with most Fleet Street proprietors. She also had a talent for making friends easily – and keeping them – which sometimes meant that she knew more in private than could be revealed in public. Years earlier, when she was writing a financial column for Jocelyn Stevens's *Queen*, she received a better offer from the rival publication *Vogue*. She lunched with Jocelyn to discuss the offer and got the full treatment. The faithful old hands were deserting him in droves and going to rival organizations. Whatever had become of old-fashioned virtues like loyalty, asked Jocelyn.

Sheila Black, who likes a moving ceremony, declined the *Vogue* offer and kept the friendship with Jocelyn, watching his climb up Fleet Street's greasy pole with amused affection. 'The wonderful thing about Jocelyn', she says, 'is that he loves to plot but there is no malice in him.'

In February 1977 Stevens related to Ms Black a story which had been successfully kept from the editor and staff of the *Evening Standard* – the negotiations with Associated, with the possibility of an evening paper closure, were on again, this time in earnest. The information was given in confidence, but Jocelyn wanted Ms Black's opinion on how long the completion of such a deal might take. Drawing on her experience as a business journalist, she suggested three months, since last-minute bids always came in to complicate apparently cut-and-dried situations. Stevens was aghast, saying that none of the directors could bear the strain for much more than a couple of weeks. In any event there was no chance of *this* deal coming unstuck – 'We're talking about two great newspaper families, you know, not a couple of paint firms.' Ms Black said he'd be surprised to find how similar they were to paint firms in times of crisis. Take-over situations are great levellers.

With the story safely in her possession Ms Black deftly set about the task of confirming it with other sources in the business world and government, some of which she had through her part-time membership of the Prices Commission. By the end of March she knew she was in possession of more than just another of Jocelyn's tall tales. She rang Stevens to say that she proposed to break the story at the earliest opportunity. Stevens hoped she wouldn't but felt in no position to argue. Journalism, after all, was supposed to be about disclosure.

In the rancorous weeks that lay ahead Sheila Black was to receive some stick from Fleet Street colleagues for allegedly writing off the *Evening Standard*'s chances of survival on insufficient evidence. But the story was accurate enough at the time and a genuine news break which blew the whistle on the secret talks. Indeed without her scoop it is hard to see how any effective opposition could have been mobilized in time.

The other 'quality' dailies weighed in with their own interpretations of what was going on. There was a lot of groping in the dark. Neither the Associated board nor the Beaverbrook board could be lured into commenting and the *Guardian* story, by Philip Jordan, recalled that Stevens had once said that anyone suggesting a merger of the two groups 'must be off his head'. But in the topsyturvy world of Fleet Street there was nothing to prevent yesterday's lunacy from becoming tomorrow's reality. Jordan extracted one quote from a Beaverbrook executive who said that anyone hearing any news of the deal might let him know, as 'I'd be fascinated to hear'.

That lone voice was speaking for quite a lot of interests. Indeed one of the main impediments to full consultation when take-overs or closures take place in Fleet Street has always been the multiplicity of interests involved in the production of a single newspaper. Most managements are obliged to deal with at least seven unions, which are in turn subdivided into numerous branches and chapels on each paper. The main ones are the Society of Graphical and Allied Trades (SOGAT), with five chapels comprising combined publishing, inside publishing, outside publishing, circulation representatives and proof pullers; the National Society of Printing and Allied Trades (NATSOPA) with eleven chapels comprising general assistants, women cleaners, clerical, commissionaires and telephonists, fire and security, night machine assistants, day machine assistants, copy readers and revisers, dark room, engineer assistants and linotype assistants; the National Graphical Association (NGA), with eight chapels, comprising the imperial chapel, case hands, lino operators, time hands, readers, telecommunications, foundry and machine managers; the Society of Lithographic and Allied Trades (SLADE), comprising the process chapel; the Electrical, Electronic, telecommunications and Plumbing Union (EETPU); the Amalgamated Union of Engineering and Foundry Workers (AUEW); and the National Union of Journalists (NUJ).

The first direct union response to the news of an impending deal between Associated and Beaverbrook came from the NUJ chapel committee of the *Evening News*. Within hours of reading *The Times*'s story Michael Rothwell, the father of the chapel (FoC), wrote to Mick Shields, the managing director of Associated Newspapers, in the following terms: 'I have been instructed by my chapel committee to write to you about expectation in Fleet Street of an imminent merger or other combination or financial arrangement with Beaverbrook group. Such expectations have hardened with the story in today's

Times. . . . .' In his second paragraph he went on to ask the management to commit itself to a policy of no compulsory redundancies in advance of any major change. He concluded by asking for a reply by 3.30 pm to put before the next chapel committee meeting.

The reply came from E. J. Winnington-Ingram, managing director of the newspaper side of Associated. It was a model of managerial reticence. After explaining that he was replying in the absence of Shields, Winnington-Ingram wrote that if a matter arose on which the unions should be advised, Associated would do so. Referring to Rothwell's request for a commitment to no compulsory redundancies, Winnington-Ingram merely stated that Associated was aware of the contents of its agreements with the NUJ.

The very blandness of the reply alerted Rothwell. He had conducted similar exercises in the past when there had been rumours of closure or redundancy, but on those occasions management had shown shocked surprise at any suspicion of concealed intentions on its part. Leafing through his chapel files Rothwell disinterred a similar exchange with Winnington-Ingram back in January 1976, when the *Guardian* had floated a rumour about early closure of the *Evening News*. On that occasion Winnington-Ingram's letter had opened: 'I was surprised as you were to read the story in this morning's *Guardian*,' and had ended, reassuringly, 'You are right in saying in your letter that if there were any substance in a matter of this kind, your Union and others involved would be among the first to be put in the picture.'

Rothwell was not a particularly cynical man but he had been around a long time. Before coming to the *News*, where he wrote about City affairs, he had spent over two years in industrial public relations, specializing in defences against take-over bids. The difference in tone between Winnington-Ingram vintage 1976 and Winnington-Ingram vintage 1977 was too ominous to be ignored. Rothwell's opinion was that something of substance was going on and that the management, for reasons of its own, wanted his union to be among the last to be put in the picture. It was not a comforting thought, and with the Easter holidays coming up there was not much time to improvise a counter strategy.

The old crusader: Lord Beaverbrook and his wife attend a banquet to honour his eighty-fifth birthday at the Dorchester Hotel in London, May 1964.

The hereditary press barons: Sir Max Aitken (*above right*), the Beaverbrook proprietor, with his solicitor and friend Lord Goodman. Vere Harmsworth (*opposite page*), the boss of Associated Newspapers, with Lord Goodman. In 1977 the two proprietors, with Goodman acting as go-between, aimed to merge part of their empires. The deal, which involved closure of the *Evening Standard*, was strongly opposed by the paper's former editor, Charles Wintour (*below left*).

The would-be saviours: among the multi-millionaires who offered themselves as rescuers of the ailing Beaverbrook empire were Sir James Goldsmith (*left*), the elegant boss of Cavenham Foods, Rupert Murdoch (*below*), the tough Australian newspaper proprietor, and Roland 'Tiny' Rowland (*opposite right*), the unpredictable chief of the Lonrho conglomerate.

Roy Hattersley: the Labour government's Prices Minister who was responsible for vetting newspaper deals.

Lord Robens: the former Labour politician who played an influential role in the take-over struggle as a Beaverbrook trustee.

Simon Jenkins: Fleet Street's youngest editor who ran the *Evening Standard* throughout the crisis that threatened to close the newspaper.

Jocelyn Stevens: Beaverbrook's extraordinary Chief Executive who was Sir Max Aitken's closest adviser after displacing John Coote (*insert right*).

The new crusader: Victor Matthews of Trafalgar House, the group that emerged victorious in the take-over battle for Beaverbrook Newspapers.

Rothwell and his chapel officials went through the motions of spreading alarm without, if possible, creating despondency. The full chapel met and was informed that 'fundamental talks' were going on that might affect all their futures. The other NUJ chapels potentially affected – on the *Express*, the *Daily Mail* and the *Evening Standard* – were circulated with reminders of the need to put up their guard. The National Executive of the NUJ was contacted and urged to bring the TUC Printing Industries Committee, which included print and journalistic representation, into the struggle. A letter was prepared and rushed round to Whitehall by hand for inclusion in the box of Roy Hattersley, the Prices Minister, as part of his holiday reading. It asked Hattersley for an assurance that if ownership of any of the newspaper titles were changed, he would refer the matter to the Monopolies Commission for full investigation.

Easter came and went without further incident, although the Sunday papers provided further grist to the rumour mill. The *Sunday Telegraph* reported that Lord Goodman had been working on the Beaverbrook/Associated talks for two months. The *Observer* reported that the sale of the *Evening Standard* was a likely outcome of the talks, and that Sir James Goldsmith and Rupert Murdoch were among the potential buyers. The *Observer* story was a good reflection of the current wishful thinking by Wintour and Jenkins but was a long way from the actual negotiators' intentions – as far as they were concerned the creation of a monopoly evening newspaper was central to the whole deal. Still, as the Beaverbrook and Associated boards resolutely refused to comment, the arithmetic of rumour was free to multiply. Newspapermen up and down the Street were fast learning not to believe all they read in the newspapers. In a statement to his chapel Mike Rothwell seriously urged journalists to distrust their own profession and 'be wary of press conjecture – which varies widely according to source'.

By the end of the holiday Rothwell had won his committee over to a policy of militancy. He had learned a key lesson during his years in industrial public relations – the employees' best defence in an unwelcome take-over situation was always to go for publicity, even at the risk of disruption. The idea behind this was simply to flush out a rival bidder, thus creating a fresh situation with new options. Until that happened employees were, willy-nilly, the prisoners of their management's intentions.

At the same time Rothwell was fully aware that the losses of the *Evening News* placed it in a highly exposed position. To be effective the policy of maximum fuss needed a broad base of support among the other journalists concerned. The most important thing to avoid was a collision between the 160 journalists on the *News* and the 150 on the *Standard* who, if the rumoured deal went through, would effectively be competing for one another's jobs. In a highly individualistic profession, Rothwell felt it was vital to develop a strategy for the defence of both papers. He was morally sure of support from journalists on the *Daily Mail*, who maintained close contact at chapel level, but less certain of the intentions of the journalists in the *Express* group. Accordingly a meeting was arranged for 8.30 pm on Thursday, 14 April, at the Old Bell pub in Fleet Street. Chapel officials from the *Sunday Express*, the *Daily Express* and the *Evening Standard* said they were ready to attend.

The only important item on the informal agenda was Rothwell's proposal that a five-chapel meeting be called as soon as possible after the NUJ's annual delegate meeting, which was to take place in Ilkley, Yorkshire, the following week. The declared object of the mass-meeting would be to show solidarity across traditional newspaper frontiers in the quest for information and consultation, drawing a line between the penmen and their paymasters. The undeclared object would be to make it a major media event, involving more than 1000 journalists. Rothwell saw it as 'a way of demonstrating to the proprietors and the public how many livelihoods were at stake'.

The Old Bell conference was a disaster. The *Express* group officials arrived two hours late, tired and thirsty after their own round of chapel meetings, and rapidly made it clear that they were averse to confrontation tactics. In their view a mass meeting was asking for trouble. It would be difficult to control and would almost certainly disrupt the production of one or possibly several newspapers. Harsh words were exchanged. An *Evening Standard* man primly declared: 'Our paper is the best in Fleet Street and we're not going to do anything to disrupt it.' The *Evening News* riposte was: 'Noble sentiments, but we're supposed to be fighting for the preservation of all titles. If we

let the management split us, none of us can expect any security.'
The combination of high passion and drink led to the raising of
inexpert fists before the bell for closing time brought the
shambles to a conclusion. The first effort to mobilize a united
front had failed.

There were logical as well as emotional reasons for the débâcle.
On an emotional level it was difficult for two groups of journalists in daily competition with one another to make common
cause. Even so this obstacle would probably have been sur-
mounted had it not been for the differing attitudes to management in the two groups. In comparison with the *Evening News*
journalists, the *Standard* editorial staff was a cosseted group.
Over the years they had benefited from what one of them
described as 'a lot of nod-and-wink agreements' with the
management. Their house and redundancy agreements were
better than those of their rivals on the *News*. Their contacts with
management, on the surface at least, had a greater degree of
intimacy. Ties of sentiment linked the humblest down-table
sub with the upper echelons of the organization. The journalists
saw, or thought they saw, friends in high places: Stevens had
used the *Standard* as a springboard for his own rise within the
company; Roy Wright, another director, had once been deputy
editor of the *Standard*; and, most importantly, Charles Wintour
was on the board, and that in itself was the best guarantee of
the *Standard*'s case being firmly made at the top. Rothwell and
his men might perceive this touching faith in the company
leadership as a snare and delusion – 'making it easier to pull
wool over the eyes of the men in a time of crisis' – but there was
method, as well as meekness, in the policy of moderation
adopted by the *Standard*'s editorial staff.

The key man on the *Standard*'s NUJ chapel committee was Ted
Simpson, an articulate loyalist who had worked on the
paper for 25 years, 'watching it change under Wintour from a
tired Tory rag to an organ of great cultural importance with a
liberal, humanistic outlook'. Simpson combined his duties as a
sub-editor with an absorption in national union affairs. He was
in his tenth year on the National Executive of the NUJ, at odds
with many of the young left-wing militants in the union but
still highly adept in the art of manoeuvre and the quiet achieve-

ment of objectives. When the crisis broke the father of the *Standard* chapel was Peter Caney, who owed his position more to personal popularity than to any vast experience in union affairs. Caney, a young man, naturally looked to Simpson for guidance. Simpson's view was that journalists' morale was the first priority. As he saw it, the paper was just edging into the black again and if the improvement was maintained its chances of survival could only be enhanced. Simpson did not basically disagree with Rothwell about the need for information and publicity, but felt that the best publicity for the *Standard* was a viable product that no management could close without risking public opprobrium. What looked like weak-kneed fatalism to Rothwell was the best strategy for survival in Simpson's book.

It made sense, though Simpson might have had more difficulty in securing support for this policy had it been realized just how close the *Standard*'s cause had come to being lost at the top. At boardroom level, Roy Wright had firmly aligned himself with the majority favouring the Associated deal and Charles Wintour was feeling increasingly isolated. Simon Jenkins had not been appointed to the board, although the editorship of the *Evening Standard* was normally considered an automatic qualification for a seat. Jenkins naturally read this as a blocking move against any increase in the *Standard* 'lobby' within the organization.

Efforts to find an alternative bidder for the *Standard* outside the newspaper industry had ostensibly drawn a blank. Jenkins had been mildly encouraged by his meeting with Sir James Goldsmith, but the Cavenham boss made it clear that he could not intervene further without some signal of approval from Sir Max. Jenkins's session with Nigel Broackes, the chairman of Trafalgar House, had also failed to produce anything concrete. Although Broackes expressed an interest in communications, he could not promise any immediate help for the *Standard*. In fact, what Jenkins read as a 'don't call us, we'll call you' attitude on Broackes's part was another link in the chain of events propelling Trafalgar towards the newspaper industry.

Nigel Broackes at 42 had outlived an early reputation as a property whizz-kid to run a broadly based company with interests in building, shipping and hotels. Although his managing director, Victor Matthews, had been disconcerted by what amounted to a rebuff from Jocelyn Stevens when Trafalgar offered assistance at the turn of the year, Broackes remained intrigued by the possibilities. At the same time he was anxious to avoid the kind of public image problems that might result from Trafalgar using its money power to muscle into the newspaper world against the wishes of the existing ownerships. In that context Jenkins's unsolicited visit had been an interesting straw in the wind, but no more than that. For Broackes timing was of the essence in take-over situations, and with Sir Max still apparently committed to a deal with Associated Newspapers the time was clearly not right for another initiative by Trafalgar. If the situation changed, Broackes would be ready.

Such calculations, however, could not be vouchsafed to the editor of the *Evening Standard*. All that Jenkins could report to Wintour was that there still seemed to be no alternative to the deal with Associated. Wintour's first move after the Easter holiday was to set down his anxieties in a letter to Stevens. As far as he was concerned there was no longer much point in pulling punches, so he wrote:

Dear Jocelyn,

At the risk of boring repetition, I do urge you to ask Vere Harmsworth what, if he buys the *Evening Standard*, he intends to do with it.

You have said that if one sells something one cannot and does not ask the buyer what he intends to do with his purchase. You may be right if you're a butcher selling a leg of lamb. You don't ask the customer how she intends to cook it.

But if you're selling even a house you may well prefer to sell it at a lower price to someone who will look after it properly rather than to a purchaser who intends to pull it down and build a block of flats.

The *Evening Standard* is a very different case. It employs 1000 men and women. The board of Beaverbrook Newspapers would look totally stone age in outlook if it was ready to sell the services of these people to another company without even asking what their fate is to be. And I can imagine the possibility of disastrous effects on the distribution and production of the *Daily Express* if such slave-owner tactics were employed.

This is not at all the same situation as Glasgow. The *Evening Standard* is produced on the *Daily Express* machines and distributed from this building. We need continuous running and I doubt if we will get it unless we can prove that we have obtained the very best deal possible for all our employees.

And remember that our *Evening Standard* employees would rather have jobs subsidized by Goldsmith than no jobs at all. . . .

In any case the stories in the *Sunday Telegraph* and the *Observer* set off union demands for a statement at the very least, and could lead to further trouble. Surely this will help you gain further information in your next round of talks.

Their need to know is absolutely fundamental to good industrial relations, to common sense and common decency.

I am sending a copy of this note to Lord Goodman.

Wintour received an emollient but scarcely reassuring letter from Goodman in response. Goodman expressed sympathy with what Wintour had written but said that the preoccupation of the negotiators was with the financial aspects of Beaverbrook. It was, he added, now appropriate that the negotiators should divert themselves a little from these aspects and attempt to get a clearer picture of the staff and editorial questions. He ended by assuring Wintour that he was to be fully advised on these matters.

Goodman's letter arrived on Friday, 15 April, the same day as Wintour received his copy of a resolution which set out the response of the *Standard* journalists to the crisis. The resolution was essentially constructive in tone, but while recognizing 'the severe problems' of the group, it called for 'prior consultation' before any major decision and 'guarantees' on editorial staff jobs. The plain fact of the matter, however, was that Wintour himself was in no position to give guarantees or to consult in any creative sense. He had scarcely any more knowledge of where the Goodman talks were heading than the chapel itself. It was not a situation he relished.

Wintour's chance to improve his knowledge of Associated's intentions came early the next week. On Monday, 18 April Lou Kirby, the editor of the *Evening News*, telephoned Simon Jenkins and suggested they should dine together at the Berkeley Hotel in Wilton Place that evening. The overture was friendly enough but Jenkins, not wishing to give away the weakness of his position, decided on a stiff tactical response.

'We should get together,' said Kirby, 'because we are going to be working together.'

'What do you mean?' asked Jenkins.

'We'll be working together in future.'

'I will not countenance any discussion which entails the end of the *Evening Standard*.'

Despite the nice line in archaic reproof, they did have dinner together. Jenkins was too curious to resist, and naturally eager to explore the strengths and weaknesses of Kirby's position. The ground rules they established were that they were independent editors discussing mutual problems. Both knew full well that if there was to be a monopoly evening paper they were the leading, and very possibly the only, candidates for the job of editor.

In the event Jenkins was agreeably surprised by Kirby's frankness about his problems on the *News*. He spoke openly about the difficulty of moving staff who had grown mediocre in entrenched positions and bitterly about his hassles with a cantankerous union. Jenkins was less cheered by Kirby's manifest ebullience about the future. Despite the refusal to talk about any possible merger Jenkins took away the strong impression that Kirby had already been promised the editorship of the new paper by his proprietor.

Next morning Jenkins, in accordance with the information-pooling agreement he had with Wintour, gave him the highlights of his conversation with Kirby. This was valuable information for Wintour, as he had just accepted an invitation from Vere Harmsworth to discuss the situation privately at his flat in Eaton Square later that day. This meeting finally brought the long-neglected journalistic aspect of the deal into focus. Harmsworth's basic proposal was that the outlines of the new evening paper should be devised by an advisory committee which, he told Wintour, 'I would like you to take on.' So far so good. Harmsworth went on to say that the committee should also include Kirby and one or two other senior journalists. Their collective brief would be to decide the make-up, character and personnel of the new paper. They would report directly to Harmsworth. Wintour felt that Harmsworth wanted David English as one of the other committee members, primarily because of the experience he had gained when the old *Daily Sketch* was absorbed into the *Mail*. Harmsworth spoke of English in the highest terms, saying they had 'almost telepathic communication'.

In general terms Harmsworth thought that the staff of the new evening should be drawn from the existing papers on a 50/50 basis but that the character of the *Evening Standard* should be dominant. In marketing terminology the paper should be directed strongly at the ABC1s (upper and middle income groups) but it should also have a good base in C2s (the skilled working class). There was a danger in going too far up-market as it might provide Rupert Murdoch, who had previously expressed interest in the London evening field, with an opening for a new publication. Harmsworth saw the new paper as being of the highest quality with Kirby as editor and Jenkins as his deputy.

For the most part Wintour was content to listen, but the editorship question produced an immediate riposte. Wintour saw it as crucial. He did not believe that Jenkins would accept the role of deputy and thought that without him key members of the staff would inevitably flake off. Harmsworth seemed genuinely surprised at Wintour's emphasis on this issue, but the meeting ended on a note of affability. Harmsworth said Wintour had given him 'a lot to think about'. Wintour agreed to think over the advisory committee proposal seriously and come back in a few days with a decision.

By this stage Wintour was convinced that the only practical way to ensure the survival of the *Standard* as he knew it was to secure Harmsworth's total support for its continued existence. This meant that the new monopoly evening should not only have Simon Jenkins as editor but should also draw the vast majority of its staff from the *Standard*. Wintour was not, in this critical situation, concerned about the *Evening News*, and he set out to persuade Harmsworth why he should share this attitude. Harmsworth's apparent openness to persuasion and the demoralization on the *News* encouraged Wintour in the belief that he had a chance. Accordingly, he set out his arguments in a five-page memorandum that was delivered to Harmsworth by hand the next day.

This craftily worded document analysed the differences between the two newspapers under a variety of headings: circulation and readership, profitability, staff morale, the editors. It noted frankly that both papers had suffered a decline in circulation over the past five years (the *News* by 39 per cent, the *Standard* by 21 per cent), but that was about all they had in common. The *Standard* had a much younger readership (50 per cent under 35) and a more up-market social profile. Sixty per cent of the *Standard*'s readers were in the ABC1 advertising categories, compared to 38 per cent of the *News* readers.

As for profitability, the *News* was reportedly losing over £4 million a year, whereas, after a bad patch in 1976, the *Standard* was now operating at a modest trading profit. Wintour argued that the disparity in profitability would be even more pronounced were it not for rate-cutting by the *News*'s advertising department, and the fact that Associated had been able to back its paper with a television campaign for its classified columns.

Staff morale on the *Standard* was 'astonishingly high' and for many years the NUJ chapel committee had accepted 'steady and moderate' leadership. On the other hand, Wintour had heard 'many reports of difficulties imposed by the *News* NUJ chapel on the editor's room for manoeuvre'.

Wintour's most hyperbolic passage was reserved for his comparison of the two editors. There was, it seemed, no comparison:

Everyone agrees that Lou Kirby is an exceptionally nice man with considerable experience. To be frank, however, he has had enough time in which to implant a character on the tabloid *Evening News*, and he has not succeeded.

Simon Jenkins, who is 33, already emerges as a person of very considerable stature. He is an extremely effective speaker; has established a major reputation as an expert on urban living; he is not afraid to think for himself; and has established very good relations with his staff. I do not agree with every change he has made in the *Evening Standard*, but owing to other management preoccupations he has been left very much on his own and clear guidance on marketing strategy may have been lacking.

Simon Jenkins may at times seem on the arrogant side but most editors of quality have more than a touch of pride about them.

Having set up the contrasts between the two papers in such Manichean terms, Wintour boldly went on to analyse the dire consequences that would follow a straight merger of such disparate enterprises:

1 If anything like a 50/50 staffing arrangement was planned I believe the result could be disastrous. If the staff of the *Daily Mail* and *Daily Sketch* barely spoke for a year, the staffs of the *Evening News* and *Evening Standard* would not speak for a lifetime.

2 In such situations the bad eggs tend to rise to the top of the chapel tree, and the bad relations at the *Evening News* could infect the *Evening Standard* men and women.

3 On a 50/50 basis the NUJ would want much bigger staffing to safeguard jobs. (This could probably be resisted.)

4 In a new newspaper, even an improved one, there is a danger of a loss of existing readership without compensating gains.

5 On any basis of political, economic, industrial and moral judgement an editorial merger would run into appalling difficulties. The *Evening Standard* is highly regarded in Whitehall, Westminster, and the rest of the media. There would be an outcry if its character was destroyed.

Wintour's proposed solution envisaged a role for the advisory committee that Harmsworth had suggested, but it would be more circumscribed and limited in its objectives. Basically, it would help to tone up the product. He wrote:

The basis of the new newspaper should clearly be the *Evening Standard*: the editor and all the members of the staff should be from the *Evening Standard*, except where it is to the clear benefit of the new paper that members of the *Evening News* staff should join the team.

But developments in the marketing philosophy, typography and general approach could well be considered by an advisory committee including Simon Jenkins, David English or Lou Kirby, and myself reporting to the chairman of Associated Newspapers.

This committee would also consider the identity of *Evening News* staff of exceptional merit. It should clearly have available such technical advice as might be necessary.

Wintour's thesis concluded on an unsentimental note:

> If Associated Newspapers want to build on the readership and character and prestige of the *Evening Standard*, then it will only succeed by building on the existing staff. Mergers are rarely happy. Closures, though brutal, yield greater efficiency and better products.

Wintour's memo provoked a rapid response: Harmsworth telephoned to invite him and Jenkins to his home for lunch and further discussion the next day, Thursday, 21 April. On the morning before the lunch the full Beaverbrook board met under the chairmanship of Sir Max Aitken to hear Jocelyn Stevens's report on the formal state of the negotiations with Associated. Stevens apologized for their protracted nature but was able to announce that the long agony would soon be over. The lawyers still had a lot of drafting to do but agreement had been reached in principle on all the main issues. Sir Max then asked whether the deal had the unanimous support of the board. The request showed all in favour except for Charles Wintour, who said he could not give his assent until the editorial side of the deal had been clarified.

Thus when Wintour and Jenkins set off for Eaton Square they both felt that the survival of the *Standard* would depend on the impression they made on Harmsworth. They were encouraged by the fact that he was apparently prepared to meet them alone. This seemed to indicate that he was seriously prepared to consider Wintour's brutalist approach to the *Evening News*.

The occasion started inauspiciously. Wintour and Jenkins arrived to find that their host was out. They were ushered in by an amiable man who described himself as Mr Harmsworth's chauffeur. He had, he explained, been instructed to look after the guests until his employer arrived. He took their order for drinks and proceeded to pour out two of the largest gin and tonics they had ever seen – brimming half-pint tumblers, half gin, half tonic. 'I assume', Wintour muttered, describing the vigil later, 'that Vere must have a slight servant problem.'

Things brightened when Harmsworth arrived 30 minutes late with his vivacious wife, Bubbles. Mrs Harmsworth was clearly thrilled by the encounter, exclaiming: 'Oh, how marvellous' it was to meet them both. She chatted gaily for several minutes about how super the *Standard* was, cheering the guests no end. The host, however, was evidently anxious to terminate the frivolities and get down to business.

Bubbles floated out of the room to be replaced by two sombre-looking men: David English, the editor of the *Daily Mail*, and Lou Kirby. Their presence indicated that Harmsworth was averse to any solution that meant ditching the interests of the *Evening News*. Their function, it soon emerged, was to 'sell' Wintour on the creative advantages of the merger he had so vigorously denounced in his memo. Harmsworth had already shown the memo to Kirby, which implied that he disagreed with it.

As they sat down to eat English did most of the talking.

His main emphasis was on felicitous parallels between the current situation and the merging of the *Daily Sketch* with the *Daily Mail*, a subject on which he was able to talk with some authority. There had been problems of course, but the merging of the two staffs had given the new *Mail* a real dynamism, and the *élan* and aggression of the *Sketch* staff in the new mix had proved vital to the success of a revitalized *Mail*. While this dissertation was proceeding Harmsworth contented himself with generalities about how wonderful things would be when they were all working together. 'I see this as a paper with the *Evening Standard* heart in it,' he said, smiling encouragement at Charles Wintour. If anything, Wintour looked more tense than before.

The chauffeur, meanwhile, busied himself with serving lunch. The fare, according to one guest, was 'cold consommé, rapidly unfrozen lamb chops that skidded as people made stabs at them, frozen peas that skedaddled all over the plate and fruit salad that dribbled as Wintour frothed. It was like a last lunch.' At one particularly tense moment the chauffeur accidentally tipped a chop and a quantity of peas into Wintour's lap.

Jenkins concentrated on pinning his own chop as Wintour let fly. Wintour expressed himself interested by David English's narrative but was unimpressed by its current application. He did not think the same transplant techniques could work in the evening newspaper context. What struck him were the differences rather than the similarities. He named three. 1. Competition between the *News* and *Standard* was much hotter than it ever had been between the *Mail* and *Sketch*, which were owned by the same firm and competed in different markets. 2. Evening papers have a faster tempo than mornings. Deadlines come so thick and fast that decisions have to be made more decisively and authoritatively. A merger would hamper this decision-making process. 3. The *Mail/Sketch* merger had had time to prove itself, but there would be no such generous margin for the paper they now envisaged. Failure in the early months would effectively let in an interloper, like Rupert Murdoch, with a new product, before the damage could be repaired.

The merger as it appeared to be envisaged by Associated would, in Wintour's view, destroy the spirit of the *Evening Standard*. If that happened he would feel compelled to resign his directorship and fight the matter publicly. The only solution that made editorial sense was the one outlined in his memorandum to Harmsworth.

In a desperate effort to find some common ground, Harmsworth suggested that the four-man advisory committee might start its work by selecting staff for the new newspaper on the basis of merit. This might well, he felt, result in an 80/20 percentage split in favour of the *Standard*. The problem of the editorship could be discussed later. It seemed to the other Associated men a generous, almost too generous, offer. They had discussed staffing ratios earlier among themselves and had decided that a new paper with an editorial staff of 180 could take a maximum of 89 journalists from the *Standard*. Harmsworth had, unilaterally, made an enormous concession.

Wintour was unimpressed. The question of the editor was fundamental and they had to begin with it. His own starting-point was quite simply that the deal was 'against all I stand for unless Simon Jenkins is the editor'. Wintour then proceeded to list Jenkins's great qualities against what he suggested were the more modest accomplishments of Lou Kirby. He was younger, abler, a better writer and better in appearance, a fact deemed relevant as editors frequently had to appear on television. Kirby, Wintour said, was not the man for the job, though he might usefully be retained as a senior editorial consultant on the new paper. As the comparison unfolded, Kirby went an even brighter shade of red; Jenkins demurely concentrated on the horrible food. Harmsworth frequently said: 'Oh dear.'

'It was', according to one of those present, 'like the assassination of Marat by the occupants of the asylum at Charenton, with Kirby as Marat.'

Not much could be salvaged after such an outburst. There was an interim agreement to differ as the lunch broke up and Harmsworth deftly invited Jenkins to dine with him the next day. In the general round of handshakes as the two Beaverbrook guests left Kirby and Wintour somehow contrived not to press each other's flesh.

The consensus among the Associated men who stayed behind was that Wintour had gone right over the top. They already knew about his exposed position on the Beaverbrook board, so he had no mandate for making such demands. He seemed to be right out on a limb, busily sawing off his last line of communication with corporate life. This assessment was only marginally altered when Wintour rang David English later that afternoon to say that he did not wish to be obdurate about the engagement of the entire *Standard* staff on the new paper. He felt an 85/15 percentage split in favour of the *Standard* would be about right. As Kirby was resolved not to start the new paper with less than 50 per cent of his old staff there did not seem to be any possibility of reconciliation. Wintour also rejected a subtle proposal by English that he (Wintour) might consider editing the new evening paper himself. As far as the Associated team was concerned, there was now no basis on which agreement could be achieved with Wintour.

Jenkins might be a different matter. He was, after all a much younger man, with fewer bridges to burn. He still had to make his way. The Associated men had all been favourably impressed by his demeanour. He had been loyal to Wintour but generally as polite and accommodating as the lunch would allow. At one stage, after venturing that the *Standard* was 'a more successful' paper than the *News*, he had readily accepted an amendment that 'less unsuccessful' might be a better description. In general, Jenkins seemed like a man who could see sense. Harmsworth was rather looking forward to seeing him unaccompanied by his stern mentor.

As for Wintour, Harmsworth was more than happy to take a break from the strain of dealing with him. When the Associated proprietor next met Jocelyn Stevens he told him that he had never been spoken to like that before – 'even by my father'. 'Is he always like that?' asked Harmsworth. 'Always,' said Stevens.

Harmsworth and the Associated men had good reason to be puzzled. Wintour was certainly not acting in accordance with any of the conventional negotiating techniques between corporations, which dictate that both sides start with tough positions and become more flexible as the bargaining develops. If anything, Wintour was developing a tougher position with each passing day. A month earlier, when asked by Lord Goodman what he considered was the 'heart' of the *Evening Standard* Wintour had replied Jenkins and perhaps a dozen key executives. Now he seemed to be defending the need to preserve not only the vital organs but also every limb down to the last toenail. English's reading of Wintour's attitude was: 'He'd made up his mind to fight and used the lunch to construct the basis of his campaign. In a way, I admired him for it.'

On his way to dinner with Harmsworth the next day, Jenkins took a long contemplative walk round St James's Park. Treating it as his Gethsemane, Jenkins pondered deeply on the options. He was not even sure whether he should have accepted the invitation. He knew he was being wooed, but for what? The editorship without most of his staff or the deputy editorship with most of his staff intact? It was hard to know, but it was possible to guess that Harmsworth did not have the fully fledged Wintour solution in mind. The *Financial Times* that morning had carried news that redundancy was now the main item on the agenda of the Associated/Beaverbrook talks and had quoted a Beaverbrook executive as saying: 'Our only option now is a deal with Associated.' Jenkins himself was inclined to believe that this was very probably true, but what did it imply as far as he and his staff were concerned? All he could do was wait and see.

On arrival, he was delighted to find that Harmsworth wanted to treat the occasion as a 'getting-to-know-you' meeting. There would be no hard decisions – these would come later. In the event they had an outstandingly pleasant two hours together, talking over general topics and discovering a mutual enthusiasm for the idea of starting a new Saturday magazine. They liked each other. So much so that Harmsworth suggested that Jenkins might care to round the evening off by going to a nightclub with him and Bubbles. Jenkins considered the possibility of being spotted by some suspicious newshound in such cosy circumstances with the rival proprietor and decided to take a raincheck on the invitation. They parted on the warmest of terms, agreeing to be in touch early the next week. Walking back to his home in Camden, Simon Jenkins looked up at the stars and reflected that he was in a highly ambivalent situation.

The journalists assembled at Ilkley for the annual delegate meeting of the NUJ had a miserable week. The current issue of the journalists' trade paper, the *U.K. Press Gazette*, provided them with the kind of advice they felt they could well do without. Under the heading 'Merging away from Madness' it gave the measured opinion:

> The trade unions have left it a little late to inquire how they can help, or help to avoid, talks on a merger plan for Associated and Beaverbrook Newspapers. They are, at least, £5 million a year too late – the combined current losses of the London Evening News and Evening Standard.
>
> The files of Press Gazette over the years record many of the warnings, the talks, the warnings of warnings, and talks about talks to end this needless bleeding to death.
>
> It can never be said that either Beaverbrook or Associated has bled in silence. Their presentations to the unions on gross overstaffing have been detailed, frightening – and largely ignored by union memberships.
>
> But not by union secretaries. They too, have the printed evidence – in 'Programme for Action' – that they have advised well; and in vain. They also may have long memories.

What amounted to an invitation to the trade-union leadership to collaborate with management in closing a title was followed by the opinion that the Associated/Beaverbrook deal could 'produce the first of a new generation of streamlined management and maximised plant'. Few delegates took the advice or the prognosis seriously, but it did nothing to alleviate the general mood of despondency. Even their own kind were turning on the idea that the preservation of titles should be the prime concern of trade unionists in newspapers.

Among the delegates from London were Michael Rothwell and Ted Simpson, both acutely aware that Yorkshire was not where the action was. 'We were supposed', reflected Rothwell, 'to represent the organized strength of the journalists at a time of crisis, but in practice we were reduced to reading the papers to try and find out what was happening to our own jobs.' He rang his chapel officers in London three times a day for news, but there was none beyond the fragmentary, speculative reports in newspapers he had already read. Still no meeting scheduled with the management, still no word from Hattersley on the monopolies (in fact Hattersley had replied promptly, but his letter had been 'lost' in Associated's internal mail).

The fresh breeze off the moors did nothing to dispel the tensions between militants and moderates. Many of the delegates wanted to put through a strong combative motion, opposing any possible merger between Associated ,and Beaverbrook. In theory Rothwell should have been delighted with such a resolution, since it widened the ambit of the dispute, but he found himself in the humiliating position of having to lobby the Executive Committee to hold back – not because he personally did not want it but because he felt it would probably be disavowed by the *Express* and *Standard* chapels. Things were bad enough already without taking the risk of publicizing the split between the journalists involved. What was required was a strategy that would unite workers in both newspaper groups, not force them apart. Although Rothwell had no knowledge of the contents of Wintour's memo, he entertained a strong suspicion that the *Standard* leadership and staff were evolving a strategy designed to save themselves at the expense of the *News*.

Ken Morgan, the NUJ's mild-mannered general secretary, was in any case strongly in favour of a moderate approach to the crisis, feeling that if the proprietors behaved badly, the journalists and other newspaper workers could score good marks by a responsible response. His own view was that the journalists should represent their case with the print and publishing unions via the TUC's Printing Industries Committee (PIC). The chairman of this committee was Bill Keys, general secretary of the Society of Graphical and Allied Trades (SOGAT), representing publishing and circulation workers, who had already gone on record to say: 'The unions are not in the business of simply adopting any plan favoured by Lord Goodman or anyone else.' But apart from some fighting talk the PIC had not made much impression; it had not even secured a formal meeting with the two managements involved. Rothwell had an uncomfortable impression that the proprietors were being allowed to dictate the timetable of events – by the time the national union leadership was drawn into the picture the deal might well be a *fait accompli*. He told Morgan privately that it was all very well being statesmanlike at the annual conference but that when they got back to London his chapel would have to act vigorously. When Morgan pleaded for reliance on the leadership of the PIC, Rothwell responded: 'Bollocks, Ken. We're going to have to do things that will horrify you. We've *got* to fight out in the open.'

In fact some horrifying things were already about to happen without any prompting from Rothwell. On the evening of Friday, 22 April, as the delegates packed their bags in Ilkley, a strange assortment of angry men occupied the boardroom of Beaverbrook Newspapers in Fleet Street. They were for the most part *Evening Standard* print workers and drivers and they wanted to know how long they would continue in those jobs. Outside in the street other van drivers blocked the entrances to the *Express* building, preventing distribution of the *Daily Express*.

The operation provided a timely reminder of the fact that there was more than journalists' livelihoods involved. One of the accurate rumours said that 2000 non-journalistic jobs would go if the deal went through. Many of the van drivers, members of Bill Keys's SOGAT, were second- or third-generation employees of the *Express* group. The journalists might be more articulate and more capable of attracting public sympathy but they had less to lose. The abler ones would soon get jobs, but the van men would have diabolical problems trying to earn their money by driving for a living elsewhere. Reg Brady, the energetic father of the *Standard*'s NATSOPA machine chapel, was not inclined to depend on the journalists, or even on the national leadership of his own union, when the chips were down.

Earlier in the day the management had announced that it was not in a position to issue a statement about the company's future until the following Thursday. Already exasperated by the delays in consultation, the print and distribution chapels on the *Standard* had decided that they could wait no longer – hence the blockade and the sit-in. The mood of militancy proved contagious. The *Standard*'s NUJ chapel met and passed its most peremptory resolution so far: ordering a mandatory (i.e. compulsory) chapel meeting for the next morning (Saturday), an unprecedented event, and 'insisting' that Wintour and Jenkins be present to provide information. The more spirited journalists then hurried from Shoe Lane to the *Express* building to join the boardroom sit-in. Various executives and directors, among them Tony Dyer, braved the motley in the boardroom with pleas of sweet reasonableness. The men were not having it.

The executive they all wanted to see was Jocelyn Stevens.

The chief executive had had a trying day, even by his own frantic standards. The morning had been spent with the Lloyd's Bank people, providing reassurances about Beaverbrook's overdraft. The company, Stevens vigorously maintained, was on course again with a chairman who was on his way back to fighting fitness, already strong enough for five hours' physiotherapy a day. Things were looking up. The bankers were mollified but less than delighted. There was, after all, no way of disguising the fact that the latest circulation figures, published that morning, showed the *Daily Express* down to a new low average of 2·55 million copies a day – public evidence of the fact that the tabloid relaunch had not worked the desired miracle. Then there had been yet another business lunch with Vere Harmsworth, bruised by his recent experience with Wintour but bucked by the success of the *Daily Mail* (the same figures showed his paper with its highest circulation since it went tabloid in 1971). More talk, more assurances and the routine insistence that they must get something in writing soon. Then Stevens was off again to the Hyde Park Hotel in

Knightsbridge for a sticky meeting with his former co-deputy chairman, Peter Hetherington, and Hetherington's solicitor to negotiate the financial terms of his departure. Stevens was still at the hotel when he received a call from his office informing him that close on 100 of his company's employees were occupying the boardroom and had indicated that they intended staying there until he made an appearance. The caller thought they meant it. Stevens said he'd be right over.

He finally made it around 9 pm, to be greeted by a rousing chorus of ironic cheers. The process of consultation had begun. Stevens conceded that talks about a merger of the two evenings were 'advanced' but insisted that absolutely nothing had been settled. At one stage he said: 'We are further from a deal with Associated Newspapers than we were seven years ago.' This was technically true, but more than a shade disingenuous – they were, in fact, exceptionally close to agreement, though the document of agreement had not yet been drafted, as it had been seven years earlier. Eventually Stevens agreed that a statement summarizing the situation should be issued to the press. It was published as a joint statement from Associated and Beaverbrook and read: 'In view of the many rumours circulating about a possible merger between Beaverbrook Newspapers Limited and Associated Newspapers Group Limited the Companies wish to declare that whilst acknowledging there have been talks about the serious problems of the evening newspapers, no agreement has been made. A meeting between the unions and the Companies had been fixed for next week.'

For most employees in both groups this was the first official information on their managements' intentions. Not much, but a start.

EIGHT

The Cloning of Charles Wintour

On the morning after the sit-in at the *Express* building, Michael Rothwell called for a strike at the *Evening News*. His week in Ilkley had lent further disenchantment to his view of what was going on in Fleet Street and he was eager to communicate his dissatisfaction. Normally Saturday is a leisurely day on the *Evening News*. The *Standard* does not publish and the paper achieves real momentum only in the late afternoon, with the pressure of sports coverage. Saturday, 23 April 1977 was an exception.

For those journalists on duty it began at 8.15 am with an emergency mandatory meeting of their chapel. The two items on the agenda were the morning newspaper reports on the Associated/Beaverbrook statement and the letter to the chapel from Prices Minister Roy Hattersley, which had been located, seven days late, the previous evening. Neither gave any cause for comfort. Rothwell himself was convinced by now that the long-awaited meeting between the two companies and the trade-union general secretaries, which had been fixed for the following Thursday, would not be consultative but decisive. The union representatives would simply be told what moves the managements had decided to make and what jobs would be lost. He told the chapel: 'We have six days – five working days, of which this is one – to force them to tell us about thousands of jobs which may be thrown away callously and without proper consultation.'

Rothwell's reading of Hattersley's letter was that it gave no grounds for assuming that the government would do anything to prevent such an outcome. Hattersley was at pains to point out that his powers were limited by statute and that any reference to the Monopolies Commission was contingent on the economic situation of the papers involved. He said that he would have to refer the matter to the Commission 'unless I were satisfied that the newspaper concerned was not economic as a going concern. Even then, if I was also satisfied that the newspaper could not continue as a separate newspaper – for instance, if closure had been announced for a certain date – I would have no option in the matter and would have to give my consent.'

Rothwell felt that Hattersley's emphasis on the circumstances in which he could not act were ominous. He told chapel members that it looked as if Hattersley had 'been got at' and was 'preparing to rat on us'. He also told them that before leaving Ilkley he had secured the backing of Ken Morgan and the National Executive Council for any initiative the chapel might take in its quest for information from the management of Associated Newspapers. He therefore proposed that the chapel should stay in continuous mandatory session – i.e. not produce a newspaper – until the management clarified its intentions. The measure might look extreme, but then so was the situation.

The debate that followed centred on the issue of numbers. There were only 32 journalists present, a normal quota for that time on Saturday, but no more than one-fifth of the staff at other times. The motion eventually foundered on this issue, with the minority present feeling unable to commit the absent majority to such a policy. Rothwell did manage to get unanimous support for two other measures designed to accelerate events – one brought the next mandatory meeting forward to 8 am on Monday, when something approaching the full staff would be present, the other pressed for an urgent meeting with Hattersley to discuss the contents of his letter. Rothwell felt that a chance had been lost to force consultation, but there might be other opportunities. At least the loss of his motion gave him time for a first-hand look at how things were going at the *Standard*. He could now accept the invitation to observe their mandatory meeting, scheduled for 10 am that morning.

The *Standard* chapel meeting was radically different in tone. As there was no paper that day it was conceived as totally non-disruptive and the main item of interest for the 120 journalists present was an address by Charles Wintour. It was still a sullen occasion. The journalists were as bitter as those on the *News* about the lack of consultation, though they still retained some basic faith in their management's intentions. Wintour tried to build on this.

He began by thanking the chapel for meeting at a time that did not inconvenience production and was full of praise for the discipline of the staff 'under fire'. Simon Jenkins was the subject of a special accolade – 'In the most difficult circumstances, he has kept his head admirably.' Jocelyn Stevens was, according to Wintour, 'very ashamed' at his failure to reply to the chapel's letter requesting information about the talks with Associated Newspapers. In mitigation of this offence, Wintour pleaded pressure of work – 'Talks with Associated often start at breakfast, or talks about talks, and usually go on for most of the day in one form or another.'

As far as information went, Wintour was scarcely more helpful than Stevens. He stressed that there was still no agreement with Associated and that it was still possible that there would be no agreement. Such talks had failed before, they might do so again. Meantime, the best way for the *Standard* editorial staff to preserve the maximum number of jobs was for them all 'to produce the most sparkling, enjoyable, entertaining newspaper you can'. On the general outlook he was bleakly frank: 'From where I sit there is no reason for the *Evening Standard* editorial to despair. Please do not read too much into this. It is not a guarantee or a promise. It is an observation. If you go away thinking all your jobs are safe, you will mislead yourselves and you could mislead others such as the *Evening News* staff.'

Wintour concluded his remarks by offering to answer questions and suggesting that he might be able to help with the wording of any statement that the meeting wanted to issue publicly – a patrician gesture that astonished the observant Rothwell. The questions, focusing on three main areas, were briefly disposed of.

'Is a merger being discussed?'
'Yes.'
'What's happening this weekend?'
'Nothing.'
'Is there an alternative offer?'
'No.'

Wintour had the respect of the meeting but the tension of the occasion made his natural terseness even more pronounced. According to one of the *Standard* executives he seemed like the unhappiest man in the room – 'Some of us felt he had been put in the position of giving notice of impending death to his own creation. When he said a few hopeful words nobody believed him and he knew that nobody believed him.'

Simon Jenkins also emphasized the importance of the staff sticking together as an editorial team. A veteran *Standard* reporter thought that his performance on this occasion called to mind Stanhope, the brave young officer in *Journey's End*, R. C. Sherriff's play about life and almost certain death in the trenches in the First World War. 'The next event for the *Standard*', Jenkins said, 'is the next editorial conference, where we shall set about producing a bloody good newspaper until such time as someone stops us.' To Rothwell this sounded at worse suicidal and at best a strategy for fighting to the last *Evening News* employee. The one thing it was not was a strategy for saving both evening papers.

Eventually Rothwell was allowed to address the meeting. He used the opportunity to revive his original idea of a mass rally of all the Associated and Beaverbrook chapels involved. It would almost certainly be disruptive, but in his view the time had come to dramatize the issues for their readers as well as the proprietors. Otherwise, Rothwell warned, 'those of you with jobs could find yourselves employees of Associated Newspapers by the end of the week.' That, he could assure them, was not a desirable position to be in. Rothwell managed to mobilize some support from the floor before the moderates, led by Ted Simpson, headed off the threat. The most they would endorse was a joint meeting that would be specifically non-disruptive, provided the other chapels agreed.

There was some discussion about whether Peter Caney, the father of the chapel, should go off on a pre-booked fortnight's holiday to Portugal later that day. It was decided that he should, devolving the leadership of the chapel on Simpson and the other committee members. Rothwell thought they must be joking.

The next day's 'heavy' Sunday papers displayed an unprecedented unanimity on the crisis. The *Sunday Times* under the headline 'Newspaper will die to save the Express', the *Observer* under ' "Standard" sale to go ahead' and the *Sunday Telegraph* under 'London papers set to merge' all boldly predicted that the deal would be done by the following Thursday when the two managements met the national union representatives on the TUC's Printing Industries Committee. The sale price was said to be £5 million, which would be used to infuse new life into the *Daily Express*. Primed by confident sources in Associated Newspapers, all three Sundays tipped Lou Kirby as the editor of the new evening, though one Associated executive was quoted as saying that the paper would be 'more like the *Standard* than the *News* but with the punch of the *Daily Mail*'. The title had yet to be decided.

William Ellsworth-Jones, who wrote the *Sunday Times* piece with Phillip Knightley, did have some qualms about the 'hardness' of the story before it was published. It was certainly true as far as his inquiries of Associated and Beaverbrook went, but he remembers having 'this funny feeling about Goldsmith'. All efforts to raise Goldsmith by telephone in Paris on Saturday morning had drawn a blank, so he had to go on the information available. His story did, however, point to the remote possibility of another outcome with the words: 'The only possible hitch to the sale could be caused by Sir Max Aitken, of Beaverbrook, deciding at the last minute that he cannot go through with a deal that humiliates his family so publicly at the hands of his arch-rival, the Hon. Vere Harmsworth, head of Associated Newspapers.' Laurence Marks of the *Observer* put it in similar terms: 'Sir Max Aitken, who is recovering from a stroke, might baulk at the last moment at surrendering his flagship to the hereditary enemy. . . . Probably, however, the brutal logic of financial retrenchment will prove stronger than sentiment.' Both Marks and Ellsworth-Jones were subsequently highly relieved at having inserted this modicum of scepticism into their stories.

The newspaper stories hardened attitudes in the Beaverbrook management. Ringing round on Sunday, Wintour discovered that Jenkins had already been active. He had just written to Harmsworth deploring the effect of the newspaper articles, which he assumed were largely based on 'leaks' by the Associated management. As far as Jenkins was concerned the editorship was still not decided and such stories made it difficult to hold his staff together. They might scatter in all directions in a way that would not help either company. Wintour already knew from a conversation with Bob Carvel, the *Standard*'s seasoned political writer, that approaches had been made to key staff by executives on the *News* with an eye to the future. Carvel had been asked to work on the new evening with Kirby as editor. Both Wintour and Jenkins were only too well aware of how quickly journalistic morale could evaporate if the staff's energies were absorbed in fighting for the available lifebelts. They needed some positive propaganda of their own in the public prints. Accordingly, Jenkins gave an exclusive interview to *The Times* to counter the fatalistic impression given by the Sundays. He told *The Times* that the disappearance of the *Standard* would 'leave a yawning gap in the political and cultural life of London', and generally painted a dismal picture of metropolitan affairs without it.

Wintour then rang Stevens, who also felt that they had nothing to lose by adopting a more aggressive attitude. He thought that Jenkins should give Harmsworth an ultimatum over the issue of the editorship, a piece of advice that ranked favourably with the apocryphal story of an editor sending a reporter to the bullet-riddled siege of Sidney Street with the injunction: 'Go and tell Peter Painter, "I'm not afraid of him." '

Emma Soames, a young writer on the *Standard*, later described the mood of the journalists in an article for the *New Statesman*:

The gloom was so intense that by the Monday morning it would not have been surprising to find the doors of the Evening Standard locked with Vere Harmsworth standing in the street holding the key. This nightmare became recurrent, as did the pattern of the days that followed. By 8.30 a.m. the place was buzzing with activity, the mood was slightly frenetic but at least the paper was making it on to the streets. As every edition hit departmental desks, incredulity mounted. The production pipeline was fraught with unions who were fully expected to stop work according to the rumours (coming in this case from Beaverbrook). They didn't and it became apparent to everyone that the newspaper itself was the only weapon we possessed in what was effectively open war against Associated.

The journalists were also upset by the fact that Wintour was not in the Beaverbrook negotiating team, as this seemed to make their position even more precarious. Wintour himself was not so concerned, feeling that a place in the team would tie him to the Associated deal and hamper his initiatives in other directions. On the morning of Monday, 25 April he decided that the time was right to activate what friends the *Standard* had in high places – it was, after all, the preferred evening paper of most MPs when Parliament was in session, and a number of them had written for him on a freelance basis. The highest-placed friend of all was Michael Foot, Lord President of the Council and Leader of the House of Commons. Foot had been editor of the *Standard* during the Second World War and a great admirer of 'the journalistic genius' of Lord Beaverbrook, despite their differences on political and social issues. Before joining the Labour cabinet he had been a regular contributor to the *Standard*'s book pages. Although he had no direct departmental responsibility relating to newspapers, his influence could be valuable.

Wintour was fairly sure Lord Goodman had persuaded the senior officials in the Prices Ministry that there was no alternative but closure for the *Evening Standard*, so Hattersley would be advised that he could not refer the matter to the Monopolies Commission. (This would have been a skilful move by Sir Max's legal adviser.) But Hattersley had also indicated that the Prime Minister had asked to be kept informed about developments. This at least suggested that he would not take a final decision without informing the cabinet. Wintour felt that Foot was the best person to keep Callaghan directly informed of the alternatives when, and if, they developed.

He therefore wrote to Foot at the Privy Council summarizing the situation as he saw it:

Dear Michael,

You might like to have some background on the *Evening Standard* situation.

Broadly speaking Beaverbrook Newspapers faces bankruptcy unless it sells the *Evening Standard*, its last remaining disposable asset. It would make more sense to an outsider if the *Daily Express* were sold but that would make the *Sunday Express* unprofitable since the total *Sunday Express/Daily Express* print cannot be produced in either London or Manchester. In fact the *Sunday Express* needs the *Daily Express* plant to survive.

It has been the view of Lord Goodman, and of our negotiating team, that Beaverbrook Newspapers is in too weak a state to lay down conditions on the editorial future of the paper. The argument has been about price, and accompanying agreements. These agreements are virtually complete.

However at the very end it was agreed that Vere should see me to discuss what he calls 'the new evening paper'. He has in mind a perfectly reasonable concept of a new newspaper largely based on the *Evening Standard*, but with a slightly broader appeal. The staff would be chosen by a four man team consisting of David English, Lou Kirby (editor of the *News*), Simon Jenkins and myself. The sole criteria would be merit. On this basis Vere guessed the outcome would be 80/20 in favour of the *Evening Standard* staff.

The problem is the editorship. It was Vere's plan that Simon should be the deputy. I told him at once that this would not work. Simon would not serve under Kirby. . . . Vere replied reasonably enough that he knew nothing about Simon. Subsequently he has met Simon alone, and they seem to have got on well. But it is my impression that Vere made some prior commitment to Kirby and that it is very difficult for him to get out of it. Meanwhile Kirby is trying to recruit *Evening Standard* staff by approaching them directly.

Meanwhile the *Evening News* editorial staff are trying to get the *Evening Standard* staff to take joint action with them, and the likely end of that could be a 50/50 split in the new paper which would be hopeless.

Are there any alternatives? If Vere pulled away from the deal, the only alternatives are Murdoch who is pretty stretched at the moment and Goldsmith who wants the *Express* for political purposes. I have myself canvassed

Barnetson, Atlantic Richfield, the Thomson Organization and the *Financial Times* – all with negative results.

In conclusion: if Vere made Simon the editor, I would support the deal and believe it is the best we can hope for. If Kirby is the editor, I will resign and oppose the deal publicly. We should know by Thursday at the latest.

The atmosphere, as you can imagine, is pretty horrific. I will keep you posted.

In fact the gap between the two sides on the journalistic mix for the new evening was wider than Wintour imagined. Lou Kirby was certainly still under the impression that he could carry at least half of his staff on to the new paper and said as much in a letter of reassurance to Rothwell that same morning. He told the *Evening News* FoC that the paper would be in the nature of an evening *Daily Mail* and 'categorically' denied that there had been any decision to give the *News* staff less than equal consideration with *Standard* staff when the merger took place.

Kirby's letter was among the documents before the *Evening News* chapel when it met for its enlarged mandatory meeting at 8 am on 25 April. It was welcome in that it appeared to dispel the worst rumours as far as the *News* staff was concerned, but it did not amount to a copper-bottomed assurance. The only man who could give such assurances was Harmsworth himself. The chapel decided to direct its energies to engaging the proprietor's attention with the strongest resolution it could devise. On the basis of its discussion, Rothwell wrote to Harmsworth as follows:

A meeting of this Chapel today passed overwhelmingly the following resolutions:

'This Chapel, fearing that the meeting arranged with the Printing Industries Committee on Thursday is likely to be no more than a formality at which Associated Newspapers and Beaverbrook Group announce firm and profound agreements they have reached, demands immediate meetings between top management and chapel officers.

'At these meetings, to be concluded to the officers' satisfaction by midday on Tuesday, 26 April, at the latest, the

Chapel requires management to disclose the extent of talks and probable agreements reached between the two sides; and insists that the Chapel has the right to be heard on possible objections and alternatives it may offer.

'The Chapel also formally gives notice to management that it will resist any attempt to impose compulsory redundancies.'

The letter went on to list six questions about the negotiations to which the chapel required prompt replies, and stated in conclusion:

This Chapel deplores the secrecy with which negotiations between Associated Newspapers and Beaverbrook Group have been conducted. For weeks these and other Chapels' reasonable requests for consultation have been rejected and neither side has treated its employees with the openness and frankness that is their due. That policy has caused grave and unnecessary suffering, and must end immediately if the *Evening News* is to be produced with the quality and continuity the Chapel wishes.

Later that day Rothwell was rewarded with a brief reply. In it, Harmsworth said he was fully aware of the concern of the chapel members and would keep them informed of significant developments. The sole aim of a merger, he said, would be to produce a distinguished and viable evening paper for the capital. This was the only way in which the interests of *Evening News* staff could best be served.

Under the circumstances it was, in Rothwell's opinion, 'a very snotty letter'. Harmsworth made things worse by giving a long on-the-record interview to Sheila Black in *The Times*. In it he answered several of the questions to which he had not deigned to reply when they were put to him by his own journalists. Although evidently conceived as an uplifting counter to Simon Jenkins's interview in the same newspaper, it had an unhappy effect on employees in both companies. Harmsworth told *The Times*:

They talk of the Evening Standard leaving a gap in London as though it were about to die. There is no question of that.

The Standard is no more about to die than the Evening News. A new paper is being born. It will have the best of both papers, and it will be produced by a combined staff, drawn from both papers.

It will be very strong culturally and will be inspired by the Daily Mail, with its breadth of appeal. There will be wide City and business coverage, plenty for women, good writers and political awareness, as regards both London and the whole nation.

The Evening Standard is very much alive, but living things have to adapt to life and the facts of life.

We have the money and the will to support the new paper. We are not buying it for purely altruistic reasons although there is an element of that.

Our jobs and our reputation are at stake. We do not want to go on losing money and they cannot buy the News or sustain a new paper. But we are buying the Standard because we want this new paper and we shall nurse it as we did the Mail, which is now largely keeping the Evening News, although when the Mail went tabloid the reverse was true.

It is completely at variance with the facts for Mr. Jenkins to imply that the Evening Standard has campaigned for all that could be best for London and Londoners and the Evening News has not. Efforts for the public good are a matter of record.

To list every successful activity of the Evening News would be a Herculean task, but its recent efforts range from active support of the arts through aggressive campaigning for social justice, to support for commuters. I can safely say that no major activity escapes the attention of the Evening News team.

It is totally unrealistic for anyone to perceive any new London evening paper that would be born as a result of a marriage between the Standard and the News as looking especially like either of its parents.

A new paper would be a new product with a new life. In short, an entirely new creation inspired by the example of the Daily Mail incorporating the best ingredients of today's Evening Standard with those of today's Evening News.

In any newspaper we will be looking for excellence wherever it is to be found.

We will not be confined by the elitist view that it exists only in the trendier parts of Camden. The capital deserves a newspaper to serve all its interests.

If ever there was a case of the right words being spoken at the wrong moment, this was it. Though the sentiments expressed were in themselves unexceptionable and might even be deemed inspiring *after* a deal had been done, all the basic assumptions were premature as far as the men who were supposed to create Harmsworth's journalistic phoenix were concerned. An interviewer on an early morning radio news show asked Rothwell: 'What's the feeling among the men?', and got a terrible earful: 'It's confusion, it's anger, it's dismay at being treated this way, in the twentieth century,' began Rothwell. 'We feel that the management have adopted the attitudes of a, say, Victorian ironmaster. Why should the men know about their livelihoods? Why should they be told? We find it intolerable that we've demanded consultation, we've asked to see the chairman, we've asked very politely. We've finally been forced to demand. We still haven't seen him, and yet in this morning's *Times* there's a huge interview with him – by another journalist.'

The *News* mandatory chapel meeting of Tuesday afternoon expressed their 'dismay and outrage' at their chairman's handling of the situation and sanctioned another angry missive to him, complaining of lack of consultation and assurances of any value.

> The final insult [it read] is that when the Chapel asked you to declare your intentions, you refused. And yet you chose to grant an interview, that same afternoon, with a journalist who represented an outside newspaper. . . .
>
> In effect, you have chosen to disclose to millions of newspaper readers what you have refused to discuss with your own staff: that is that a new paper is to be born, and that this will be achieved by making redundant scores of journalists from the *Evening Standard* and *Evening News*.

The only factor preventing an immediate walk-out was the continuing uncertainty about the fraternal support of the Beaverbrook chapels. The editorial FoCs of Associated and Beaverbrook had met again at the Old Bell the previous afternoon and failed to establish a united front. The fact that no fists had been brandished this time was evidence of increased solidarity, but they still could not agree on a common strategy, though Ted Simpson, on behalf of the *Standard*, was now quite ready to entertain the idea of a non-disruptive rally. The stumbling block this time had been the attitude of the *Daily Express* chapel officers, representing the largest of the five chapels concerned, who saw no reason to move until after the Thursday meeting with the general secretaries. By now there was enough information available to indicate that *Express* jobs were not at stake.

Harmsworth's interview in *The Times* had different consequences at the *Evening Standard*, where most of the journalists had still been hoping the problem would go away. The spectacle of Harmsworth speaking publicly as if he was already their proprietor seemed to make such hopes illusory. Tuesday afternoon's mandatory meeting at the *Standard* was the ugliest so far and the chapel committee had a tough job in holding the staff to the policy of working together. They emphasized that they had no confirmation from their own management that the developments outlined by Harmsworth would in fact take place, but there was an undercurrent of suspicion about members of the staff having already made private deals with Associated. The general mood was not improved by a typical Fleet Street rumour that Bubbles Harmsworth was going round London appointing her friends to the diary column of the new evening paper. 'Several people had a few wines,' recalled Ted Simpson, 'and had to be shut up. But everyone seemed tense, unhappy and bitter.'

Sir Max Aitken was also feeling tense and unhappy. Tuesday, 26 April was his first full day back in his office at the *Express* building since his stroke and he fell to brooding on the weight of his family history. His son and Jocelyn Stevens had been locked since breakfast time in the last stages of the negotiation at Lord Goodman's flat, where the deed of agreement was being drafted with Harmsworth and Associated's lawyers. The Beaverbrook chairman was evidently oppressed by this reality. At about 3 pm he asked his long-time secretary, Mrs Anne Westover, to send Charles Wintour in to see him. Wintour found him sitting in a darkened office, looking thoroughly miserable.

Sir Max said: 'Charles, I don't want to sell the *Evening*

Standard, and particularly not to the Harmsworths. Do I have to sign? Is there *any* alternative?'

Wintour said that he had personally explored what looked like all the realistic alternatives and come up with nothing. On the other hand, he had heard that the heiress Olga Deterding might be interested. There had been a gossip paragraph to that effect in the *Guardian* that morning and she had already made some approaches to Simon Jenkins about helping the *Standard*. Had Sir Max heard of her interest? The chairman said he had not, but he did know that she had plenty of money. It was at least worth sounding her out. As Wintour left on this assignment Sir Max said: 'If she makes an offer make sure it comes to me. Jocelyn doesn't show me everything.'

Tuesday was also the day on which the journalists' representatives finally got to see Roy Hattersley. The issues involved were not new to the government, which had been kept informed on how the talks were progressing since early March. The two sides to the negotiations, with Wintour dissenting, had not concealed the fact that they wanted to avoid any reference to the Monopolies Commission on the grounds that further delay could only put more jobs at risk. They also thought that there were no legal grounds for any such reference – under section 58(3)b of the Fair Trading Act 1973 the minister had no powers of reference if the managements could show that a closure was impending. As the government at that time was highly sensitive about any suggestion of ministers acting above the law this was a telling point. (In February the Attorney-General, Sam Silkin, had been censured by the Court of Appeal for such an alleged offence, though the decision was reversed by the Law Lords later in the year.)

Most of Hattersley's information about the talks came from the ubiquitous Lord Goodman, but he had also asked his own lawyers to review the legal situation. Their report concluded that if a 'special emergency' case was made out there was nothing Hattersley could lawfully do to delay the deal going through. The report was circulated to Michael Foot and other ministers who were concerned about the possible disappearance of the *Standard*. Initially Hattersley had been inclined to think that a 'special emergency' situation existed. Shortly after the case came to him he had told a table companion at a Prices

Commission lunch that, in the absence of other bidders, it was difficult to fault the logic of an Associated/Beaverbrook deal. Asked about Wintour's objections, Hattersley had replied: 'It's not so much what's good for the newspaper industry. Wintour just wants us to do what Wintour wants.'

Hattersley was certainly no enemy of the newspaper industry – he was an NUJ member himself – but, rather like the union general secretaries, he had come to believe that there was no alternative to the proposed merger. This was very much his frame of mind when he received the journalists' deputation at 1 Victoria Street on Tuesday evening. The deputation comprised three members of parliament, all NUJ members, and chapel officers of the *Daily Mail*, *Daily Express*, *Evening News* and *Evening Standard*. The key people were Georgina Walsh of the *Standard*, who was also chairperson of the London evening papers branch of the NUJ, and Mike Rothwell, who put the journalists' case for a reference to the Monopolies Commission.

Hattersley emphasized, as he had in his letter, how little discretion he had in the matter, though he said he would welcome any information that the unions could provide which might alter his view of the economic situation of the two groups. When Rothwell said that they needed time to open the situation up, as the Associated offer was, 'in City terms, a shut-out bid' (i.e. a deal that was available only to one party), Hattersley replied that his information was that no one else was interested in buying the *Standard*. The minister went on to say that if someone thought he had made a case under section 58(3)b of the Act and Hattersley delayed the deal for a week, he could find himself in court. There could not be any period of procrastination.

At this point Rothwell decided to bore in hard on the precise role of Sir Max Aitken's solicitor, who, he felt, must have been reading the Riot Act to the minister.

'Lord Goodman', Rothwell told Hattersley, 'is dilating loopholes in the act and causing a dangerous precedent. In future, any proprietor could put a newspaper into an economic emergency if he wanted to sell it without reference to the Monopolies Commission.' Hattersley smiled but refused to rise to the bait. 'There are no loopholes,' he said. 'It's a bad Act. It was not well drafted.'

After the meeting the journalists rehearsed the old platitude about 'full and frank discussions' for the benefit of the waiting television camera crews and concealed the fact that their hopes of government intervention had been disappointed. Rothwell said the time had come for the workers involved to take up 'battle positions'.

By this stage any hope of an aggressive intervention by the union general secretaries was fading rapidly. They were concerned about redundancy terms but offered scant leadership to those opposing the deal in principle. It was no secret that the national leadership of the two most powerful print unions, the NGA and SOGAT, were fundamentally out of sympathy with many of their members in Fleet Street. Both unions had moved their headquarters out of London – SOGAT to Southend-on-Sea, the NGA to Bedford – some years earlier and in both places it was often said that Fleet Street 'provides less than 5 per cent of our members and 90 per cent of our headaches'.

Olga Deterding, a single lady in her late forties, was no stranger to the newspaper business. She had inherited a fortune at the age of ten from her father, Sir Henri Deterding, one of the founders of Royal Dutch Shell, and had been a natural object of gossip columnists' attention ever since. As a young woman she had escaped the journalistic stereotype of 'poor little rich girl' by going to work in Albert Schweitzer's leper colony at Lambaréné, but she found it waiting for her on her return. Her romances were highly publicized (particularly her long-term attachments to Alan Whicker, the television personality, and Jonathan Routh, the fun-loving presenter of 'Candid Camera'). She came to know many journalists personally and to like them. She was a large woman, of strong character but fragile emotions, and eager to find a new purpose in life. She travelled a great deal but had recently displayed a desire for a stake in the British publishing business. She had put in a bid for the *Observer* before it was taken over by Atlantic Richfield and had toyed with the idea of putting money into *Encounter* magazine. She still had a great deal of money, though just how much was one of the few secrets she managed to keep. Estimates varied between £3 million and £23 million. When she was in London she lived in a penthouse flat in Mayfair, ordering her affairs with a see-through perspex telephone and surrounded by a magnificent array of sub-tropical plants.

Charles Wintour arrived at the penthouse at about 8 o'clock on Tuesday evening with a proposition. He guessed that the *Evening Standard* could be saved with an immediate injection of £2 million and a guarantee covering losses of up to £1 million per annum for the next three years. He stressed that these were his own figures which would need checking and that they were not bargaining at this stage. Was Miss Deterding interested? She was, but she would also like to know the price of buying the *Standard* outright. Wintour was intrigued to learn that she had written to Sir Max Aitken as long ago as December 1976 offering 'talks about talks' to help the *Standard*. Her only reply had been a verbal one from Jocelyn Stevens, thanking her for her interest. Either the letter had not reached Sir Max or he had forgotten her offer. Wintour promised to remedy the situation by trying to get a price for the *Standard* by the following morning.

During their conversation Wintour found Miss Deterding quite shrewd on financial questions, if sometimes eccentric on other matters, though this was scarcely a disqualification for press proprietorship. Wintour thought her interest well worth encouraging. Immediately after the meeting he rang Lord Goodman's flat in Portland Place, where Jocelyn Stevens was still in negotiation, and told his chief executive what he had done, acting on the authority of the chairman. Stevens undertook to follow it up.

The follow-up was extremely swift, though not exactly along the lines that Wintour had in mind. Shortly before 11 o'clock that night Miss Deterding, who had known Stevens since childhood, received a call from him asking whether she had something light for supper. She said there was some caviar handy. Stevens said he would be right over, accompanied by young Maxwell Aitken, to talk newspapers. Over the lady's caviar at midnight, Beaverbrook's chief executive told Miss Deterding some astronomic untruths: the price of the *Standard* would be around £10 million and she should be prepared to lose £2·5 million a year for the next three years. Having effectively scared her off, he was back at Portland Place within the hour for further negotiations. Stevens and Maxwell Aitken eventually left Lord Goodman's flat at 3 am with the draft of an agreement with Associated ready to be typed up. It had been an exceptionally gruelling breakfast.

When Charles Wintour called on Miss Deterding on Wednesday morning he naturally found her less keen on investing in the future of the *Standard*. She told him Jocelyn had persuaded her the sums involved were so large that 'it just was not on'. On his return to the office Wintour penned a dry note to Stevens: 'The lady was obviously put off by your midnight visit and I did not press her to change her view as I felt it would be unfair to her. . . .'

Stevens was unrepentant about scotching Miss Deterding's interest. 'Olga was a very old friend,' he said later. 'But she did not have *that* much money and she was really not up to operating with the sharks that infest these waters.'

The national newspapers on Wednesday morning all saw the Associated/Beaverbrook deal as imminent, though Wintour's latest comments on the situation were dutifully recorded. He had kept his contacts with Miss Deterding a secret but felt free to tell the press of his meeting with Sir Max Aitken. 'There has been no signature,' Wintour said for quotation. 'I have just been talking to him [Sir Max]. Negotiations are not complete. You have to believe that.' The *Daily Telegraph*'s able industrial correspondent, Blake Baker, described Wintour's efforts as those of a man 'fighting a rearguard action'.

This was also the impression of an increasingly large number of *Evening Standard* journalists. Within the NUJ chapel the policy of bringing the paper out come hell or high water was under attack from dissident members. Ted Simpson and Charles Catchpole, the deputy FoC, went to see Wintour to tell him that the editorial cohesion was beginning to fragment and could collapse entirely without some action by the management. They handed him a letter setting out the latest chapel resolution requesting information and covering the main areas of complaint. It also indicated that they could no longer act as cheer-leaders without more concrete support from the top. The key passage read:

The strain on our people, caught in a sea of rumour and uncertainty, is now becoming unbearable. Over the recent

period, as responsible Chapel officers, we have addressed
letters and resolutions to important sections of Group management. We have had no <u>written</u> replies setting out the assurances which are so clearly necessary for the Chapel's morale.

Wintour forwarded the letter to Stevens's office with an
accompanying memorandum of his own:

> ... it is very hard to keep the *Evening Standard* working when
> you will not reply to a single note addressed to you. Surely
> it is possible to at least indicate the arrangements for redun-
> dancy and pensions if a merger is contemplated. In my letter
> to you dated 12 April I said that 'Their need to know is
> absolutely fundamental to good industrial relations, to
> common sense and common decency'. It has still not been
> met and there is a great wave of bitterness building up on
> both sides of Fleet Street at the moment.

Part of the evidence for this bitterness was a leaflet being
distributed on the streets of London by *Evening Standard* van
drivers. Under the cudgelling head: 'MURDER OF A NEWS-
PAPER? WHICH ONE?', its language was more direct and
uncompromising than that used by the journalists:

> Any person who murders another could get life imprison-
> ment. What will the Associated News or the Beaverbrook get
> for murdering a newspaper?

> Talks have been taking place with a view to merge or sell
> a title of a newspaper without the employees, many with
> long and loyal service to their employers, being consulted.

> *Remember they said 'It's what living in London is all about'.*

> If the Beaverbrook Newspaper Group and Associated
> Newspapers have their way we will not be able to say that
> much longer. In an atmosphere of secrecy a deal is being
> made to merge the Evening News with the Evening Standard.
> It will be a sad day for London when its population of seven
> million people will have no choice on what evening paper
> to buy.

Freedom of the Press

Once again a few people will decide what you can or can not read, and in the process make thousands of workers unemployed. We say they should not be allowed to take such a decision without you, the people of London, the public, having the opportunity of expressing a point of view.

We therefore request you to:

Write to your Member of Parliament;

Write to the Press;

Write to the two companies concerned;

Demand the Government puts such plans reached by the two newspaper groups before the Monopoly Commission under Section 58 of the Fair Trading Act.

If you are a member of a printing union write to your union representative demanding resistance to the moves.

The Secretary of State for Prices and Consumer Protection, Mr. Hattersley, would be doing the Newspaper Industry, and the reading public, a disservice if he were to act merely as a rubber stamp for this or any other proposed deal.

ACT NOW BEFORE IT IS TOO LATE!

Reg Brady, who organized the leaflet campaign, told Wintour that no evening papers would be delivered for an 'indefinite' period if the deal went through. Wintour took the threat with a grain of salt but passed it on to Jocelyn Stevens. The threat was probably not empty – at that stage some chapel officers feared an even worse outcome. According to one FoC, 'Some vans were likely to get burnt, if not buildings.'

That afternoon Charles Catchpole was called from an acrimonious chapel meeting to take a call from Stevens. He returned to inform members that the chief executive had confirmed that no deal had yet been signed. Stevens had also told him: 'We are not so damned stupid as to think in this day and age that things can be done without agreement.' Armed with this fragile assurance the men returned to work.

The journalists at the *Evening News* were already on strike, with the qualified blessing of the NUJ. Mike Rothwell had telephoned

Ken Morgan with news of the strike vote – 107 for, 17 against, 2 abstentions – after Wednesday morning's mandatory chapel meeting. He emphasized that without any response from Harmsworth the chapel felt it had no alternative, though the strike was not strictly constitutional as the NUJ had a disputes procedure which should be gone through before any stoppage. Morgan's immediate response was: 'The whole damn thing is unconstitutional, particularly the attitude of the management.' As general secretary of the union he felt obliged to warn the chapel to be wary of any 'overreaction' that might play into the management's hands, but he had no quarrel with the strike as it 'took full account of the justified level of emotion'.

Despite the strike, Lou Kirby and his deputy, John Leese, managed to put a paper together, working from agency copy and with a handful of stringers. Kirby might not be a philosopher-editor in the Wintour mould but he was a master of the nuts and bolts of the business. He also had the motivation of knowing that Harmsworth wanted him to edit the new evening paper. The proprietor had formally asked him to take the job the previous day and Kirby had accepted. (Jenkins and Wintour had been wrong in assuming that Kirby had been promised the job much earlier, though within Associated it was always assumed that he would get it.)

While Kirby was earning his money the hard way, his erstwhile rival for the new post was being entertained at the Savoy by Colin Owen-Browne, the managing director designate of the new paper. Owen-Browne was an advertising man in his late thirties, renowned in newspaper circles for the pugnacity of his salesmanship and his corner-cutting methods of doing business. He had originally risen to prominence in the Beaverbrook organization under the patronage of Jocelyn Stevens, and had been advertising director for a while. Earlier in the year he had fallen out with his patron and others over the new tabloid *Daily Express* and had disappeared ignominiously from the scene, only to pop up a few months later as a close confidant of Vere Harmsworth. It was generally agreed that Owen-Browne was irrepressible. Charles Wintour could not stand him. At the Savoy, acting as Harmsworth's plenipotentiary, Owen-Browne drew a glittering word picture of the career prospects that would open up for Jenkins as deputy editor of the new evening paper. Jenkins listened politely but said that he had already made it clear that he could not serve under Kirby and that Owen-Browne should make this clear to Harmsworth as time was running out for everybody concerned.

Owen-Browne also indicated that the new paper would need to have a lot more sex in it than the *Evening Standard*. Back at Shoe Lane, Jenkins reported the conversation to Wintour, who noted that Owen-Browne was still 'his old bullshitting appalling self'. At Associated Owen-Browne told his colleagues about the meeting and the continued intransigence of young Jenkins. Among them Jenkins became known as 'Wintour's clone'.

Shortly before 4 o'clock on the Wednesday afternoon, Wintour went to Sir Max Aitken's office to report the negative results of his encounter with Miss Deterding. The chairman seemed no happier than he had been the previous day as he listened to Wintour's account of how his chief executive and his son had throttled an option. Wintour knew that Sir Max's antipathy towards Sir James Goldsmith had previously ruled him out as a bidder, but that had been at a much earlier stage of negotiations with Associated. Judging that the moment was now right, Wintour now posed what was for the chairman a choice between two evils – sign with Harmsworth, or sanction an overture to Goldsmith.

Sir Max, studiously avoiding the names, said: 'We must both explore every alternative, and above all we must be *seen* to explore every alternative.'

Wintour took this as his authority to go and see Goldsmith. The meeting with Sir Max continued with some desultory conversation about the Associated deal, from which it emerged that the chairman was not at all clear about the intentions of his own board. He asked: 'What are they going to do with all that money? Put it into the *Daily Express*?' Wintour informed him that he thought something like £2 million might go to the *Daily Express* and some of the balance would perhaps be used to diversify the company. Within an hour of leaving Sir Max, Wintour was having tea with Sir James Goldsmith at the head office of Cavenham Foods in Leadenhall Street. Sir James poured, from a silver teapot.

No two men could have been more eager to do business but there were trying complications – the main one being that neither could be confident of support from his own board of directors. Sir James confided a great liking for the *Evening Standard* and said that if he had been dealing with his own money he would happily have bought it outright. It did not, he modestly maintained, much matter to him whether he made £43 million a year or £45 million a year. However there was no industrial logic in taking over the *Standard*, or even a slice of it, as far as his company was concerned. The Beaverbrook group as a whole was a different matter and he might well be able to sell that idea to his directors. In fact he already had a proposal forming in his mind that might suit Cavenham's shareholders. The shape of it was a £5 million guarantee for the Beaverbrook overdraft, plus Cavenham underwriting a rights issue of £5 million for new working capital.

Sir James asked Wintour how such an idea might strike Jocelyn Stevens, whom he had come to regard as a 'volatile' figure. Wintour confessed his current impression that Stevens was now so deeply into the deal with Associated that he would not wish to draw back. But Wintour undertook to go back and take a new reading.

Wintour was agreeably surprised to find that Stevens instantly warmed to the possibilities of Goldsmith's intervention. Although it was less than three months since he had denounced him as hostile, Stevens had, following the attempted coup against him, returned to the enthusiasm he had had for his old schoolmate when Goldsmith first bought into the A shares in January. When subsequently reminded of this apparent *volte face* Stevens saw no inconsistency – he had previously been obliged to denounce Sir James because of his chairman's attitude. Now that Wintour had told him that Sir Max's view had changed, however temporarily, he was free to re-embrace the Goldsmith option openly. Sir James, like Olga Deterding, was an old friend, but the Deterding objection happily did not apply. Goldsmith apparently had the money and was thoroughly at home in shark-infested waters. Stevens had already been considering drawing him into the action again but had felt unable to move without Sir Max's authority. Wintour's independent efforts had removed that constraint: he could now see Goldsmith and talk of company affairs 'without having to play the traitor'. As it happened Goldsmith had arranged to see

Stevens that very evening at a dinner given by David Metcalfe, a mutual friend. Stevens would let Wintour know what happened. After dinner Stevens told Goldsmith he could deliver Beaverbrook Newspapers but he must have an offer by 11 am the next day.

That evening Simon Jenkins had another engagement in Eaton Square. Vere Harmsworth was in an expansive mood, evidently confident that the deal would be complete within 24 hours. He displayed the various kingdoms of Associated Newspapers and offered Jenkins anything he wanted, with one exception – the editorship of the new evening paper. That post, Harmsworth told him in confidence, *had* to be reserved for Lou Kirby.

'What,' asked Harmsworth, 'are you going to do?'

'Have a very long drink,' Jenkins replied. He went on to say that he would probably take a break from newspaper power games and write books. Harmsworth seemed incredulous.

Jenkins walked round Belgravia for an hour torn between preserving the confidentiality of the discussion and the terms of his agreement with Charles Wintour to share all information of importance to the future of the *Evening Standard*. Eventually he decided that informing his superior in the organization could not really be considered a breach of confidence. He rang Wintour from a call box on the edge of Belgrave Square to say that their strategy had failed and that he was effectively out of a job. Kirby definitely had the editorship. Wintour, working on the 'all's fair' principle, promptly leaked the story of Kirby's appointment and Jenkins's rejection of the deputy editorship to *The Times*.

At 1.20 am Wintour was woken by a call from Stevens. The dinner with Goldsmith had been fruitful, though the time left was perilously short. There was still hope of keeping the *Standard* intact, and Goldsmith would make a move some time in the morning. Fortunately, the lawyers for Associated had still not typed up the final draft of the deed of agreement.

Early on the morning of Thursday, 28 April Wintour wrote a letter of guarded optimism to Michael Foot, explaining the new situation:

Dear Michael,

Just to keep you informed, there is a very slight chance that we may have a solution which will keep the *Evening Standard* alive as a separate entity.

This depends really on Sir James Goldsmith. He might either be ready to inject several millions into Beaverbrook Newspapers on certain terms which will include a management restructure and certain promises of assistance from the trade unions involved; or alternatively he might make an outright bid for control by offering a substantial sum for the voting shares now owned by the Beaverbrook Foundation. . . .

. . . Goldsmith's conditions would in no way affect the editorship of the *Evening Standard* for which I am glad to say he has a high regard. If such a development occurs – and time is running out fast – I hope very much that it would receive your blessing even if you may not find Goldsmith the most welcome newspaper owner.

The sad fact is that Sir Max is a very sick man . . . and I think it would be best for his health if he were to relinquish all responsibilities for the newspapers. . . .

NINE

High Afternoon at the Bonnington

THERE WAS NO mention of a possible intervention by Goldsmith in the morning papers of Thursday, 28 April. The quality press concentrated its attention on the terms of the deal with Associated, on the assumption that it was only hours away. The most detailed story, by Blake Baker in the *Daily Telegraph*, estimated the cost of redundancies at around £9 million, to be shared by the two newspaper groups and the State Redundancy Payments Fund. Some 2000 print and distribution workers and 150 journalists were expected to lose their jobs. The only important item missing from his story – and those of the other newspapers – was exactly where the sentence would be announced. The setting of the long-deferred meeting between the top brass of the two groups and the national union officials was still a well kept secret.

Tom Pocock, one of the *Standard*'s most seasoned reporters, graphically recalled the mood of that morning: 'We were like men with the black bags already tied over our heads, waiting for the long drop.'

The prospect of being about to be hanged wonderfully concentrated the minds of the various chapel officials. All along the efforts to oppose the deal had been hampered by division and mutual distrust between the men most likely to be affected. Communication between the diverse unions in the newspaper business is always hazardous, but most national newspapers have a federated house structure in which the chapels representing each craft can confront common problems. At the *Evening News* nobody had been able to create a federated house. As the crisis developed Mike Rothwell had tried to establish a dialogue with the other chapels, but met with little success. He was even, as he put it, 'given a severe bollocking' for trying to build alliances with union members on the rival paper. On the *Evening Standard* a federated house existed but the journalists had withdrawn from it some years earlier after a dispute over alleged interference with editorial matter by the printers. In consequence, there was never a point at which those threatened with redundancy could speak with one voice. Indeed the loudest voices were sometimes raised against co-employees rather than the employers. At one staff meeting the *Standard*'s forceful theatre critic, Milton Shulman, had launched a tirade against the restrictive practices of print and distribution workers that made even his own executives wince. 'It might have been true,' said one, 'but it was not exactly politic, when we were all trying to make common cause.'

On Thursday morning these internecine squabbles assumed a less serious aspect as FoCs and chapel officers from Beaverbrook and Associated assembled for a strategy meeting at St Bride's Institute in Fleet Street. The television cameras had been invited, the idea being to make it a major media event with 'community action' as its theme. There were rousing speeches – 'If one goes down the road, we all go down the road' was greeted with wild applause – and many professions of solidarity. For the first time in anyone's memory a public platform was being shared by union representatives of both the *News* and *Standard*. Under the vigorous chairmanship of Reg Brady, the meeting overwhelmingly endorsed the following propositions:

1   That this meeting of FoCs and union representatives of Associated Newspapers and Beaverbrook Newspapers agrees to resist any proposed merger or selling of any title between Associated Newspapers and Beaverbrook Newspapers which would result in unemployment for any of our membership, and would be detrimental to the reading public in London. Our aim, therefore, is to maintain two evening newspapers.
2   That a liaison committee be formed from the two groups for liaison, and to seek to maintain the maximum unity possible.

Despite the ringing resolutions, there was an undercurrent of frustration. For all those present the next scheduled meeting with their respective managements was at 6.30 pm, when they would be told what had already been decided elsewhere. Rothwell remembers thinking that they had finally achieved a united front, but too late to make much difference. Then, as the meeting was winding to a close shortly after midday, Reg Brady was handed a note with the intelligence '2.30 pm Bonnington Hotel' – an alert printer had extracted the information that this was where his general secretary would be from a switchboard operator at union headquarters. Brady read out the note and was greeted with a chorus of 'Where's the fucking Bonnington?' Someone knew it as a medium sized hotel in Southampton Row just north of Holborn tube station, about a mile away. They finally had a fix on where the climax of the secret talks was to take place. Brady announced that the first action of the liaison committee would be to round up as many members as possible and picket the hotel.

By 2 o'clock, when the senior management and national union representatives were starting to arrive for the secret summit, Southampton Row was chock-a-block with raucous, placard-waving print workers. The slogans were calculated to give offence: 'Don't lower your standards, Sir Max'; 'You opposed dictatorship once, Sir Max'; and a reference to his Battle of Britain exploits, 'Are we the first of the few, Sir Max?' Lord Goodman had to be escorted through the throng by policemen, pursued by a man carrying the banner 'Headlines, deadlines – then breadlines'. Other demonstrators jostled him, shouting: 'No sell-out'. Once inside the foyer of the hotel the visiting dignitaries were directed to a basement conference room booked in the name of Associated Furniture Investments. The stage was now set for what Ken Morgan later described as 'the most Gilbertian day in the history of Fleet Street'.

Associated had assembled a large cast for what was presumed to be its hour of triumph, though Stevens had warned Vere Harmsworth earlier in the day about the approach from Goldsmith. Prominent among Harmsworth's entourage were his managing directors, Mick Shields and John Winnington-Ingram, and Colin Owen-Browne. Also hovering in attendance were lesser employees charged with looking after the projector that was to be used to present Associated's cinematic vision of the new monopoly evening paper. Owen-Browne, at his most clubbable, was soon chatting up the leading union bigwigs, Bill Keys of SOGAT, Joe Wade and Les Dixon of the NGA, Owen

O'Brien and his brother Teddy of NATSOPA. With Lord Goodman present everyone seemed anxious to exhibit his best behaviour: Morgan likened his influence to that of the cavalry in battle, 'adding tone to what would otherwise be seen as an unseemly brawl'.

Considering that the meeting's purpose was to axe a newspaper, it began in amicable style. Most of the important union leaders, like Keys and Dixon, were by now reconciled to the inevitability of the deal. In private contacts with the two managements before the meeting they had been led to believe that if the *Standard* were allowed to survive the *News* would have to go. As far as the preservation of both titles was concerned it seemed they could not win, so their main objective had been to extract the best possible terms for those who would be made redundant. The managements had agreed to follow the generous guidelines on voluntary redundancy set out in 'Programme for Action', which had been endorsed by all the general secretaries earlier in the year (though it was later rejected by union memberships, with the exception of the NUJ). Having extracted a pledge of redundancy payments of three weeks average earnings per year for those under 60 (four weeks for journalists), the general secretaries felt there was little more they could do. The meeting, as Rothwell and the militants had suspected all along, had not been designed to be a negotiation but to enshrine a *fait accompli*.

The only impediment to the opening pleasantries between the parties was the fact that Lord Goodman appeared to be the only representative of the interests of Beaverbrook. Sir Max had not been expected to attend because of his health, but the time for the start of formal proceedings came and went without any sign of Stevens or Maxwell Aitken. Despite Goodman's assurances that the deal would go through, the union leaders began to get restive. Bill McLoughlin of the Engineering Union (AEUW) wisecracked: 'I don't know whether I'm in a funeral parlour or an intensive care unit.' Teddy O'Brien bet Goodman £10 that there would be other bidders by the next day. A phone call to the *Express* building established that Stevens had not forgotten the meeting; he had had to sort out some last-minute problems and was on his way.

Stevens had been having a lovely day. At 9.30 am, Goldsmith rang from his car to say that he was formally interested in acquiring a larger stake in Beaverbrook Newspapers. His offer was to look at the facts and figures of the Beaverbrook empire to see, as an independent observer, if there was a solution that would avoid a merger and save the *Standard*. Stevens's response was that he would need something in writing before the Bonnington meeting. This was to strengthen his hand as there was still no document from Harmsworth. Stevens then collected his shadow, Maxwell Aitken, and swished off to see Lord Robens, the boss of Vickers Armstrong, in his office at the top of Millbank Tower overlooking the Thames. Lord Robens was a trustee of the Beaverbrook Foundation, which controlled most of the shares in the three newspapers. He was the only trustee who was not either related to Sir Max Aitken or an employee of the company and it was thought that he had a strong influence on Sir Max, though this was not invariably the case. Stevens had arranged to see him in order to go through the details of the Associated deal. When informed of the Goldsmith intervention, Robens appeared to be favourably impressed.

At 11.15 am Stevens checked with his own office and was told that a letter from Sir James Goldsmith had already been delivered. He at once telephoned Harmsworth and told him of Goldsmith's intervention.

'Too late, we have a deal,' said Harmsworth.

'No we haven't,' said Stevens.

At Harmsworth's invitation Stevens and Maxwell Aitken agreed to call on him at his office on the way from the Vickers Tower to Fleet Street. When they met, Stevens repeated his conviction that the Associated deal could not now go through automatically. Goldsmith's proposals would have to be considered by the Beaverbrook board and, very probably, by the government. They none the less agreed that while the situation remained unclear the plans to meet at the Bonnington should not be cancelled.

Stevens and Aitken then went to meet Goldsmith in the boardroom of Grand Metropolitan Hotels where he was having a business lunch. David Karr, who had originally been drawn into Beaverbrook's affairs to defend the company from Goldsmith, was also there to advise on his intervention. One of the main subjects of discussion was the amount of money Goldsmith was prepared to put up.

Sir James himself was most concerned about the role of Lord Goodman, whom he regarded as a key opponent of his Fleet Street ambitions. He was most anxious to have no further problems with the former head of the Newspaper Proprietors Association. From his point of view, the most vital part of the exercise was to have Lord Goodman firmly identified with the Associated deal as the only option in front of the assembled union representatives with 'no time to turn on a sixpence and change'. The object was to destroy Goodman's credibility with the trade-union leadership.

Stevens arrived at the Bonnington late but with brilliant timing at 2.50 pm. The hairiest part of the operation was getting past the angry placard-wavers in the street and the chants of 'Judas Jocelyn'. Once inside the conference room he had a rapt audience.

Smiling his apologies, Stevens explained that he had just been in contact with another party regarding the future of Beaverbrook Newspapers and went on to identify the party as Sir James Goldsmith. Lord Goodman seemed stunned, Harmsworth looked rueful, while the faces of the union leaders struggled with a congestion of emotions – outrage at being lured together on what now appeared to be a fool's errand and thoughtfulness at what the new initiative implied for their members. As nobody knew how to proceed and Lord Goodman disclaimed responsibility for further conduct of the meeting, the gathering broke up into small groups with the main focus around the trolley of drinks, provided by Associated Newspapers for celebratory purposes.

The Harmsworth men huddled and decided that, under the circumstances, there was no point in going ahead with the presentation they had prepared. One of the junior executives piped up: 'Do we need the projector any more?'

'Not unless someone has some holiday snaps to show,' growled a voice from the vicinity of the drinks trolley.

In the general mêlée Harmsworth managed to engineer a brief encounter with Stevens and utter words of reproach – 'You've used me as a stalking-horse for Jimmy Goldsmith.' The

Beaverbrook chief executive looked his most wide-eyed and demure.

From the general secretaries there emerged something approaching a consensus. It went as follows: if Goldsmith was going to make a bid or put forward a plan, the sooner they all saw him the better. There was no time like the present. Stevens said he would try to arrange a meeting with Goldsmith later that day. Some of the union men said they had other business to attend to in the meantime but it was agreed that they should reconvene at the Bonnington at 5.15 pm to see what further developments had occurred. As Ken Morgan dodged out through the hotel lobby he was cornered by a journalist covering the story and asked whether he was going on to another meeting. 'I'm just going to buy *two* evening papers,' was the cheerful reply.

Morgan was also going back to Acorn House, the NUJ head-quarters, where he was expecting to meet Mike Rothwell and other chapel officials. As soon as they received the news Rothwell and his deputy, Tony Grantham, rushed back to their newspaper, where another mandatory chapel meeting was scheduled to begin. It was pelting with rain and there were no cabs to be found. 'We got back wringing wet,' Rothwell re-called, 'bursting to be first with the glad tidings, but they already fucking knew.' A flash on Goldsmith's intervention had already come over the agency tapes in the *Evening News* office.

But it was still an invigorating meeting with tremendous applause for the efforts of the chapel committee. In the general euphoria, Rothwell attempted to sound a modest note of caution. The strategy of flushing out a rival offer had worked but all that gave them was time for a more serious bidder to emerge. Nobody could afford to relax until that happened. Rothwell went on to quote odds against Goldsmith emerging as the eventual winner, mainly because 'he will only be bidding with paper'. When asked later how he could make this assertion, before any details of Goldsmith's offer had emerged publicly, Rothwell drily replied: 'Because I'm a City journalist.'

At the *Evening Standard* the chapel was well into a long mandatory session when the news arrived. The main item before the journalists was a fighting letter from Simon Jenkins urging the staff to stick together at this, the darkest hour in the newspaper's 150-year history. His peroration ran: 'I must tell the staff that irrespective of my own position I honestly do not believe the new paper to be a worthy successor to the *Evening Standard*. It will not be our kind of paper. . . . We must not let this ship sink.' These sentiments, combined with the knowledge that their editor had just turned down handsome offers from Associated, raised his prestige to new heights. Another item on the agenda was a proposal, supported by the chapel committee, that the journalists effectively bury the hatchet with the print and publishing chapels by rejoining the federated house. The motion was fiercely debated, as many journalists evidently still feared interference with editorial independence, but was eventually carried by 58 votes to 45. Then Ted Simpson was called to the telephone. He returned with the news that the caller had been John Devine, the president of the NUJ, relaying a message from Ken Morgan. It ran: 'All the bets are off. Goldsmith has intervened and wants six weeks to complete his study.'

The journalists, accompanied by their editor, promptly adjourned to the Poppinjay public house in Fleet Street, next door to the *Express* building, where they spent the rest of the evening noisily digesting the news. As Simon Jenkins dispensed interviews to rival newspaper reporters catching up on the story, horny-handed printers from the *Express* came by to pump his fastidious hand and tell him what a fine young fella' he was. 'There was', Ted Simpson recalled, 'great rejoicing.'

Meanwhile back at the Bonnington most of the cast had reassembled, with the exception of Lord Goodman, whose services were now largely redundant. Stevens had done his part and informed the general secretaries that he had fixed a time for them to meet Goldsmith at the Cavenham offices in Leadenhall Street later that evening. There was also discussion of a strong rumour that 'Tiny' Rowland, maverick head of Lonrho, the British-based multinational trading company, was interested in acquiring the *Standard*. Vere Harmsworth asked diffidently whether there was anything more he could do for anybody and heard 'Fix a meal.' The long-suffering proprietor duly had the hotel organize impromptu food in a room abutting the kitchens downstairs. Around 6 o'clock the Associated contingent discreetly started to melt away, leaving the union men to devise a strategy for their meeting with Sir James.

At 6.30 Harmsworth and Winnington-Ingram had a date with heads of department and FoCs of Associated in the Beaver Hall in the City, where they had intended to break the news of the deal and show their marketing film. In the event only Winnington-Ingram went along, apologizing for the absence of the chairman who had been 'with general secretaries all afternoon'. Flanked by Lou Kirby, Winnington-Ingram shouldered the disagreeable task of formally disclosing the plan for a monopoly evening paper after it had come unstuck. He bravely spoke up for the deal, though his discomfiture was apparent. One problem, he said, was 'that tension had built up in the media' – a back-handed compliment to the methods that had been deployed, in different ways, by Rothwell and Wintour.

Over at the *Express* building the Beaverbrook management pondered the seriousness of the Lonrho interest. There could scarcely be any doubt about the company's capacity: with pre-tax profits of £92 million on a turnover of more than £1000 million, Lonrho was clearly capable of digesting the entire Beaverbrook empire. Tiny Rowland, a highly individual businessman whose operations had earned the epithet of 'the unpleasant and unacceptable face of capitalism' from Edward Heath, had earlier declared a willingness to join any Goldsmith attempt to gain control of Beaverbrook Newspapers. But Rowland expressed interest in a lot of things.

His latest intervention had been characteristically bizarre. It emerged that he had called the *Standard* switchboard at 7 o'clock that morning wanting to speak to City journalist Jim Levi, who had asked a mutual friend to sound Rowland out the previous day. Levi wasn't in, but Rowland delivered a diatribe against the sale of the *Standard* to Associated to one of his colleagues and then hung up without giving his name. Levi, when told of the anonymous caller, guessed that it was Rowland and called back. Rowland expressed interest in intervening to save the *Standard*. Levi told Jenkins and at lunchtime, while Goldsmith and Stevens were conferring in the Grand Metropolitan boardroom, Rowland telephoned the editor at the Serpentine restaurant in Hyde Park to make his interest known. Jenkins thought he was serious.

*　　*　　*

The union leaders met Goldsmith at 8 o'clock at his offices in Leadenhall Street with Jocelyn Stevens and Maxwell Aitken in attendance. The boss of Cavenham immediately made it clear that he was not making a formal bid for Beaverbrook, but was rather offering 'an intention, a plan, a hope' for the future. He wanted a period of six weeks to look at the figures to see if there was an alternative that would keep the *Standard* alive. He also proposed to conduct his study and discuss his findings with the unions and management jointly.

First impressions of Goldsmith were good: 'He was', said one of the general secretaries, 'a one-sheet-of-paper man. Three figures here. Four figures there. It will work or it won't.' They liked that. Goldsmith also talked about the need for the *Standard* as a contribution to press diversity, saying that its loss would be a blow to democracy. They liked that too.

Stevens was clearly promoting Goldsmith to the union leaders, though the attitude of young Maxwell Aitken, who scarcely uttered a word, was hard to discern. Stevens also gave a firm pledge that the *Standard* would remain in business whilst the study was in progress. It was essentially a friendly meeting, mellowed further by Goldsmith's generosity with his Scotch, but there were moments when old animosities rose to the surface.

Stevens and Bill Keys were old sparring partners and at one time, during the Glasgow closure, had almost come to blows in the street. Keys, the son of a newspaper casual worker from the Elephant and Castle, liked to illustrate the class gulf between himself and the Beaverbrook boss by recounting a Panorama programme in which they had appeared as representatives of the two sides of Fleet Street. The programme had listed the wedding presents they had given their wives. Stevens's gifts included a diamond tiara and an expensive car. Keys had given his wife an alarm clock so that she could wake him the next morning to get him off to work on time. Stevens, Keys would often say, was 'a man who couldn't run a bath'. He delivered the message in a different way at the Leadenhall Street meeting, after catching Goldsmith's eye.

'The first thing I'd do would be to sack him,' said Keys, jabbing a finger in the direction of the Beaverbrook chief executive. Stevens laughed and said, 'You don't really mean that, Bill', but nobody could be quite sure. In any event, there were no dissenters from the view that Goldsmith should be given a chance, though it was hoped that the Harmsworth offer would remain on the table, if only as a safety net.

At about 10 o'clock Stevens and Goldsmith moved to an upstairs office to watch the news. The programme carried an item on Tiny Rowland's interest in the *Standard* and reported the progress of 'tense negotiations' on the paper's future in the Cavenham office of Sir James Goldsmith. At that point the main action at Cavenham was the sound of relaxed laughter emanating from the general secretaries' room. Tensions by now had thoroughly eased after the end of what seemed a successful meeting. Stevens went back downstairs, happily contemplating the discrepancies between appearance and reality in the news business. Outside the general secretaries' room he was confronted by the burly figure of Bill Keys at his most mock-menacing.

'How many times have I told you, Joss,' he said, motioning the chief executive to one side. Stevens waited, breath bated for some ominous development.

'How many times have I told you', Keys jokingly went on, 'not to give the lads drink?'

Stevens, Aitken, and Goldsmith decided that it was their duty to put Vere Harmsworth in the picture and inform him of the attitude of the general secretaries. At Eaton Square, the Associated proprietor, courteous to the last, allowed Goldsmith to use his telephone to call Tiny Rowland and find out what he had in mind. Rowland affirmed that his interest was genuine and thought they might have lunch together to see what could be done. Harmsworth uncomfortably watched the architecture of his great deal being dismantled in his own sitting-room. He made one last offer to Stevens. How much more do you want to complete the deal, he asked. '£5 million,' said Stevens. In the general confusion a man came in carrying a crumpled brown paper bag – the proprietor's take-away Chinese supper. Stevens, Aitken and Goldsmith left just before midnight, to round off the day at Annabel's nightclub.

At the *Express* building someone asked Charles Wintour if it was really true that he was the only Beaverbrook director to oppose the deal with Associated Newspapers.

'Not any more,' replied Wintour.

TEN

Menopausal Millionaires

Vere Harmsworth counter-attacked on the day after the Bonnington débâcle: while his top executives searched the City take-over code for some just cause or impediment to Goldsmith's designs on Beaverbrook Newspapers, the chairman of Associated Newspapers addressed himself forcefully to the chairman of the TUC Printing Industries Committee. His letter to Bill Keys, dated 20 April 1977, read:

> I would be grateful if you would convey to your colleagues the following most serious warning that I feel I must record to protect the goodwill of our industrial relations.
>
> Associated Newspapers Group Limited may not be able, for commercial reasons, to renew their offer to acquire the *Evening Standard* and meet the redundancies thus incurred at a rate in excess of the statutory level unless it is possible to launch the new merged evening paper by the end of May.
>
> I am informing you of our position as I am well aware of the difficulties that you and your colleagues will face in enabling negotiations to be completed so quickly in the event of Beaverbrook renewing their approach to us.

The message was clear enough: the unions could no longer look to Associated for redundancy pay-offs at generous 'Programme for Action' levels if they got themselves bogged down in fruitless negotiations with Goldsmith. Keys evidently took the threat seriously. On 1 May the *Sunday Telegraph* quoted him as saying:

> It could finish up that we have no evening newspapers in London. This four to six week situation could mean that if at the end, Goldsmith says no, the Standard is a dead duck.
>
> At the same time the Evening News is haemorrhaging away to such an extent that it might not be possible to put money

185

into restructuring it, particularly in the summer months which are no time to launch a new paper. These are my fears.

The reaction further down the union ladder was more combative. A statement issued jointly by all union representatives at the *Evening Standard* denounced Harmsworth's 'intended blackmail' and declared that 'every opportunity should be given to any interested person who seeks to maintain newspaper titles . . .'. Harmsworth's letter was, none the less, firm evidence of Associated's intention not to give up without a fight.

Further evidence was provided by the announcement that Associated had retained S. G. Warburg, the City merchant bank, to act on its behalf. Warburg's had an impressive record of success in publishing take-over struggles, having previously acted for IPC, Reed International and the Thomson Organisation.

Lord Rothermere returned to England from his home in Florida to oversee the next phase of the campaign. Though now 79 years old, Esmond Rothermere was still an active man and retained the chairmanship of the Daily Mail and General Trust which held over 51 per cent of Associated Newspapers shares. His Lordship was reported to be displeased by his son's failure to consummate the deal with Beaverbrook.

There were father-and-son problems at Beaverbrook too where young Maxwell Aitken, along with other members of the family, marshalled an attempt to persuade Sir Max to relinquish his executive power on the grounds of ill-health. It was argued that he should keep the honorary title of president while a trusted lieutenant assumed his executive authority. Among the candidates fingered for such a role was a Beaverbrook non-executive director from the Aitkens' Scottish homeland, Sir Iain Stewart. A former chairman of Fairfields shipyard on the Clyde, a director of the Eagle Star Insurance Company and of the Royal Bank of Scotland, Sir Iain seemed suitably qualified for the emergency. Sir Max was having none of it.

At the first meeting of the Beaverbrook Foundation in May he opened the proceedings by saying: 'If anyone wants me to pack up, let me hear it.' All he heard were words of praise.

Although it had been Sir Max's expressed wish that the

company should seek alternatives to the Associated deal, he was less than happy with the alternative that now confronted him. As Goldsmith moved ever closer to the centre of Beaverbrook affairs, Sir Max's jibes about him became increasingly bitter. His appetite for Cavenham Foods was not much improved by the type of deal Goldsmith had in mind. Goldsmith's general ideas had been embodied in a press statement drafted soon after the Bonnington meeting. The statement was never issued but the offers and conditions it contained remained the basis of his approach throughout.

It began by proclaiming: 'The *Evening Standard* should be saved'; and then broadened the rescue net to cover all Beaverbrook's newspapers. It offered a guarantee of Beaverbrook's bank debts and the underwriting of a rights issue on the stock exchange to raise new capital, if this was needed. The conditions followed: union agreement to 'an effective reorganization of the company', enfranchisement of all Beaverbrook shares on the principle of one share one vote, enlargement of the board to reflect shareholders' interests. As a sweetener, voting shareholders were promised 'fair compensation' for the loss of their exclusive privilege, in the form of a free issue of new shares.

Essentially Goldsmith was offering to keep the *Standard* alive and to use his management skills on the *Daily Express* in return for the enfranchisement of Cavenham's 35–40 per cent holding of non-voting shares. There would be guarantees and underwriting of a share issue, but there would be no cash as such. It would be a paper deal *par excellence*, with the drawback, for the Aitken family, that they were being asked to sign away control for a price which, however 'fair', was unlikely to recompense them for the loss of their heritage.

Sir Max's reservations about Goldsmith were shared by his son and other members of the family and close friends. John Coote, who had remained close to the Aitken family even after he ceased to be an executive of Beaverbrook Newspapers, was an important critic of the intervention. He regarded Jocelyn Stevens as 'a Trojan Horse' for the Cavenham boss. Lord Goodman was still implacably opposed to Goldsmith, and Goodman's advice was reckoned to be crucial in any ultimate decision by Sir Max.

It was mainly the recognition of this fact which led to a remarkable exchange of letters in *The Times* initiated by Mike Rothwell. As a strong trade-unionist, the *Evening News* journalists' FoC disagreed with another of Goodman's concerns at the time – the campaign he was helping to orchestrate against the NUJ's attempts to get a closed shop among journalists throughout the newspaper industry. Rothwell thought that as long as Goodman was on the scene there was a strong possibility that the Associated/Beaverbrook deal would go through. 'I also thought', he said, 'that a really hard kick in the groin would get him out of the fight.'

On Wednesday, 4 May *The Times* published the following letter from Rothwell:

Sir, You have published, and I applaud you for it, a series of letters deploring the possible closure of the Evening Standard. They reflect a sadly elitist view – because I suppose, they come from the elite.

The protests of the far greater readership of the Evening News (which sells, incidentally, vastly more copies in London alone than does your fine newspaper nationally) have been muted. Perhaps that is because the management of the News can hardly egg on similar support for their paper's preservation when it is currently their policy to try to sustain a dubious commercial case for killing it.

Public interest demands the fullest possible debate on the two papers' futures. It looks for expert guidance.

But the very man who could be expected to give opinion a lead stays silent.

He is a champion of the arts. He is a campaigner for the rights and freedoms of the journalist. He has fought a mighty public battle, over the last several years, for the continued existence of the widest range of publications. And in all these matters he has claimed to be acting in the interests of the public. I refer, of course, to Lord Goodman. Can it be that fatigue has prevented him from lifting his pen? He must, after all, be very tired. In the past few weeks he has been the honest broker between Beaverbrook and Associated Newspapers.

Had he been successful in concluding the deal last

Thursday, the cultural world would not now be calling for the survival of the Evening Standard, but lamenting its sudden death. Well over a million other evening paper readers would be mourning the Evening News. As many as 150 journalists would be unable to enjoy press freedom because their employers would be flinging them out of work.

And the people of London, who have been consulted as little in this matter as have the thousands of newspaper workers who stand in peril of redundancy, would be given limited choice of an evening paper – either a new one that patently no one but Associated Newspapers' management wants, or none at all. Too tired to enter the lists, Lord Goodman? Or too embarrassed?

On Thursday, 5 May *The Times* published a reply from Goodman who, while acknowledging that he was indeed tired, said friends had urged him to answer a 'particularly poisonous allegation'. His silence, he wrote, had been caused neither by fatigue nor by embarrassment but by respect for the confidential nature of the Beaverbrook/Associated talks. Now, however, Rothwell's letter had stung him into getting the agreement of the negotiating parties to refute its 'monstrous untruth'.

Goodman's answer to Rothwell was that he had, in fact, made the negotiating parties agree to consult before they concluded any deal. This, he added, was in keeping with the NPA's practice during his chairmanship that 'nothing affecting the interests of union membership was put into operation without full, free and frank discussion with union leaders.'

Goodman's defence then became puzzling for anybody not privy to the discussions in the inner sanctums of Associated and Beaverbrook just before the Bonnington meeting. Rothwell's letter had not protested about the failure to clinch a Bonnington deal – indeed, it would have been extraordinary if it had. But Goodman wrote that a complaint about his activities was that he had not permitted the deal to be concluded and had left a state of uncertainty as a result. 'If these results have ensued,' he added, 'I must plead guilty but without shame or compunction. There are certain risks that must be preferred to others.'

What the readers of *The Times* could not know was that Goodman had, at a late stage, informed Jocelyn Stevens that he had given an undertaking to consult the unions about the deal, as Stevens recalled later. The two negotiating parties were not keen on the idea, according to Stevens, because the union leaders would have to have been openly hostile to the closure of the *Standard*. The Beaverbrook side guessed that Goodman's undertaking on consultation was linked to the need for political clearance for the deal. At the final meeting before Bonnington, Stevens felt that Goodman's hand 'kept itching to phone Downing Street'. It was, none the less, something of an unreal debate. The union general secretaries were already aware of the intentions of the two managements. In any case, consultation with union leaders did not necessarily imply consultation with the workers most affected by the deal. As far as the workers were concerned, Stevens's view was that the two managements had to announce the proposed agreement first and consult later if they were to have any chance of getting the results they wanted.

That was certainly Michael Rothwell's understanding of the managements' position, as he made quite clear in a second letter to *The Times*, published on Friday, 6 May:

Sir, I am disturbed by the actions of Lord Goodman's friends. They have goaded him into a display of spleen and paranoia which, far from protecting his reputation, can only harm it.

Writing in great haste, and on his own confession suffering from fatigue, he has accused me (Letters, May 5) of uttering a 'monstrous untruth'. I trust that when, in his words, his batteries are recharged, his judgement will also be restored and he will withdraw that silly slur. For it cannot be taken seriously.

Thousands of Fleet Street workers know that their pleas for consultation on the Beaverbrook/Associated talks have been rejected. So, too, does the nation – which has witnessed our indignation and sympathised.

The attitude of management (those 'negotiating parties' who led Lord Goodman to yesterday's extraordinary out-burst) has been that everyone, from employees to readers, must be kept in the dark. My own chapel's files hold a series of demands for talks; each turned down with the clear implication that we shall be told what is happening once it has happened, and until then will we kindly shut up.

I could quote extensively from correspondence with Mr. Vere Harmsworth, chairman of Associated Newspapers, and other directors. If I did so, perhaps Lord Goodman would be surprised. He would realize that – whatever his stated intentions – the parties for whom he has been acting have resolutely refused 'full, free and frank discussion'.

Their attitude was given with awful clarity to a meeting of fathers of chapels and heads of departments on Thursday, April 28. Mr. E. J. Winnington-Ingram, a director closely concerned in the talks, said then that 'It was everyone's intention to discuss the proposals when they had been finalised.'

That same evening as I understand, Mr. Jocelyn Stevens told a meeting of print and journalists' general secretaries that, had not Sir James Goldsmith just intervened, he would have been announcing to them the death of the Evening Standard – 'a miserable solution because it would have involved a loss of a title and loss of jobs . . . a solution we arrived at with a very heavy heart and the greatest possible reluctance.'

In other words: hang them first, let them appeal afterwards. Perhaps, when Lord Goodman is feeling less fatigued and has checked his facts – and a host of others with which I would gladly supply him – he will realize the enormity of the exercise in which he has been engaged.

Meanwhile, sleep well, sweet Lord. And please wake in a better temper. The public are surely entitled to a more reasoned answer to my original, reasonable letter.

There was no reply from Lord Goodman.

Rothwell's apparent victory in the war of words did not, however, achieve his objective. Though Lord Goodman refrained from further public utterance on the affairs of Beaverbrook Newspapers, he remained as active as ever behind the scenes.

Sir James Goldsmith, meanwhile, was trying to win friends and reduce animosities. For those who earned their living by writing the blackest mark against him was the outstanding criminal libel action against Richard Ingrams, editor of *Private Eye*. Stevens told him he must settle. By the end of the second week of May through the help of Charles Wintour and Simon Jenkins the action had been composed with an agreed public apology by Ingrams. At the same time Goldsmith underwent a crash course of meetings with union leaders at both national and chapel level. Although his main priority was to see what staffing cuts could be achieved to make the Beaverbrook group viable, his decisive approach to problems made a good impression. He promised an end to the strategy of milking the *Sunday Express* and the *Evening Standard* to feed the *Daily Express*. In Goldsmith's mind this amounted to 'starving the strong pigs to feed the weak, a bad policy'.

Some noticed striking parallels between the Cavenham boss and the tycoon who had founded the newspaper group. Both Goldsmith and Lord Beaverbrook made their money by using financial acumen to merge and build up companies before turning to the press. Both came from a mixed national background – Goldsmith Anglo-French, Beaverbrook Canadian-Scottish. Politically, they were both maverick High Tories, outsiders of a right-wing, radical stamp distrusted by the conservative British establishment. Both had been involved in controversies over political peerages. For both of them the route to influence lay through the press rather than the House of Commons. Personally, they shared dynamism and natural charm, which they exploited to the full. They also shared a liking for travel and a lack of humbug about their private lives. There was even an echo over more than half a century through the food cupboard – Beaverbrook had bought the controlling holding in the *Daily Express* from the then owners of Bovril; Goldsmith's Cavenham Foods now owned Bovril.

Charles Wintour wrote to Michael Foot on 2 May: 'Goldsmith, if he wins, would leave the *Evening Standard* alone. He likes it. But he would not leave the *Express* alone: he would like to see it crusading again. (He has a great admiration for Lord B.)'

On 9 May he wrote to Foot again:

Our real problem is the health . . . of Sir Max who, despite pressure to elevate himself to a non-executive Presidency, won't give up. And he changes his mind all the time.

The Harmsworth deal is probably better for shareholders. The Goldsmith deal is better for employees and, in my view, the public.

Foot's reply recognized Wintour's role in helping to bring about a settlement of the *Private Eye* action: 'Good luck with Goldsmith and congratulations on the *Private Eye* interment. We should make you Foreign Secretary.'

As Goldsmith's credibility as a proprietor improved, so did the mutual esteem of those who had fostered his intervention. Jenkins wrote to Wintour complimenting him on his 'fighting spirit and brilliant tactical manoeuvring'. Wintour wrote back returning the compliment: 'The plain evidence that the paper is now in the hands of an outstanding editor . . . has given me the greatest glow of happiness and satisfaction.' Wintour was also encouraged by expression of interest in the *Standard* from a Midlands newspaper group and a Middle East consortium represented by Lord Shawcross. It looked as if he might still be able to mobilize alternatives to a deal with Associated even if Goldsmith's initiative failed.

While the bouquets were flying round the Goldsmith camp, Vere Harmsworth was quietly improving his position. Associated discreetly built up its stake in Beaverbrook Newspapers until it held 113,850 of the ordinary shares, representing a little over 7 per cent of the voting rights, and 300,000 of the non-voting A shares. The *Evening News* was strengthened by the arrival of two senior Beaverbrook journalists, Robin Esser, formerly of the *Daily Express*, and David Henshall, formerly of the *Evening Standard*. The feeling at Associated was that more men would have joined the exodus from Beaverbrook had the NUJ not imposed a ban on recruitment between the papers for the duration of the crisis. Harmsworth also dusted off a project which Associated had previously put on the shelf for some time. Known by the code name of 'Operation Barge', the plan concerned the launch of a small circulation, up-market evening paper aimed at the West End and the City of London.

The idea had been thoroughly researched but no murmur of it had been heard during the weeks of negotiations in which Beaverbrook, Associated and Lord Goodman had worked on the presumption that there was room for only one evening newspaper in London. Two weeks after the Bonnington meeting, however, Associated was ready to throw Operation Barge into the pot. Having waved the stick at the unions with his letter to Bill Keys, Harmsworth unveiled his carrot in an interview with the advertising trade weekly *Campaign*.

The details emerged in its issue of Friday, 13 May.

The up-market paper envisaged by Associated was to be the *Evening Standard*. Simon Jenkins's paper would, Harmsworth said, 'be turned into a very high quality paper with a restricted circulation in central London and a higher than normal cover price'. Its proposed style was compared with the staid French newspaper *Le Monde*. At the same time as it moved the *Standard* into a 100,000 circulation high-quality niche, Associated proposed to produce a mass-market evening paper selling 750,000 copies a day – 'an Evening Mail, a broader Evening Standard or a more quality Evening News', in Harmsworth's all-encompassing description. Such an arrangement, he told *Campaign*, would mean 300 to 400 fewer redundancies than the 1700 lost jobs which he estimated would result from a straight *News/Standard* merger.

David English, who had been foreign editor of the *Daily Express* before moving to Associated, was given the task of re-establishing personal contact with Sir Max Aitken. Over lunch at the Howard Hotel by the Temple, Sir Max told him that he was disturbed by the Bonnington episode. The message he gave English to be retailed to Harmsworth was: 'I don't want Vere to be angry with me. I want to get back to a deal with him. He understands newspapers. The others don't.' Harmsworth was naturally encouraged, the more so since he had just returned from a trip to Paris, where he had guardedly exchanged views on the Beaverbrook situation with Goldsmith. In his opinion the Cavenham boss was more vulnerable to a counter-attack than most of the current newspaper reports were ready to acknowledge.

Harmsworth had let it be known that Associated were ready to mount a full take-over bid for Beaverbrook should Goldsmith decide on a similar course of action. This threat effectively probed the weakness of Goldsmith's position. The one thing he most wanted to avoid was a bidding contest with other contenders, though his public comments gave no hint of any great concern. In an interview with Ivan Rowan of the *Sunday Telegraph*, published on 15 May, he enthusiastically described the newspaper industry as 'creative, amusing, challenging – that's the extra dimension. The extra dimension means a lot to me.' When asked why he should seek so daunting a challenge Sir James replied lightly: 'The male menopause.' The condition did not, however, seem likely to impair his financial judgement.

Apart from an understandable disinclination to pay out hard cash for a business as uncertain as Beaverbrook Newspapers, Goldsmith was labouring under twin problems born of broader ambitions for Cavenham and himself in the spring of 1977. These involved a major restructuring of his British operation. Earlier in the year he had told the *Financial Times*: 'I think I've been Chairman of public companies long enough and I haven't enjoyed it.' The way to remove this irritant seemed simple enough in theory. The French holding company, Générale Occidentale (GO), in which Goldsmith was the majority shareholder, already held 51 per cent of Cavenham. GO could buy the remaining 49 per cent from the minority British shareholders and Goldsmith and his associates would then, as he put it to the *Financial Times*, be 'paddling our own canoe'. The geographical switch of ownership of Cavenham from London to Paris would, Goldsmith said at the time, mean nothing because 'the power of command stays with me'.

If the theory was simple, the practice was rather more complicated. In March the British minority shareholders, led by the Prudential Assurance giant, turned down the initial offer, worth £60 million. The price was not high enough. One rejection was not going to put Goldsmith off, but it underlined the need for care when he made his next approach. To reinforce his revised offer, he planned to raise £50 million on the Paris capital market. The French financial world had confidence in him – but as a financier and not as the prospective owner of an ailing newspaper chain.

As Goldsmith recounts his thinking in May 1977, he was afraid that an outright bid by Cavenham for Beaverbrook would shake that confidence. His purchase of *L'Express* could be seen as a pardonable diversion – all the more acceptable given the French magazine's leading circulation position and its fat advertising revenue. Purchase of Beaverbrook Newspapers, on the other hand, might be viewed as fundamentally changing the nature of Cavenham and his capital-raising operation could be compromised as a result. He was also aware of possible problems for his buying in of the minority Cavenham shares in Britain. The British shareholders had been awkward once and could be again. If a purchase of Beaverbrook brought down Cavenham's share price he would undoubtedly be accused of using the newspaper acquisition in order to buy in the food company more cheaply.

These twin dangers, in Paris and London, were prime reasons for caution. Goldsmith saw himself as navigating between rocks which might wreck a ship more important to him than Beaverbrook Newspapers. So he had to steer a roundabout course. It was, he felt, safer for his overall interests than an actual take-over bid. It was also a great deal cheaper.

In piloting his roundabout course Goldsmith encountered other hazards. One of his first moves had been to set the leading accountancy firm of Deloitte's to audit the Beaverbrook books to unearth the financial details he wanted before making a formal offer. Almost immediately the review ran into problems.

The difficulty stemmed from Cavenham's status as a holder of Beaverbrook shares. Although its holding might now be around 40 per cent, Cavenham was not, under stock exchange rules, entitled to any more information than any other owner of Beaverbrook A shares. Goldsmith wrote to Rothschild's, Beaverbrook's financial advisers, to say that he was not asking for any exclusive information and added: 'Should any third party come forward with a constructive plan better than my own for Beaverbrook and for its newspapers, I would be happy to co-operate with this party.' But that was not the snag as far as Rothschild's were concerned. It was not a question of keeping Goldsmith and some putative third-party bidder on an equal footing. The difficulty was that Goldsmith, who had not made any kind of formal offer so far, had to be treated like any other Beaverbrook shareholder. If financial information beyond what was in the annual accounts was given to one shareholder, it would have to be provided to all, including Associated. Beaverbrook was naturally anxious not to give any wider currency to its financial situation than it had to.

Although Goldsmith was put out at the limits set on his examination of the group's affairs, this reticence was probably not a major drawback. For one thing, Goldsmith himself had doubts about the quality of financial information which was available to him. It was not until early May that Beaverbrook started drawing up revised, 12-month forecasts to see if fresh finance was in fact needed. Charles Wintour, who had become Goldsmith's main cheerleader at boardroom level, commented at the time: 'It seems odd that this was not done before.'

A much more serious problem for Goldsmith was the need to synchronize his interest with that of Lonrho's Tiny Rowland, who had been welcomed into the lists by a Beaverbrook journalist as 'the least unacceptable of the unacceptable faces of capitalism'. It was not clear why Rowland was interested in Fleet Street. Lonrho had press interests in Africa and Scotland but involvement in the more risky, and much more financially demanding, Beaverbrook Newspapers did not seem to fit logically into Lonrho's existing scheme of operations. It was also puzzling that Rowland should be thinking of plunging in at a time when his company was making moves to reduce its borrowings through a rights issue on the stock market. But people had given up being surprised by the unexpected from Tiny Rowland. He had a knack of going off at an apparent tangent, only to turn up with handsome profits a few years later. And Lonrho, in the first half of 1977, seemed to be in an acquisitive mood. It was, one government minister commented, like a child playing monopoly, buying up properties all over the board.

Rowland did not seem particularly well briefed about the British newspaper industry. In a conversation with Sheila Black of *The Times* he said that he wanted to buy the best and biggest London evening newspaper. She had to point out that, while it might be the best, the *Standard* was certainly not the biggest. Nor did Rowland appear very sensitive to the attitudes of the journalists he was proposing to save from Associated's grasp. Simon Jenkins asked him how the editors of Lonrho's African papers were selected. Rowland replied that the last time such an appointment had had to be made, Lonrho had simply called the local Ministry of Information for a list of suitable candidates. The *Standard* man was not sure that he was joking.

Contemporary press reports assumed that Rowland was interested only in the *Evening Standard* and that he and Goldsmith had been working in close harmony. Neither was strictly true. The two financiers were acquaintances but not specially close. Some evidence of the distance between them was the fact that Rowland had been a leading contributor to *Private Eye*'s 'Goldenballs Fund', which had been used to finance its defence against Goldsmith's legal onslaught. At their first meeting after the Bonnington episode, Goldsmith found that Rowland was interested in the Beaverbrook group as a whole and was prepared, if necessary, to mount a full take-over operation.

Rowland, always on the move, proved a difficult man to pin down on details. One story that went round at the time had it that Goldsmith went to the Lonrho offices to talk to Rowland. After they had spoken for a while, Rowland got up and left the room without explanation. Goldsmith waited for a decent interval and then went to look for him. He asked a secretary where Rowland was. She didn't know. Goldsmith went to the front hall and asked the commissionaire if Rowland had left the building. Yes, the commissionaire said, he had driven away in a car. After some delay, Goldsmith got on to Rowland's chauffeur on the car phone. The chauffeur said Goldsmith couldn't speak to Rowland. Why not, Goldsmith asked. Because he's just got on a plane at Heathrow, the chauffeur replied. When the story was relayed back to Goldsmith many months later, his comment was: '*Si non è vero è ben trovato.*' It did not in fact happen but it could have quite easily.

Eventually the two financiers agreed on a joint approach, though it was the Conservative politician Edward du Cann, a Lonrho director, who finally signalled his company's acquiescence. Goldsmith sent the formal offer to Rothschild's on 18 May.

The scheme Goldsmith had evolved was a judicious blend designed to attract Lonrho by offering a cheap way into Beaverbrook and, at the same time, to cage Rowland so that he could not use his cash muscle to dominate Goldsmith. The two financiers would be partners, but unequal ones.

It provided for Cavenham and Lonrho – hereafter known in their united guise as 'Cavhro' – to form a joint company which would buy Cavenham's voting shares in Beaverbrook. The Beaverbrook board and the holders of voting shares, meaning the Aitken family and the Beaverbrook Foundation, would agree to enfranchisement of the non-voting shares. Cavrho would then underwrite a rights issue on the stock market to raise £5 million. It would also guarantee Beaverbrook bank loans up to £3 million and a lease on the Aitken House development, so that Beaverbrook could arrange a sale and lease-back of the property to raise more cash. Goldsmith would join the Beaverbrook board as chairman. Rowland would come in as his deputy. Two other new directors, one each from Cavenham and Lonrho, would also join the board. Sir Max would be offered the position of life president.

The proposal did not envisage any major change in the executive structure of Beaverbrook Newspapers. In this respect Goldsmith was shrewdly ministering to the survival instincts of the existing management team. Although it did not constitute part of the offer document, he told Jocelyn Stevens and Maxwell Aitken that their full-time services would be required for another five years, under contracts worth £250,000 and £225,000 respectively. Both men formally declared this interest to other board members.

On Thursday, 19 May the Cavrho offer went before the Beaverbrook board and met a hostile reception from Sir Max. He was strongly in favour of outright rejection of the Goldsmith/ Rowland alliance. Other directors, with some difficulty, persuaded him that negotiations along the lines of the Cavrho proposals should be maintained, even though the terms as they stood were inadequate. Sir Max accepted the board's decision but did not see it as one that precluded other initiatives. He therefore met Vere Harmsworth and reopened negotiations with Associated.

This was also the day on which Tony Dyer, under the conditions imposed after the failure of the coup against Jocelyn Stevens, formally resigned from the Beaverbrook board and his position as deputy managing director. Sir Max was evidently upset to see him go.

Six days later Sir Max invited Dyer to Marsham Court for a

private chat. He said that Jocelyn Stevens would have to go and asked if Dyer would take his place. Dyer replied with understandable caution that in the event of Stevens going he would be prepared to hold the management together for a few weeks, but no more. Sir Max did not raise the matter again. Dyer assumed that he had changed his mind. Dyer remained on the staff of Beaverbrook Newspapers for another eight months before moving to another job – managing Vere Harmsworth's provincial newspaper group.

ELEVEN

A Night's Rest for the Beaver

═══════

ON FRIDAY, 20 MAY 1977 the *Evening Standard* celebrated its 150th birthday with a bumper 64-page edition printed on pink paper. Its tone was pardonably self-congratulatory. Among the famous names who recalled their past association with the newspaper were Michael Foot, Kenneth Tynan, Malcolm Muggeridge and Dame Rebecca West. In a message of support Margaret Thatcher called the *Standard* 'required reading', while James Callaghan expressed the hope that 'you will be able to maintain your standards'. All in all, it amounted to a resounding display of sentiment at a time when the *Standard*'s existence seemed to be menaced once more by an Associated Newspapers take-over. But it did not much alter the realities of the situation.

These realities were, however, radically changed by the contents of another newspaper. On 19 May the *Daily Mail* broke what looked like a sensational exclusive story under the headline 'World-Wide Bribery Web By Leyland'. A subsidiary strapline read: 'Exposed – the amazing truth about Britain's State-owned car makers.' The story included the transcript of a letter allegedly written by Lord Ryder, chairman of the National Enterprise Board, to Alex Park, chief executive of British Leyland, the nationalized car firm, which detailed arrangements for 'contract padding' overseas sales.

The following day's front-page headline read: 'Slush Money: The Secret Bank Deals.' The strapline was: 'The documents that prove the case.' Among the documents paraded in evidence was a facsimile of the alleged letter from Lord Ryder to Alex Park, the keystone of the *Mail*'s revelations.

Within hours the story began to crumble. Errors in the letter were rapidly spotted, exposing it as a fake. Further interviews with the man who had supplied it, a Leyland executive called Graham Barton, revealed that it was a clumsy forgery. The *Mail*'s great scoop ended on 21 May with the ignominious headline: 'Ryder Forger Confesses.'

In other circumstances the *Mail*'s mistake might have been passed over as one of the misjudgements which newspapers inevitably make from time to time and which generally cost them dear in the libel courts. But the *Mail*'s right-wing stance and the spotlight cast on newspapers by the imminent publication of the Royal Commission report on the press all served to magnify the significance of the blunder. The political row intensified when it emerged that the *Mail*'s editor, David English, had had his offer of resignation refused by Vere Harmsworth. James Callaghan, in a reference to the 'contemptible' *Mail* stories, described them as having 'reduced journalism to a lower level than I can remember for many years'.

Other Labour politicians with longer memories visited the sins of the pre-war *Daily Mail* on its current leadership. The equivocal relationship of Vere Harmsworth's grandfather with the Fascists in the 1930s was recalled, as was the *Mail*'s part in publicizing the Zinoviev letter, a notorious forgery which helped ensure the electoral annihilation of Ramsay MacDonald's first Labour government in the 'red scare' campaign of 1924. Over 100 MPs signed a motion condemning the *Mail*'s 'tactics in pursuing smear campaigns' and called for the editor's resignation. (Ironically Stewart Steven, the *Mail* executive immediately responsible for seeing the 'slush fund' story into the paper, was a staunch socialist.)

David English accepted public responsibility for the lapse, though his energies had been divided for many months by the negotiations with Beaverbrook. His private estimate was that he was spending 60 per cent of his working time on matters relating to the merger and only 40 per cent editing his own newspaper. Had he been editing full-time he might have viewed the 'evidence' for the Leyland story with more suspicion. As it was, the story that was designed to enhance the *Mail*'s reputation for investigative flair and expertise had the reverse of the desired effect.

For Harmsworth's opponents at Beaverbrook the *Mail*'s gaffe was a gift from heaven. Previously the Labour government had not particularly differentiated between Beaverbrook and Associated. Both firms ran stridently right-wing morning newspapers and Sir Harold Wilson had bracketed them together as twin persecutors of the Labour Party in his evidence to the Royal Commission. Callaghan had previously taken a hands-off attitude towards the prospect of an Associated/Beaverbrook deal. He was not interested in getting involved. At one stage Harmsworth had managed to get him on the telephone, but Callaghan had said he had nothing to say and that it was up to Roy Hattersley to decide whether to make a reference to the Monopolies Commission. Harmsworth's call, Hattersley said later, 'was an absolute waste of 2p'.

After the 'slush fund' episode any immediate expansion of Associated Newspapers' press interests was bound to run into trouble from the Labour Party. John Coote, whose job as director-general of the British Film Production Association brought him in touch with senior political figures, was astonished at the strength of the hostility engendered by the *Mail* story. He told Vere Harmsworth privately that three senior cabinet ministers were implacably opposed to any merging of Beaverbrook and Associated interests. Roy Hattersley, who had previously pursued a course of studied neutrality in accordance with Callaghan's wishes, let it be known privately that there was no chance of an Associated/Beaverbrook merger going through without reference to the Monopolies Commission. The deal had become a political minefield.

Harmsworth incautiously raised the temperature even further by linking Callaghan's reaction to the *Mail* story with the recent row over the appointment of his son-in-law, Peter Jay, a former economics correspondent on *The Times*, as British ambassador in Washington. The Associated proprietor said in self-defence: 'I reject utterly Mr Callaghan's allegation of vindictiveness, despite my understanding of his feelings, as this deplorable but honest mistake has followed so closely upon the furore occasioned by the appointment of Mr Peter Jay.'

Charles Wintour heard a radio report of Harmsworth's remarks on the morning of Wednesday, 25 May and felt they should be answered. He had accepted an invitation to speak at the Automobile Association's annual lunch later that same day. His speech, already prepared, was a light account of recent events at the *Standard* couched in the language of the second-hand car trade. After amusing his hosts with the prepared text, Wintour abruptly changed gear:

> I had intended to say no more about the current situation in Fleet Street, but Vere Harmsworth's statement today calls for comment.
>
> On the exposure of the Ryder forgery David English honourably and immediately offered his resignation.
>
> Mr Harmsworth, rightly in my view, rejected it. But today Mr Harmsworth, in attempting to answer the prime minister's description of the *Daily Mail's* conduct as contemptible and a display of political spite, drags up the appointment of Mr Peter Jay to Washington.
>
> In other words he is smearing the charge of nepotism against the name of the prime minister.
>
> Why is Mr Vere Harmsworth chairman of Associated Newspapers? Why is he in a position to squander millions of his shareholders' money in an effort to force the *Evening Standard* out of business? Why has he been able to sell his evening paper at an uneconomic price, to offer cut rates to advertisers who switch from the *Evening Standard* to his own paper, to start up costly and uneconomic ventures in the suburbs, and to maintain an uneconomic circulation area – all, I believe, with the aim of compelling his competitor to surrender?
>
> May I suggest that the only reason why Mr Vere Harmsworth is chairman of Associated Newspapers is that he is the son of the second Lord Rothermere. And the second Lord Rothermere had the job because he was the son of the first Lord Rothermere. And the first Lord Rothermere had the *Daily Mail* because he was the brother of a real newspaper genius, Lord Northcliffe.
>
> Mr Jay is acknowledged by all to be a most brilliant man who is earning large sums entirely as a result of his own talents. Mr Harmsworth however is in a position to endanger the jobs of 1700 people in Fleet Street purely through a mere accident of birth.

Some people who inherit great responsibilities handle their duties soberly, wisely and responsibly. I am all in favour of a mixed newspaper ownership. But I think it is about time that Mr Harmsworth was called to account for his conduct in London over the past few years. If the Royal Commission [on the press] does reconvene to examine this forgery case, let it not forget that his is the publishing house that even now is still attempting to take over the *Evening Standard.*

I call on Mr Harmsworth to put his own house in order before he tries to expand his inheritance any further.

It was, by any standards, an extraordinary attack for a senior newspaper executive to make on an established proprietor, and was widely reported. The effect on most Beaverbrook employees was immediately bracing. The Imperial Father of the *Express* federated house chapel sent congratulations for a speech that 'echoed the views of all Beaverbrook employees'. Ted Simpson reported: 'Morale has now gone up a few more significant notches.' Michael Foot's letter of congratulation, invoking the shade of Lord Beaverbrook, read: 'What a speech! I'm sure it is the first time for months that the old man in his grave can have had a night's sleep.'

Vere Harmsworth naturally saw the matter differently, and responded by savaging Wintour in the correspondence columns of *The Times.* His letter, published in the issue of 31 May, read:

Sir, I write regarding certain remarks about me made by Charles Wintour in his speech at the AA luncheon as widely reported in the press. As to the rest of his remarks I consider that the character of his speech is self evident.

Mr. Charles Wintour alleges that I set out to 'eat the Evening Standard alive'. I wish to state that the negotiations were freely entered into by Beaverbrook Newspapers; that the choice to sell the Evening Standard was theirs; that every detail of the arrangements was agreed by them including the follow up joint printing operation designed to ensure the survival of newspapers, not their demise. So far as I know the negotiations were fully approved by the Beaverbrook board of which Mr. Wintour was and is a member.

It was always fully understood that no arrangement would be sought to be imposed on either company except by mutual agreement. Hence the wholly inappropriate nature of the phrase 'eaten alive'.

Since I have been the subject of his personal attack I feel I must record that I offered Mr. Wintour the post of chairman of a selection committee to consist of himself, Mr. Simon Jenkins and Mr. Lou Kirby to choose from the staffs of the Standard and the News those to serve on the proposed new paper and further that he should advise on the style and character of this paper. Mr. Wintour declined the offer and said that the entire staff of the Evening Standard must be retained from the Editor to the most junior journalist and that the whole editorial staff of the Evening News could be, so far as he was concerned, made redundant. I argued with him –

1. That he ignored the important Evening News readership and service to the London community;

2. That his attitude was immoral in that it took no regard for hardship, length of service or merit;

3. That it was commercially foolish to lose an opportunity to concentrate the best elements of two newspaper staffs;

4. That it would be dishonourable for me to do any such thing, and

5. That even if I so wished the unions would never permit it.

Mr. Wintour dismissed all these arguments but conceded that he would be prepared to advise the taking up of 15 per cent of the best of the News staff as super-numeraries.

I am also accused of playing with 1,700 jobs. I must point out that if the advice given in Mr. Wintour's speech were followed not 1,700 but over 4,000 jobs would be lost.

It is astonishing that Michael Foot, who personally I like and admire, has so closely associated himself with the hysterical utterances of Charles Wintour.

It was of course true that Wintour had advocated closing the *News* if a choice *had* to be made between the two papers, but he was also against the deal that made such a choice necessary. He reminded Harmsworth of this salient fact in a letter of reply, published in the next day's *Times*:

Sir, Mr. Vere Harmsworth (Letters, May 31) implies that as

a member of the board of Beaverbrook Newspapers I approved the sale of the Evening Standard and every detail of the scheme for a merged evening newspaper.

This is not so, as the minutes of Beaverbrook Newspapers board meeting on April 21 fully confirm.

One other tiny point. Mr. Harmsworth says I alleged he set out 'to eat the Evening Standard alive'. It wasn't me, actually. He is referring to a leading article in the Evening Standard (which I no longer edit) commenting on the Daily Mail case which said, 'It makes it no easier for us to comment on the case, that the Daily Mail owners a month ago tried not just to bite the Evening Standard but to eat us whole'. This epidemic of false attribution seems catching at Associated Newspapers.

The *Evening News* journalists set the seal on a miserable fortnight for Harmsworth by seizing on the first public revelation of the editorial selection committee in his letter to *The Times*. Mike Rothwell passed on a chapel resolution demanding 'an assurance that never in the future shall the Associated Newspapers Group chairman or his representative enter into the kind of squalid and inequitable arrangement he claims to have offered Mr Charles Wintour of the *Evening Standard*'.

Sir James Goldsmith alertly chose the period of Harmsworth's maximum discomfiture to improve his offer to Beaverbrook. The terms of the second Cavrho offer were set out in a letter to Rothschild's dated 26 May. As well as underwriting the raising of £5 million through a rights issue in return for enfranchisement of non-voting shares and guaranteeing £3 million in bank loans, Cavrho now proposed to back Beaverbrook's credit with its suppliers up to £4 million. On the rights issue, Goldsmith said he understood that the Aitken family and the Beaverbrook Foundation would not take up their entitlement. If they did, however, the rights issue would be increased by the amount of their participation. Theoretically this could boost the capital raised by the rights issue as high as £8·3 million – in the unlikely event of the Aitkens and the Foundation being willing and able to plough money back into the firm.

The rest of the new proposal provided for the appointment

of three 'independent directors of stature'. No names were mentioned, but two of the people Goldsmith was thinking of were Edward Heath and Lord Robens. He also added a pledge that there would be no staff redundancies without full consultation, though everyone would have to agree to co-operate 'to phase out inefficient practices in the group, no matter at what level these become apparent'.

The one negative change between the two Cavrho offers was the dropping of the Aitken House sale and lease-back scheme, because the property had already been put up as security for one of Beaverbrook's major loans.

The Associated camp tried to make political capital out of the fact that Cavenham's revised corporate structure could, if Goldsmith's bid were successful, effectively make Beaverbrook a foreign-owned company, but this was not a successful ploy. There was in fact a tide of opinion for Goldsmith in the higher reaches of the Labour Party, though the reason for it was curious. One political observer illustrated the point by quoting President Lyndon Johnson's rugged rationalization for keeping J. Edgar Hoover as FBI boss – 'I'd rather have him in the tent pissing out, than outside the tent pissing in.' Roy Hattersley told a friend, in less colourful terms: 'Goldsmith has *élan* and energy and is determined to have political influence. So it's much better to have him in the open as a newspaper proprietor where we can all see him.'

On 25 May Goldsmith had told Stevens and Wintour, his main supporters on the Beaverbrook board, that Hambro's, his bankers, and Rothschild's were now much closer than they had been in previous weeks. He also told them that he believed that Evelyn de Rothschild, who was a close friend – Goldsmith was godfather to his son – would recommend his offer to the Beaverbrook board.

He was wrong.

Rothschild was among a group of directors who were actively seeking some way out of an *impasse* which involved a choice between Harmsworth, who was unwelcome to most Beaverbrook employees, and Goldsmith, who was unwelcome to Sir Max Aitken and most of his family.

On 28 May Rothschild combined his interest in horses with

a renewal of City contacts by going to Sandown Park race-course. Trafalgar House was sponsoring the day's card. Victor Matthews, the managing director of Trafalgar, was a racing enthusiast. Amid the horse talk and the pleasantries of the afternoon, Rothschild had a brief but serious word with him. Rothschild outlined the Beaverbrook situation and said that if Trafalgar wanted to get into the action, it would have to start moving. Matthews, who had not had any serious dealings with Beaverbrook since his abortive meeting with Stevens and Hetherington at the turn of the year, was intrigued. He undertook to speak to his chairman, Nigel Broackes, about the possibility of a new initiative. Matthews went off in search of Broackes, but by the time he had been located and brought back to the stewards' enclosure, Rothschild had left.

They had more success three days later, on Derby Day, when Rothschild, accompanied by two banking colleagues, went round to the Trafalgar headquarters bearing a photograph of the finish of the race as a gift. The Rothschild men then had a productive discussion about the problems of Beaverbrook with Broackes, Matthews and the third member of Trafalgar's executive trio, Eric Parker.

The next day's meeting of the Beaverbrook board, on Thursday, 2 June, was a deeply confused occasion with tensions of personality close to the surface. Sir Max had been thoroughly displeased by Wintour's attack on Harmsworth, partly because it constituted yet another impediment to a deal with Associated and partly because Wintour's acid remarks about Harmsworth's qualifications for proprietorship might apply as directly to the chairman of Beaverbrook Newspapers. He was also displeased by the necessity of having to consider another scheme from Goldsmith. Apart from a discussion of the terms of the Cavrho offer the key motion before the board was that it should recommend to the trustees of the Beaverbrook Foundation 'that they consider as a matter of urgency the enfranchisement of the non-voting shares and/or a change in the control of the Company'.

Confusion was caused by the fact that the board had not been supplied with a written statement of the latest Cavrho offer. And some of those present found Evelyn de Rothschild's oral presentation insufficiently enlightening. Stevens thought the new offer sounded as if it was worth something like £12 million in new money – £2 million more than was considered necessary – but other directors were not so sure. The fact that Goldsmith had proposed the appointment of three independent directors was not mentioned.

Rothschild was firmly in favour of the enfranchisement proposal, which would make the company more attractive to all potential bidders, but did not link this with any endorsement of Goldsmith's plan. Indeed he made a strong point of the fact that the Goldsmith/Rowland offer amounted to a demand for control of the company through the enfranchisement of the A shares. Sir Max took little part in the detailed discussion but made what seemed like an ominous reference to the need for a change of management.

Although the motion recommending enfranchisement was eventually passed the meeting left most directors as baffled as before about which direction the company should take. Wintour expressed his exasperation in a letter to Rothschild, written immediately afterwards. After detailing what he considered unnecessary points of confusion about the Cavrho offer, he wrote:

> From our long-standing and entirely happy relationship I am totally and sincerely convinced that you are solely concerned to give us the best possible professional advice in an intensely difficult and delicate situation.
>
> But the whole position is very political. It would be disastrous if anyone could suggest that any vital facts were withheld.
>
> I am sure you realize that I do not now feel I can be entirely objective about the matter. It is my belief that Sir James Goldsmith, with his *élan*, commercial instinct and new-found enthusiasm for publishing, is more likely to make a success of Beaverbrook Newspapers than any consortium or non-publishing concern, and certainly would do more for the employees and the newspapers than a take-over of control by Associated Newspapers.
>
> It is especially for that reason that I hope that in any future discussion we should be given a written statement of what Goldsmith is offering. And I hope that we could have that statement in advance of our next Board meeting, so there is time for us all to examine the facts, and to take a

view away from the personal tensions that are felt in the Boardroom.

On the next day, Friday 3 June, Wintour wrote to Michael Foot, attaching a copy of the enfranchisement resolution:

Dear Michael,

You may like to know that the Board of Beaverbrook Newspapers yesterday passed the attached resolution with one abstention – John Junor. This could clear the way for Goldsmith or Associated or anyone else so far as the Board is concerned.

However Sir Max, with the support of two other directors, made it absolutely clear that he favours a deal with Associated rather than the revised Goldsmith proposals (which Jocelyn Stevens and I much prefer). There are other directors, notably the chairman of our merchant bankers, Evelyn de Rothschild, who are searching for a third bidder. The names of Trafalgar House and Trust House Forte have been mentioned.

The problem is that the trustees of the Foundation can now turn down the recommendation of the Board. (This could lead to ructions, particularly from the unions, but under present legislation there seems nothing we could do about it.)

Alternatively the trustees might say they wish to sell their controlling shares to someone. Presumably if it was Associated, the Monopolies Commission would have to report, which would allow the Goldsmith/Lonrho proposal to be ventilated properly. . . .

It is an indication of the state of mind and state of health of our chairman that he is now going away until 15 June.

Wintour's frustration was understandable enough, but he had misread the revived energy of his chairman and with it his capacity to affect events. Sir Max had made some key decisions, though the form in which they had been vouchsafed to the board had been so oblique as to pass almost unnoticed. It was not until the *Sunday Times* issue of 5 June hit the streets that most Beaverbrook directors realized just how actively involved their chairman had been.

Sir Max, it then transpired, had decided to speak out publicly about his problems for the first time since his illness. The forum he chose was a lengthy interview published in the *Sunday Times*'s gossip column, 'Atticus', jointly written by Anthony Holden and Alison Miller.

Some of his reflections were historical: 'The fact is they took me for dead. I got ill. I had a stroke – and the ship fell apart. As soon as I got out of hospital, it was up to me to get the ship right. And now I'm feeling better, that is what I want to do.'

Some personal: 'The only people I trust are Lord Goodman, my secretary and myself.'

Some sentimental:

> If newspapers are to survive they must support each other. It is the only way for the industry, and in fact the only way through life, really. I was as surprised as anyone at Wintour's attack on Harmsworth. I have always liked Vere. He is a good man. And the suggestion that the Rothermere line of proprietorial descent is any different from that of my own family is fanciful. I inherited from my father and my son Maxwell follows from me. His son Maxwell, just a few months old . . . is as far ahead as any of us can look.

But the most newsworthy aspect of Sir Max's reflections was his comment about the future: 'Now that I'm recovering, I want to bring some morale back into the situation. I know what it is like to be without energy, and it is only with energy that we will survive. If you ask me if I'm going to sell the Daily Express, the answer is no. The Sunday Express? No. The Evening Standard? No. Beaverbrook Newspapers? No.'

It seemed, under the known circumstances, an astonishing statement to make. There had been some improvement in the price of Beaverbrook shares on the stock exchange and some talk, mainly from Jocelyn Stevens and Maxwell Aitken, of the possibility of a go-it-alone strategy if all else failed, but all the directors were convinced of the desperate need for new money. And that seemed to imply the loss – or at least the dilution – of control by the Aitken family.

The clue to Sir Max's thinking emerged dramatically on the news pages of the *Sunday Times*, where Holden and Miller reported exclusively on an apparently fruitful contact between him and Rupert Murdoch. Murdoch was reported to be considering a capital injection of £10 million into Beaverbrook Newspapers in return for a percentage of any future profits and the right to appoint new senior managers to the group. The existing managers most likely to be affected were, according to the story, Jocelyn Stevens and Charles Wintour.

Details of this unusual scheme had been discussed at a secret meeting between Sir Max and Murdoch during one of Murdoch's visits to London earlier in the week. The story went on to quote Murdoch, speaking from his New York office, as saying that the Cavrho offer was 'no money at all'. He was also quoted as saying: 'I think it's fair to say that I am thinking about how I can help. I am a friend of Sir Max's and want to stay so. I have told him that if at any stage there is a question of closing down titles, and I can help in any way to avoid it, I would be happy to do so.'

While the Beaverbrook directors were digesting details of their chairman's new plan for the company's survival from the columns of a rival newspaper, Sir Max set off on a two-week holiday, leaving the Royal Hotel, Deauville as a forwarding address. He was going to try out his new £70,000 ocean racing yacht called, appropriately enough, *Knockout*.

TWELVE

The Wizard of Oz

RUPERT MURDOCH HAD made a public point of turning his back on Britain after the failure of his attempt to take over the *Observer*. His existing British press interests were doing well – the *News of the World* still dominated all the other Sundays in terms of circulation, while the *Sun* was poised to top the 4 million mark and take over from the *Daily Mirror* as the best-selling daily. But certain aspects of Fleet Street had lost their charm. In November 1976, shortly after his arrival in New York, he told an interviewer that his prime reason for leaving Britain was frustration with 'the daily bloody arguments with chapels, broken agreements and endless fights'. A secondary reason was his impatience with 'the old-school-tie system'.

Initially, at least, Murdoch found the United States a great deal more congenial. In Britain, he reflected, the monopolies legislation would probably have hindered any further expansion. In the United States, on the other hand, 'you could buy a newspaper a week and nobody would notice.' In fact his North American acquisitions in the early weeks of 1977 attracted sufficient notice to warrant his being featured on the cover of *Time* magazine garbed as King Kong. After taking over the daily *New York Post*, he gobbled up *New York Magazine* and the radical weekly *Village Voice*, to add to a transatlantic empire which had started earlier with the more modest *San Antonio Express and News* and the tabloid *National Star*.

The intellectual salons of Manhattan emitted many a piteous cry when they learned that a substantial portion of their reading matter had fallen into the hands of a man previously characterized as the 'Dirty Digger' and Rupert 'Thanks for the Mammary' Murdoch. Alexander Cockburn, a *Village Voice* columnist, reflected their anguish when he wrote of the terrible prospects of being taken over by Murdoch or the other main contender, the *Washington Post*. Life under the establishment *Post* company would, Cockburn reflected, be rather like torture by Ottoman Turks who crushed a man's testicles between silken pillows; to be subsumed by Murdoch was like being an unwanted chieftain in New Guinea who had his testicles smashed with a flat rock.

Murdoch ran his newspapers as well as owning them. His skill at clinching spectacular deals was celebrated from Australia to Texas, where he had bought his first American newspapers with an $18 million cheque during an airport stop-over. But, for Murdoch, the purchase was only the start – he was the kind of proprietor whose presence was felt in the newsroom and printing plant as well as the boardroom, juggling the mix of sensation, news, sex and sport to meet his central aim of giving the public what it wanted.

In his early days in Australia Murdoch's close involvement in the practical business of running newspapers sprang from necessity as well as temperament. It was not simply romanticism which sent him out on to the Canberra tarmac in his pyjamas to urge pilots to fly out copies of his paper through the night fog. In New York he amazed printers by turning up at dawn to watch production of his newly bought *Post*, and got on the telephone himself to complain to the Associated Press about its lateness with a story the paper wanted. His call was directed to the agency's editing desk where it would have an immediate effect, rather than to the more prestigious executive levels at which newspaper owners normally commune.

Murdoch, still a boyish-looking 46, was characteristically taking the American newspaper world by storm, as he had done the British a decade earlier and the Australian a decade before that. It was widely assumed that he would have his hands too full in New York to pay much attention to the crisis at Beaverbrook Newspapers.

In fact, Murdoch had been watching the Beaverbrook situation with considerable interest. His reasons were partly sentimental. Murdoch had done a stint as a sub-editor on the *Daily Express* while learning the business as a young man. Subsequently he and Sir Max had become good friends after his purchase of the *News of the World* in 1969. The Beaverbrook proprietor had been one of the few established newspaper barons to welcome the new arrival.

After the breakdown of the Bonnington meeting Murdoch's interest had become more specific. He had sent word to Sir Max that he was ready, as a friend, to provide 'assistance' if necessary. His contacts with Beaverbrook Newspapers at that stage were informal and at the highest level, with Sir Max himself and with Lord Goodman. Goodman had told him frankly that he was beginning to give up hope of ever achieving an agreement between Sir Max and Vere Harmsworth. In Murdoch's words, 'He could not get them to a decent marriage.'

Goodman was also eager to erect a bulwark against the possibility of a deal with Cavenham Foods. Goldsmith's efforts to ingratiate himself with the Beaverbrook leadership had apparently had no effect on the attitude of Goodman, who was also keenly aware that a policy of drift by the Beaverbrook board might leave it without any positive alternative to the Cavrho affair. 'What slightly frightens Goodman is that Goldsmith doesn't give a damn,' said a Labour minister who had dealings with both men. 'Goldsmith is essentially cavalry. Arnold is dug in for the winter.'

From his various dug-outs near the centres of the establishment Goodman sniped away at the Cavenham boss. He told Roy Hattersley that Goldsmith was not a fit man to own a British newspaper. At a dinner given by Princess Alexandra's husband, Angus Ogilvy, Goodman told Duke Hussey, the managing director of Times Newspapers, 'We've got to stop this man getting Beaverbrook', reiterating his belief that Goldsmith was not a fit man to run a great British newspaper. Embarrassingly for Hussey, Goldsmith himself was sitting a few places away talking to the industrialist Arnold Weinstock about his problems over Beaverbrook. As Goodman bent *The Times* boss's ear in one direction, Weinstock pointed up the table towards Hussey and suggested that Goldsmith should ask him for advice. It was a piquant moment.

Murdoch's offer of assistance seemed to provide a way out of Goodman's dilemma. In contrast to Goldsmith, Murdoch was the kind of person with whom Sir Max felt at home. Pointing up the difference in crude terms, one long-time Beaverbrook employee said: 'Murdoch is an Oz. Max can understand him. But Goldsmith is a foreigner.' More importantly, Murdoch had a proven record of success in the British newspaper industry, whereas Goldsmith was a stranger to the business.

When Murdoch and Sir Max met for dinner in the first week of June the Beaverbrook boss was 'very bullish' about the idea of the Australian coming in. He also said that he did not feel able to trust anybody working for him any more. The deal they discussed in outline envisaged Murdoch supplying a new top management team for the company and £10 million of working capital.

Although both men were keen to consummate a deal, little more could be done in advance of the next Beaverbrook Foundation meeting, which was obliged to discuss the enfranchisement proposal put up by the Beaverbrook board. Murdoch's own offer shrewdly avoided any suggestion of change in the ownership structure. The next meeting of the foundation was scheduled for 21 June, after Sir Max's return from his sailing holiday.

In Sir Max's absence Jocelyn Stevens joined the list of participants in the Beaverbrook saga who had taken to the correspondence columns of *The Times* to make their case. What had provoked him into print was a story in *The Times* by Sheila Black on 7 June which spoke of sapped energy and desperately low morale at Beaverbrook Newspapers. Stevens's anxiety to 'match a few facts to your correspondent's imagination' led him to spray his letter with financial disclosures which technically contravened stock exchange rules by giving readers of one newspaper information which should have been made known to all Beaverbrook shareholders at the same time. In the six weeks since the Bonnington meeting, he wrote, the three Beaverbrook newspapers had produced a trading profit of more than £1,150,000. All three had broken advertising revenue records. The *Daily Express* circulation, having bottomed out at 2·3 million, was rising. The *Standard* had won its biggest share of the London evening market for 12 months. The *Sunday Express* had made more than £850,000 profit. That, Stevens added, was 'not bad for energy'.

But his enthusiastic claims for Beaverbrook's new-found profitability were somewhat undermined when the company issued a formal statement the following week about its trading results between 24 April and 4 June which confirmed the profit figure Stevens had given in his letter, but made clear that non-trading items such as depreciation, interest charges on its borrowings and tax had not been taken into account. As a result, the *Financial Times* commented, 'in terms of earnings, the figures are worth very little'.

If it were to cope with the crippling burden of indebtedness, Beaverbrook still needed a saviour. It was now up to the Beaverbrook Foundation to determine who that saviour might be. Although the board could propose, it was ultimately the foundation which had to dispose. For some people on the board, who considered the foundation flawed in terms of organization and personnel, this was not an appealing prospect.

The foundation's structure, which Lord Beaverbrook had devised in the 1950s to safeguard his fortune and perpetuate his name, certainly had some unusual features. Originally there were three separate foundations – one in Canada and two in Britain. The Canadian foundation, which held Lord Beaverbrook's non-newspaper assets and 3 per cent of the non-voting shares of Beaverbrook Newspapers, was the rich one. The two British foundations, later merged into a single body, had as their only major asset a 58·5 per cent holding of voting shares in Beaverbrook Newspapers. The objects of all three foundations were similar – to disburse the income from their assets for charitable purposes, with an emphasis on the Presbyterian Church and the encouragement of links between Scotland and Lord Beaverbrook's home province of New Brunswick.

In his last days, Beaverbrook had spoken of his 'standing army' waiting in Canada to march to the help of his British newspapers if they got into trouble. But the 'army', well fed on the fortune Lord Beaverbrook had built up outside the newspaper world, was not available under the conditions that he himself had laid down. A newspaper firm in Britain could hardly be regarded as the proper recipient of money from a Canadian charitable foundation. At one stage of the crisis Maxwell Aitken flew across the Atlantic to talk to the trustees of the Canadian foundation. They were friendly and wanted to help but, under the terms of the trust, could not contemplate liberating funds on the scale required by the founder's newspapers.

From a rigorous business point of view, the fact that the bulk of Lord Beaverbrook's money was tied up in a charitable foundation out of reach of his newspapers should have made no difference. The newspapers should have run themselves at a profit, or perished, without looking longingly at the Canadian assets. But in a volatile business where almost every other Fleet Street firm could depend on outside backing of some kind, the inaccessibility of Lord Beaverbrook's pot of gold could only appear as a final act of mischief from beyond the grave.

While the British foundations enjoyed the prestige of a controlling interest in the newspapers they did not enjoy much in the way of funds. After the two British foundations merged in 1974 their combined value was listed as £819,826, including £27,500 for a former house of Lord Beaverbrook's in Fulham. In their returns to the Charity Commission the Beaverbrook Newspapers shares were listed at book value. The sums given to charity varied sharply, dropping below £1000 some years and reaching around £40,000 in others. Donations in the early 1970s showed a fairly wide spread – children's organizations, health institutes, the RAF museum, press charities and the Battersea dogs' home. The main beneficiaries of the merged foundation were the King's College Hospital Liver Research Unit and the Ocean Youth Club.

Although some foundation members were also senior managers of Beaverbrook Newspapers their formal interest as trustees lay only in safeguarding the charity's income and deciding who to give it to. Business matters relating to the newspapers were rarely discussed at meetings of the trustees.

Charles Wintour's comment on the ten trustees, in a letter to Michael Foot, was: 'A less suitable group to decide the fortunes of a firm employing 7000 people, with a turnover of £100 million and publishing three newspapers that claim to have an important effect on the nation's destiny, could scarcely be devised.'

They were, none the less, a reasonably faithful reflection of the interests of the Aitken family. Five of the ten trustees were members of the family itself – Sir Max, his son Maxwell, his daughter Laura, his wife, Lady Violet, and his stepmother,

Lady Beaverbrook. One, Lord Robens, was a close friend of Sir Max. Two had devoted their careers to the personal interests of the family – Anne Westover, Sir Max's secretary, and George Millar, who had been Lord Beaverbrook's personal assistant. The remaining two – Jocelyn Stevens and John Junor – were long-serving Beaverbrook directors. Lady Beaverbrook had also been a director of the company but had never played any significant role in its affairs. She was better known as a racehorse owner and dog lover. Her concern for animals was once spectacularly displayed when she paid £9000 to charter an airliner to ensure that two dogs accompanying her on a trip to Canada had enough room to run about on the way.

To help them in their deliberations the foundation solicited the advice of the Hill Samuel merchant bank. The use of another merchant bank was a clear indication of the fact that the trustees viewed their interests as being separate from those of the Beaverbrook board, which was advised by Rothschild's. The meeting of Tuesday, 21 June 1977 which considered the enfranchisement issue was to confirm the width of that separation.

The arguments for opening up the company that had been so effective in the Beaverbrook boardroom cut little ice with the foundation. From the viewpoint of the trustees, enfranchisement of the A shares amounted to a surrender of control to Goldsmith without any immediate return for the family or the other voting shareholders. While other alternatives were still in the offing it seemed unreasonable to take such a precipitate step. Even though three of the trustees present had voted at boardroom level for consideration of the enfranchisement proposal, there were no dissenters from the foundation's decision against enfranchisement. Goldsmith's initiative had effectively run into a brick wall.

Later that same afternoon Rupert Murdoch had talks at his Bouverie Street office with representatives of Hill Samuel and Rothschild's to discuss the scale of the cash injection required by Beaverbrook. Goldsmith valiantly told the *Daily Telegraph* that Murdoch's chances of getting control of the Beaverbrook group were 'about as great as my becoming prima ballerina at Covent Garden'. The compelling mental image of the large, cigar-smoking entrepreneur in a tutu could not conceal the fact that Murdoch's chances were immeasurably improved by the Beaverbrook Foundation's stand against enfranchisement.

It had, however, also improved the prospects of a group that had yet to surface publicly as an interested party. On Wednesday, 22 June, the day after the foundation's meeting, the board of Trafalgar House met formally to consider a proposal to initiate a full take-over bid for Beaverbrook Newspapers. Much of the groundwork had already been done by Nigel Broackes and Victor Matthews, in consultation with Evelyn de Rothschild. They knew that Sir Max was ready to encourage their interest, though it was impossible to be sure what he would decide at the end of the day. One of the channels of communication with him had run through Peter Hetherington, who had friendly links with both Sir Max and Matthews. Despite his abrupt departure from the Beaverbrook group, Hetherington was still Sir Max's personal tax adviser.

The Trafalgar board decided to endorse their chairman's recommendation for a full take-over bid, though no publicity should be given to the offer unless and until it seemed certain of success. Jocelyn Stevens was told of Trafalgar's interest after the meeting and informed that if the take-over were successful Victor Matthews would become the new executive chairman of Beaverbrook Newspapers.

Matthews's credentials as a potential newspaper proprietor were not immediately apparent, though like Sir Max Aitken he was a firm believer in capitalism, conservatism and patriotism. They also had in common experience as promising amateur centre forwards and had lived through immediate physical danger in the Second World War. Otherwise, they were as different as the British social and business systems could make two men. Even their superficial points of resemblance underlined the gulf. Millionaire's son Max Aitken scored his goals for Cambridge University and cut a dashing figure as an RAF fighter ace. Elementary schoolboy Victor Matthews played his soccer in the plebeian surroundings of Highbury and sailed in the Dunkirk and Dieppe operations as a frequently seasick able seaman.

Born in Islington in 1919, Matthews was reticent about his early life. He had lost his father in the First World War and been brought up by his mother. While the Aitkens had survived the slump in fine style, Matthews still carried vivid memories of the working-class hardships of the 1930s. When he left the navy in 1945 his first priority had been to find a steady job. He was taken on by the construction firm of Trollope and Colls and stayed with them until 1960, when he took over a small South London building firm, Bridge Walker, and boosted its turnover from £250,000 to £2 million in four years. His success attracted the acquisitive eye of Nigel Broackes, the boss of Trafalgar House. In 1967 Trafalgar, expanding from its original base in property, took over Bridge Walker and Victor Matthews became Broackes's right-hand man and managing director.

The contrast between the self-made rough diamond and the urbane solicitor's son was to become a frequently noted feature of the British business scene. It was the living embodiment of a well-loved cliché – the thoughtful, cultured chairman and the businesslike manager from the wrong side of the tracks. Broackes and Matthews certainly made a formidable team as they took Trafalgar through construction companies, including Trollope and Colls, into shipping and hotels.

Matthews might not know much about newspapers but his company's record of success in previously unfamiliar fields was undeniably impressive. With annual profits of more than £40 million in sight for 1977, Trafalgar was suffering from an ailment most firms would have welcomed – a surplus of cash. The prospect of paying mainstream corporation tax loomed on the not-too-distant horizon if the company could not find enough firms worth buying. This fact alone should have been enough to give Matthews a luminous quality in the eyes of Jocelyn Stevens.

There were also personal considerations that lent a glow to the Trafalgar House initiative at that stage. Unlike the Murdoch offer, which had been sprung on the chief executive without his knowledge, it had comforting implications for Stevens and the existing management. With no previous experience in the publishing world, Trafalgar was bound, initially at least, to depend on the management skills of the Stevens team.

Murdoch, on the other hand, had deliberately avoided any contact with Beaverbrook's top management. In conversation with Simon Jenkins, Murdoch had made a point of the fact that while he intended to preserve the identity of the *Evening Standard* he would make radical changes elsewhere. The minimum he envisaged was a new chief executive, half a dozen new top managers and a new editor for the *Daily Express*. Although this intelligence was not conveyed directly to Stevens, Murdoch remarked later: 'Jocelyn did not have any illusions about his future.'

Stevens was, however, in the process of establishing much firmer control of the present. On Thursday, 23 June, the chief executive told the Beaverbrook board that Trafalgar House was preparing an outright bid of £12.5 million for the group. He also reported that the latest information from Carmelite House showed that Associated Newspapers was still intent on keeping its options open. On the one hand, Associated offered a sweetened version of the original plan, which would keep the *Standard* alive and speed up payments to Beaverbrook for printing facilities; alternatively, Stevens told the board, Associated might start negotiations for a merger of the two groups. The Goldsmith offer still remained on the table.

When it came to an assessment of the Murdoch offer, Stevens could only say that he had had no contact with the boss of News International. It was Sir Max who formally told the directors that Murdoch would like to take management and editorial control of Beaverbrook without launching a full take-over bid. There was general agreement that a decision would have to be made soon, probably within the next week.

Rupert Murdoch, meanwhile, was busy re-establishing contact with the unions. On the surface the newspaper trade unions had no reason to love him, since his feelings about Fleet Street labour practices were as plain as the nipples on page 3 of the *Sun*. But the national union leaders were themselves increasingly frustrated by the activities of their London chapels and Murdoch's credentials were boosted enormously by his success in rescuing the *Sun*. According to NATSOPA's Owen O'Brien: 'There was a feeling among us for Murdoch because of his track record. He delivered.'

For the union leaders, delivery of commercial success meant

preservation of jobs, and safeguarding employment was very much at the front of their minds after the rejection of 'Programme for Action'. The Royal Commission report on the press, then at the printers, was to speak of the possible disappearance of 9000 Fleet Street jobs through rationalization and new technology.

Bill Keys, who had already been told by Sir Max privately that he was 'prepared to embrace Murdoch', was also disposed to look favourably on the News International offer. The prospect of a new management broom at Beaverbrook was perhaps the most pleasing aspect for a man who had publicly labelled Sir Max's team as 'the most inept in Fleet Street'.

Although Murdoch made no secret of the fact that he would look for manning cuts in Beaverbrook Newspapers, the union leaders were persuaded that it was worth the price if the operation brought a new professionalism to the group as a whole.

Murdoch's other main target was the trustee who might be the most influential voice, after Sir Max, in making up the foundation's collective mind – Lord Alfred Robens of Woldingham.

Strangely, in view of Robens's obvious importance in the final decision, Murdoch was the only one of the four contenders who took the trip up to the 29th floor of the Vickers Tower by the Thames. Sitting in the deep yellow armchairs of Robens's office, with a panoramic view over London, Murdoch and his managing director, Bert Hardy, spoke of their plans. They made it plain that they were perfectly aware of the probability of a Monopolies Commission veto if News International bid for ownership of Beaverbrook. They assured Robens that, in view of this, they would leave ownership in the hands of the foundation. Then they unfolded their management control scheme. Both men left with a strong impression that Robens would be on their side when the final decision was made.

Murdoch also approached other trustees whose views might weigh heavily in the final decision. John Junor, the editor of the *Sunday Express*, who had played a complex role throughout as director and trustee, was attracted by the Murdoch proposal. Initially he had seemed keen on Goldsmith's intervention, but had subsequently cooled to the extent of being the only director who did not vote for the enfranchisement proposal. It was not clear whether this was because of Sir Max's hostility to Goldsmith or because the Cavenham boss had been so warmly taken up by Stevens and Wintour. Apart from his dedication to the *Sunday Express*, Junor was clearly intrigued by Murdoch's strategy of going round the Beaverbrook board directly to the foundation to achieve his objectives. Murdoch naturally gave him an assurance that he would not interfere in the running of the *Sunday Express*, except in the positive sense of making it less of a pack-horse for the whole group.

Murdoch also spoke to Maxwell Aitken. Even after six months on the Beaverbrook board the proprietor's son was still very much an unknown quantity. At some times, particularly during the abortive coup attempt against Jocelyn Stevens, he seemed eager to assume the proprietorial role as part of his birthright. At other moments he seemed diffident about com-miting his future to newspapers. When Murdoch approached him Maxwell's feeling was not particularly dynastic. As he told it later: 'I felt the proprietorial hierarchies of Fleet Street weren't going to go on for ever. One's whole life wasn't neces-sarily going to be devoted to running the *Daily Express*, the *Sunday Express* and the *Evening Standard*.' Murdoch got a clear message on those lines when he lunched with Maxwell to talk about the future. It was not an impression shared by everyone, but Murdoch had no doubts: 'He wanted the money, he wanted to have the money for a comfortable life – those were his words,' Murdoch recalled.

Although the Murdoch offer, as it stood, did not envisage any direct cash inducement to Maxwell, the News International boss had plans that would ensure a handsome provision for his father.

Murdoch's impression from his mini-canvass of the trustees was that he would get strong support from Robens and Junor if Sir Max held firm. He was not so sure about Maxwell.

Friday morning's *Daily Telegraph* publicly identified Trafalgar House as the fourth contender but highlighted Murdoch's offer of £10 million and a management contract under the headline: 'Murdoch favourite in race for Beaverbrook.' The Trafalgar group was upset by what it considered a premature 'leak' of its interest but decided to press on. Victor Matthews spent a pur-poseful morning with Stevens at Rothschild's modern office in New Court.

The subject for discussion was the difference in the prices which Trafalgar would offer for Beaverbrook's voting and non-voting shares. Clearly the ordinary shares, because of their voting rights, commanded a premium over the powerless A shares. Reflecting this, the stock market price of the A shares was standing at just under 60p while the ordinary share price was around 225p. The natural course seemed to be for Trafalgar to offer prices for the two classes of shares which corresponded with this ratio of around 4:1.

However natural that course might appear, it was bound to be strenuously contested by the biggest holder of A shares – Cavenham Foods. In opposing the apartheid of enfranchised and non-enfranchised shareholders, Goldsmith was in accord with contemporary City opinion as well as acting in his own interests. In Beaverbrook's case the 13·6 million non-voting shares dwarfed the 1·6 million voting shares in the company's equity base. The situation was aggravated by the fact that the foundation and Sir Max Aitken held 79 per cent of the voting shares as an inheritance in which they did not normally trade. As a result the price of the voting shares was not determined by the operation of full open-market forces and, Goldsmith's argument went, it therefore did not represent an objective basis on which to determine the division of the money Trafalgar was offering. As if to back up Goldsmith's view, the price of the voting shares behaved very oddly, shooting up to 300p in quotations after the stock exchange had closed for the weekend, although it was clear that nobody was going to offer anything like that amount for them. It did, however, serve to widen the apparent disparity in value between the voting and the A shares.

Friday, 24 June was also the day on which Sir James Goldsmith finally secured a personal interview with Sir Max Aitken. An arrangement for them to meet alone at Marsham Court the previous day had been cancelled at the last minute by Sir Max. Instead they met for tea in Lord Goodman's flat in Portland Place.

In the reassuring presence of his legal adviser and guide, Sir Max listened as Goldsmith summarized the events of the past six months and stressed his belief in the profit potential of Beaverbrook's three newspapers. He said he wanted the firm to remain independent and specifically criticized Murdoch's offer before producing his one new card – a proposal that, if his offer was accepted, Sir Max should stay on for one year as non-executive chairman, with Goldsmith as his executive deputy. It was, Goldsmith later recalled, a perfectly friendly occasion. Sir Max actually told Jocelyn Stevens afterwards that Goldsmith seemed 'a nice chap'.

It was not, however, nearly enough to swing events Cavenham's way.

Over the weekend Rupert Murdoch quietly improved his position by sending a letter to Sir Max. In addition to the £10 million load and management contract. Murdoch was also ready to secure Sir Max's own finances by buying all his personal 20 per cent holding of the voting shares for considerably more than he could expect from any other contender. Inside the envelope he tucked a cheque made out to Sir Max personally for £1·4 million.

THIRTEEN

Trafalgar Expects

THE FINAL WEEK began with a firm prediction in the trade press. The *U.K. Press Gazette* of Monday, 27 June, asserted that Beaverbrook Newspapers needed men with national newspaper expertise as much as they needed the money. Such a requirement pointed to the strong likelihood of a deal with Associated Newspapers or News International. The *Gazette* reported: 'The idea of the Daily Express joining Cunard's QE2 as a second flagship for Trafalgar House Investments was not taken too seriously in Fleet Street last week.'

It was, however, being taken extremely seriously by Sir Max Aitken, whose breakfast guests at Marsham Court that morning were Nigel Broackes and Victor Matthews. It was also being taken seriously by Jocelyn Stevens, who lunched that day at the Mirabelle restaurant in Mayfair with Peter Hetherington.

The loser in the April power struggle was able to inform the winner on the background to the Trafalgar offer. Stevens was surprised to learn that Sir Max had asked Hetherington to talk to Trafalgar on his behalf almost a month earlier. Whatever might be alleged about Sir Max's indecision, he could hardly be said to have been inactive.

After lunch Stevens drove from Mayfair back to Fleet Street, but instead of going to the *Express* building he turned south through the congested streets towards the Thames and dropped off at the headquarters of Associated Newspapers. In the chairman's office, Stevens sat down with Vere Harmsworth and Mick Shields and told them that it was only a matter of days before a final decision would be made on Beaverbrook's future. He also reckoned that the minimum price for Associated's participation in that future had to match

Murdoch's offer in monetary terms. An interest-free loan of £10 million might do the trick.

Stevens's dinner engagement that evening was with the Harmsworths in Eaton Square. It was intended to be a purely social occasion, but Vere and Jocelyn could not pass up the chance of talking newspapers. Huddled in a corner of the drawing room they continued their afternoon conversation. Stevens warned Harmsworth of the danger which Trafalgar could represent to him if it got into Fleet Street. The advent of Matthews and Broackes could undermine the whole of Associated's long-term strategy. When one of the other guests quizzically commented on the presence of Beaverbrook's chief executive at the Harmsworths' table Stevens replied with a smile: 'I've had some very funny meals in my time.'

With a Beaverbrook board meeting fixed for the afternoon of Wednesday, 29 June the next 36 hours saw the four contenders reacting with varying degrees of alacrity.

Sir James Goldsmith's rearguard action took the form of an intensified campaign against the 4:1 price ratio between the voting and non-voting shares which Trafalgar seemed likely to offer. First he wrote to the City Takeover Panel to say that such a disparity would be totally unfair and unacceptable to holders of A shares. He then sent a letter to Rothschild's in which he repeated Cavrho's willingness to work with others in a concerted rights issue operation to save Beaverbrook as an independent public company. Referring to a Trafalgar House statement that it would not integrate Beaverbrook with the parent company, Goldsmith added: 'Indeed if Trafalgar House, as they state, are principally concerned with the maintenance of Beaverbrook as an independent group, then they should also be invited to join this syndicate.'

Warming to this theme, Goldsmith added:

We believe that this type of proposal is better, not only for the publishing interests of the company but also for its shareholders. The net tangible assets of Beaverbrook, at balance sheet value, are 128 pence per share. This is a conservative valuation. We know from the negotiations with Associated Newspapers that the goodwill of the *Evening Standard* is worth at least £5 million, and this figure should be added to the 128 pence per share. The value of the goodwill of the *Sunday Express* would be even greater. According to the negotiations with Associated Newspapers, even the value of the plant and machinery would throw up a surplus. So a bid today for all the shares of the company would not, in our view, be to the ultimate benefit of shareholders.

I realize that you, as merchant bankers, tend to prefer a quick and final solution which eliminates any on-going responsibility. In this case, we believe that it would be wrong. The public interest, the interests of those within Beaverbrook and the interests of shareholders would all be better served by maintaining the company as a strong, independent company, capable of developing and improving its fortunes.

But Evelyn de Rothschild, who was himself a substantial shareholder in Beaverbrook Newspapers, was apparently unmoved by this reasoning and responded by inviting Goldsmith to make a full bid in direct competition with Trafalgar. Although Tiny Rowland favoured this option, Goldsmith judged that Beaverbrook Newspapers, with its underdeveloped property interests, would be worth more to Trafalgar than to Cavrho. Unwilling to engage in a losing battle, Goldsmith retired to Nice with an unseasonal attack of 'flu.

Victor Matthews sent a letter to Sir Max attaching the Trafalgar offer in the form of a draft press statement. It was worth £12·5 million, conditional on the foundation and Sir Max agreeing to sell all their shares to Trafalgar, and on the Beaverbrook directors recommending the offer to other shareholders. The proposed split was 221p per voting share, 65p per non-voting share and 60p each for the relatively unimportant number of cumulative preference shares. Trafalgar promised a further 'substantial cash investment' in the newspapers and pledged to keep all three titles going, subject to profitability. Sir Max would resign from the board and become life president. Matthews would become executive chairman. No other changes at boardroom level were currently envisaged.

The Rothschild team, which included Anthony Vice, a former editor of the *Sunday Times Business News*, was becoming steadily more enamoured of the Trafalgar House initiative. The attitude of the trade unions was more problematic. Although Matthews had no direct contact with the print unions, Jocelyn Stevens rang Bill Keys and other key leaders and acquainted them with the terms of the Trafalgar offer. He emphasized that it contained the two pledges in which they were most interested: no compulsory redundancies and preservation of the three titles. He took the added precaution of tape-recording the union leaders' replies.

'Ian Fleming couldn't have written it,' said Bill Keys later. 'It was real cloak-and-dagger stuff.'

Associated Newspapers forwarded a new plan to Beaverbrook refining its interest in a joint printing facility and designed to circumvent any problems with the Monopolies Commission. The proposal, based on discussions with Stevens and Maxwell Aitken, envisaged the creation of a new subsidiary, Fleet Street Printers Ltd (FSP), jointly owned by the two groups. Associated would buy into the new company at a price based on 50 per cent of its asset value and guarantee half of the Finance Corporation for Industry's £8 million loan to Beaverbrook. The objective was to achieve within three years 'a rationalized single-centre production' for all the Associated and Beaverbrook titles in London. There was no mention of closure of any title; and no mention of any interest-free loan.

Rupert Murdoch packed his bags and flew back to New York, content with an offer that gave the Beaverbrook proprietor 'his money and his pride'. He reckoned there was nothing more he could do. Sir Max had not cashed his cheque for £1·4 million, but he had not returned it either. Murdoch thought his chances were still good, but he also thought that Sir Max's final decision would depend ultimately on which old friend was the last to influence him. He very much hoped that friend would be Lord Robens.

The business of processing Murdoch's formal offer was handled by merchant bankers Morgan Grenfell. Their letter to Rothschild's indicated that News International was prepared to subscribe up to £10 million (or possibly more if required) for a new class of management shares in Beaverbrook.

The subscriptions would be spread over a period to meet the cash flow requirements of the company. Murdoch's New International would exercise management control through an executive committee and enjoy the right to appoint a minority of the Beaverbrook directors.

At 4 pm on Wednesday afternoon Stevens presented the range of possibilities to the Beaverbrook board. As it stood, the Associated offer of a joint printing venture did little to ease the company's cash crisis, but if it were to be combined with a £10 million loan there were distinct possibilities in the proposed alliance. Compared with the original plan, the *Standard* would be saved and the cash Beaverbrook received would be increased. The managements of the two firms believed that their five London-based newspapers could all be printed on the Fleet Street site within three years. If there were quick union agreement, the *Evening News* could be brought across the road within 12 months. Once that move was achieved, the way would be open for savings in the distribution costs of the two evening newspapers. A deal restricted to joint printing would, Stevens told the board, not be referred to the Monopolies Commission.

On the other hand Stevens considered that Rupert Murdoch's proposal would almost certainly have to be referred to the Commission, despite an assurance in the Morgan Grenfell letter that this would not be compulsory. Evelyn de Rothschild, who was by this time strongly identified with the Trafalgar House offer, described the News International plan as a variation on the Goldsmith/Rowland Cavrho proposal. Both aimed for effective control without an actual take-over bid. In Beaverbrook boardroom slang, Murdoch became bracketed with Goldsmith as the 'Stealth' parties, as opposed to the 'Wealth' of Associated and Trafalgar.

Faced with the alternatives, the board decided not to decide. But it did try to narrow down the field. Rothschild's was instructed to have urgent talks with Trafalgar to try to improve the price being offered. Stevens was told to seek a minimum commitment of £10 million from Associated. The Trafalgar and Associated proposals were, in the board's estimation, the only ones which merited serious consideration at that stage.

There was of course no guarantee that the trustees would come to the same conclusion.

As well as coming down in favour of the 'Wealth' parties, the board set a final deadline for the revised offers of 11 am the next day. With that settled, Stevens and Rothschild wrote a laconic dispatch to the outside world:

29th June 1977 (1750 hours)
The Board of Beaverbrook Newspapers Limited met this afternoon to consider the various proposals open to the Group. They will continue their deliberations tomorrow, and a further statement will be made as soon as possible.

That evening Rupert Murdoch telephoned from New York to ask his managing director, Bert Hardy, how things were going. Hardy's information was that whatever the board might think, Sir Max and Robens were holding firm and that Lady Violet and her daughter, Laura, would probably follow their lead. With John Junor and one other, possibly Maxwell Aitken, they would have a majority of the trustees. Bill Keys had a similar understanding of the position. Murdoch felt he was still in with a chance.

FOURTEEN

A House Divided

JOCELYN STEVENS'S DAY began in the headquarters of his main rival. Associated Newspapers had just two hours in which to pledge the £10 million loan that could seal an alliance between the two groups.

Stevens had hoped to meet Associated's chairman, but Vere Harmsworth was not in his office when Stevens arrived at 9 am and did not show up in the following half hour. Instead Stevens met Associated's managing director Mick Shields.

Back at the Beaverbrook headquarters Stevens found his own proprietor in an agony of indecision. Although Sir Max seemed reconciled to the fact that Thursday, 30 June, would be his last day as a fully independent proprietor he was still unsure which bid to favour. For Stevens, however, the absence of any concrete financial commitment from Associated had reduced the options. Trafalgar House offered, to his mind, the quickest and most clear-cut deal for shareholders and employees alike, with enough money to ensure the survival of the newspapers.

Stevens's opportunity to express this view came when Sir Max asked him directly for his opinion. It was a crucial moment and Jocelyn Stevens has a suitably dramatic recollection of the exchange that followed.

'Who do you want to win?' Sir Max asked.

'Trafalgar.'

'If that is so, so do I.'

Despite the mistrust that had sprung up between them over the preceding months, in the end Sir Max's commitment to Stevens proved stronger than other attachments. With the decision made Sir Max called his secretary and dictated a letter to Rupert Murdoch in Stevens's presence. He said he was returning the cheque for £1·4 million and turning down Murdoch's offer of assistance 'with tears in my eyes'.

At 11.10 am the Beaverbrook directors took their places round the long table in the boardroom on the third floor of the *Express* building. Stevens told the others that there was still no word from Associated. It seemed possible that Vere Harmsworth had lost any taste for eleventh-hour interventions after being on the receiving end of one at the Bonnington Hotel. More probably he assumed that any inflation of the Associated offer would simply be used as a lever to raise the price offered by Trafalgar. In any event, the long-lived Associated option died a silent death.

When Sir Max reported that Trafalgar House might be willing to improve its original offer there seemed to be only one option. The straightforwardness of the Trafalgar proposal, compared to the others, appealed to those directors most concerned with finance. For those more interested in editorial matters, such as Charles Wintour and Roy Wright, Trafalgar's financial strength seemed to promise a safe haven for the *Evening Standard* and the *Daily Express*. There was also an unexpressed but general sense of relief at the prospect of being able to make a new start. The Aitkens had had their day. The only sticking point was the purchase price, and that seemed capable of remedy.

The board gave unanimous approval to a motion put forward by John Junor that Sir Max, together with his son, Rothschild and Stevens, should immediately go to see Trafalgar House to try to negotiate an improved deal before the foundation met that afternoon. The motion also empowered Sir Max to accept on behalf of the board any improved offer which satisfied him.

At Trafalgar's Berkeley Street headquarters the Beaverbrook delegation found themselves pushing against a door that was already ajar. Broackes and Matthews were indeed ready to raise their company's offer – from £12·5 million to £13·69 million for all the voting and non-voting shares in Beaverbrook, plus £900,000 for the 1·5 million preference shares. The new offer put the price of each of the 1,632,000 voting shares at 252p, an increase of 31p over the original proposal. The 13,685,600 non-voting A shares would be valued at 70p each,

5p more than in the first offer. It meant that the Beaverbrook Foundation would get £3 million and Sir Max over £1 million. Jocelyn Stevens felt confident he had an offer the foundation could not refuse.

While he waited for Beaverbrook's response Victor Matthews shared his thoughts with a television interviewer. He told Sally Hardcastle of the BBC programme 'The Editors', which was recording the day's events: 'Yesterday evening I thought we had the price right, and discovered it wasn't right. This morning I thought that perhaps the price they wanted would be too high for us, and at this very moment in time I am encouraged.' He also said that, for all his experience of take-overs, there was still something about buying a new business that was 'very special and exciting'. The excitement, in fact, was far from being over.

Going into the trustees' meeting Stevens might feel a nostalgic pang for the Associated deal and remain intrigued by the thought of what Goldsmith would have done with the *Daily Express*, but there was no doubt in his mind that Trafalgar was best for the company and for his chairman. Encouragingly, Sir Max had not wavered from their joint resolution of that morning. It looked as though the foundation meeting would be a formality. A simple majority of six of the ten trustees would be enough to ratify the sale.

The meeting started according to plan. Sir Max spoke for Trafalgar. He gave the trustees four reasons for selling the foundation's shares to Trafalgar: the offer was the most straight-forward one for all Beaverbrook's shareholders; it was the best for the general security of employment for the company's employees; it was the best in terms of monopolies legislation; and it was 'the best for the country'.

Sir Max looked round the table, seeking the opinions of the trustees. As he did so two other options sprang back into life. One was the Murdoch option which had been discarded at the previous day's board meeting; the other was an extension of the go-it-alone strategy which had not even been discussed.

The spokesman for the first alternative was Lord Robens, supported by John Junor. The spokesman for the second was Maxwell Aitken, supported by his mother and sister. Their combined effect would be sufficient to block any deal with Trafalgar.

In pleading Trafalgar's case Stevens wisely decided to concentrate his fire on the Murdoch proposal. He began with some cautionary remarks about Murdoch being a competitor. If News International gained control by a management contract they could run the *Daily Express* into the ground, to the greater profit of the *Sun*. It was an unlikely prospect, rendered all the more improbable by Murdoch's plan to move his top editor, Larry Lamb, to the *Express*, but a theoretical possibility all the same. According to Stevens's recollection, Robens then advanced the proposition that Murdoch enjoyed union support. Stevens hit back by offering to produce tapes he had made of conversations with Bill Keys of SOGAT and Owen O'Brien of NATSOPA. These, Stevens claimed, showed that the Trafalgar deal also enjoyed union support. Stevens then played the boardroom card. He pointed out that the directors had effectively rejected Murdoch the previous day and had not even discussed his proposal at their meeting that morning. If the trustees now resurrected News International, the whole matter would have to be taken back to the board.

Stevens was answering the Murdoch supporters, but he was really speaking to Sir Max. The crucial question was whether the chairman would be swayed from his earlier resolution, either into supporting Murdoch or into a new round of uncertainty. As the meeting wore on Sir Max continued to back his chief executive.

In the face of Sir Max's resolve, Robens and Junor shifted ground and allied themselves with the four other trustees who expressed a preference for Trafalgar – Stevens, Lady Beaverbrook, George Millar and Mrs Westover.

But Sir Max's wife and two children continued to oppose his wishes.

According to Maxwell Aitken their opposition was not so much dynastic as commercial. 'It was', he recalled, 'a sale with only one person in the auction room, which was wrong.' Maxwell's argument at the meeting was that there had been a recent improvement in the group's fortunes which should, if sustained, allow them all more time to solicit further bids before deciding on a final sale. Indeed, Maxwell's commercial appreciation was more acute than it seemed at the time. Over the next few months the fall in the value of the dollar, which arrested the rise in price of newsprint, and a general improvement in advertising revenue were to make conditions easier for Fleet Street as a whole. Beaverbrook was, in fact, selling out at the very moment when a go-it-alone policy was becoming a realistic strategy, rather than a desperate one.

Against Maxwell was the fact that Trafalgar had set a definite time limit for acceptance of their revised offer – noon the next day. After so many months spent coaxing what seemed like an adequate bid into existence, most of the trustees were clearly reluctant to risk the consequences of further delay. In the end the opposition to Trafalgar was reduced to the absence of three family signatures from the agreement to sell the foundation's shares.

At 2.30 pm, when Sir Max formally announced the trustees' decision to the directors, he looked over at his son and said: 'This is a hard decision to take and it is particularly hard on young Maxwell.'

At 2.50 pm Jocelyn Stevens called Victor Matthews at Trafalgar House to tell him the result. Matthews wasted no time in inspecting his new domain. Accompanied by the BBC television team he got into his Rolls-Royce, registration number TRA 1, and headed for the *Express* building. On the way Sally Hardcastle interviewed him about the Beaverbrook tradition:

HARDCASTLE: 'Do you feel any affinity with Lord Beaverbrook?'
MATTHEWS: 'Oh yes, very much so. Very keenly, I believe in the things he believed in, otherwise I don't feel one could do this.'
HARDCASTLE: 'What kind of things?'
MATTHEWS: 'Well, his was the empire. We haven't got the empire and so to me it is Britain now and that is the most important thing and why I feel very strongly about it.'
HARDCASTLE: 'Can you tell me when you talk about Britain, what kind of British things do you mean?'
MATTHEWS: 'Well, I believe very much in a country that enables a person like myself, and I wouldn't

over-emphasize this, but I am just like any other chap that we see walking across the street now who has got to the top and if that can happen in a country, in a straightforward, ordinary way, by hard work, then I am very anxious to maintain that.'

After identifying himself with the Beaverbrook philosophy of personal enterprise and ambition justly rewarded with success, Matthews stepped out into Fleet Street. Jocelyn Stevens greeted him at the wide glass doors of the *Express* building and took him upstairs into the boardroom for a press conference.

While Stevens's smile flashed in the television lights, Charles Wintour was at his most cool and precise. 'We now have a rich and powerful parent,' he said. 'I believe that from now on Beaverbrook Newspapers will be a more effective fighting force in the newspaper industry, play a more vigorous role in the life of the country and also find a much more prosperous future.'

Sir Max Aitken walked out to the pavement and got into his waiting car. Before he was driven off, he was asked if he felt sad that the Aitkens no longer owned newspapers. 'Well, no,' he replied evenly. 'I've given up because I got ill. No, I am not disappointed.' But what would his father be saying if he was still alive? 'I think he would have sold up long before,' said Sir Max.

In the *Daily Express* newsroom the 'back bench' went to work on a celebratory issue. The massive headline – 'YOUR EXPRESS: A NEW HORIZON' – covered half the front page. Beside it, a message to readers from Matthews promised a competitive, exciting and, above all, successful future.

The BBC television team were given a more sceptical perspective by the union general secretaries. They were most perturbed by Victor Matthews's pledges of support for the existing management team. Bill Keys said bluntly that it could not produce the necessary improvement for the future. He was vigorously seconded by Owen O'Brien: 'I would say not to change is a recipe for disaster. All we are going to do is to defer the crisis of Beaverbrook Newspapers another couple of years.' The most laconic reaction came from a Beaverbrook van driver who was asked for his opinion of the new situation: 'Trafalgar

House bought it so we've still got a job,' he replied and drove off. Like everybody else, he was mistaken.

In fact, Trafalgar still did not actually have an undertaking to which the Beaverbrook Foundation could be held. The problem lay in the wording of the document that had been passed round for signature at the end of the foundation meeting. In the bustle which had followed the meeting nobody had noticed that the document was not correctly worded, and therefore not legally binding. The first person to see the fault and bring it to Stevens's attention that afternoon was David Bucks of Hill Samuel, the foundation's merchant bankers. By that time, Victor Matthews was in the middle of his press conference.

After passing Matthews a note outlining the situation and urging him to go on as if nothing had happened, Bucks and Stevens went hunting for the dispersing trustees with a correctly worded document. Lady Beaverbrook had gone racing. Lady Violet and her daughter had left for the South of France. George Millar was on his way to Devon. By early evening they had rounded up most of the remainder, though Maxwell Aitken hesitated when confronted with the document. 'For Christ's sake, sign it,' said Stevens. All that remained was to get Sir Max and Mrs Westover to sign.

At Marsham Court Sir Max was sitting with Mrs Westover in front of his television set watching Wimbledon. It was an epic match, a men's singles semi-final between Bjorn Borg and Vitas Gerulaitis stretching into five sets. Sir Max sat in semi-darkness, his head moving from side to side with the ball. He greeted Stevens and Bucks and asked if they would have a drink.

'Yes please,' Stevens replied, 'and I have this thing for you to sign.'

Sir Max took the document, read it and looked up at Stevens. 'Does this mean we haven't sold?' he asked.

For one paralysing moment Stevens thought that the question might be the preliminary to a change of heart on Sir Max's part. But it proved to be only a matter of curiosity. When the situation was explained to him Sir Max signed and went back to watching the tennis.

Epilogue

SOME OF Victor Matthews's early pronouncements as Fleet Street's new crusader gave cause for concern. He declared that his editors would enjoy freedom so long as they agreed with the policy laid down. He also said that he would find himself in a dilemma about whether to report a British Watergate affair because of the national harm it could cause – although that might not have appeared too untraditional to anybody remembering Beaverbrook's role in ensuring press silence about Edward VIII and Mrs Simpson during the Abdication crisis.

He got Jocelyn Stevens's name wrong on television; he did not know what the initials NPA stood for; he spoke of Bill Keys as coming from 'the National Union'. But apart from the ignorance pardonable in a man new to the business his commitment was impressive. Matthews moved promptly into the *Express* building and dealt crushingly with any notion that Trafalgar might be more interested in Beaverbrook's properties than its newspapers.

For a total cost of £14,592,560 Trafalgar had acquired fixed assets valued at £37,204,000. When Beaverbrook's liabilities, including £11,079,000 of borrowings, were taken into account, the net tangible assets were £21,169,000. Beaverbrook's freehold, land and buildings were in the books at £26,266,000 and the sight of the decaying property occupied by the *Evening Standard* behind Fleet Street was enough to quicken the heart of any developer. But not Victor Matthews's. 'This is Cunard all over again, you see,' he said on BBC radio. 'When we took Cunard over, the suggestion was that we were going to sell off all the ships and asset stripping, y'know that's the name of the game, that's what Trafalgar is all about. But that's fundamentally wrong. Every company we've taken over, we've gone into the field, whatever it's in, and made a success of it and that's exactly what we intend to do with Beaverbrook.'

Trafalgar's commitment to 100 per cent ownership was rapidly discharged. The Beaverbrook Foundation received £3,015,464 for its voting and non-voting shares. Sir Max got £1,218,523 and his son £98,700. The Canadian Foundation was paid £301,000 for its holding of non-voting shares. The amount of stock held by Beaverbrook directors varied widely. Stevens received £76,230 and Evelyn de Rothschild £70,560. John Junor was paid £13,570 for his shares, Charles Wintour £3976 and Roy Wright £700.

On the other side of Fleet Street, Trafalgar paid £496,902 to Associated Newspapers for its voting and A shares, giving Vere Harmsworth a little more financial fuel for the next round in the traditional battle. Sir James Goldsmith quietly swallowed his objections to the offer and decided to be 'a good loser'. He was rewarded with £3,574,900 for Cavenham's holding of the A shares – an agreeable return for the £1,566,264 expended less than nine months earlier.

Matthews also maintained his pledge to keep Stevens and his management team, with two amicable exceptions. Five weeks after he took over Roy Wright was replaced as editor of the *Daily Express*. His successor, Derek Jameson, was a highly regarded tabloid expert from the *Daily Mirror*. Jameson, who shared a Cockney background with Matthews, had entered Fleet Street at the age of 14 as a messenger boy at Reuters. His appointment appeared a natural consequence of Matthews's concentration on circulation and his declared belief that what the *Express* needed was more headlines and less small print. Wright left philosophically. Taking his substantial cash settlement with him, he moved across the road and settled in as senior assistant editor of the *Daily Mail*.

The other early departure was made by Maxwell Aitken, three weeks after the take-over. 'He has left with the utmost goodwill between us,' said Matthews. 'There is no bad feeling at all. He did not see himself in the newspaper world after the family had given up control of Beaverbrook.' Taking £45,000 in settlement of his contract, the one-time heir to the Beaverbrook empire moved into the property business, operating out of a modest office in Mayfair.

Within a year the Beaverbrook inheritance became no more than a memory as far as Fleet Street was concerned. Though Sir Max remained life president of the newspapers he played no active part in their affairs. Even the proud name had gone. The company became Express Newspapers and the men from Trollope and Colls took down the Beaverbrook name from the front of the big glass palace.

Close friends of Sir Max said that he sometimes regretted the deal that so completely excluded him from the affairs of the company he had owned. But there was no turning back.

Critics of Trafalgar's victory made much of the fact that the group had no previous experience in newspapers and that Matthews appeared to see himself in the role of an old-fashioned proprietor ready to intervene at every level of the business. However, in the long run the combination of these elements may well turn out to be a recipe for revival.

The conventional wisdom in Fleet Street has focused for too long on the need for more professional management while tending to dismiss the proprietor as an outdated and almost irrelevant figure. Many contemporary proprietors are almost unknown to their staffs and frequently live abroad. This fact has undoubtedly enhanced the function of newspaper managements but it has not conspicuously increased their competence.

Like it or not, the history of Fleet Street – and, in particular, that of Beaverbrook Newspapers – suggests that vigorous owners are crucial to the development of vigorous newspapers. Management and marketing strategies, however greatly refined, have never been a substitute for personality at the top. If Trafalgar's victory represents the re-emergence of the involved proprietor it could bring benefits to Fleet Street that extend far beyond the frontiers of Express Newspapers.

Select Bibliography

Lord Beaverbrook, *Success*, 1921.
——, *Men and Power*, 1956.
Russell Braddon, *Roy Thomson of Fleet Street*, 1965.
Nigel Broackes, *A Growing Concern*, 1979.
Arthur Christiansen, *Headlines All My Life*, 1961.
Tom Clarke, *My Northcliffe Diary*, 1931.
Graham Cleverly, *The Fleet Street Disaster*, 1976.
Hugh Cudlipp, *Walking on the Water*, 1976.
Tom Driberg, *Beaverbrook. A Study in Power and Frustration*, 1956.
David Farrer, *G – for God Almighty*, 1969.
——, *The Sky's the Limit*, 1943.
Paul Ferris, *The House of Northcliffe*, 1971.
Harold Hobson, Phillip Knightley, Leonard Russell, *The Pearl of Days*, 1972.
Fred Hirsch, David Gordon, *Newspaper Money*, 1975.
Simon Jenkins, *Newspapers. The Power and the Money*, 1979.
Charles Loch Mowatt, *Britain Between the Wars*. 1955.
Reginald Pound, Geoffrey Harmsworth, *Northcliffe*, 1959.
Simon Regan, *Rupert Murdoch. A Business Biography*, 1976.
Royal Commission on the Press, 1947–9.
——, 1974–7.
A. C. H. Smith, *Paper Voices*, 1975.
A. J. P. Taylor, *Beaverbrook*, 1972.
——, *English History 1914–45*, 1965.
C. M. Vines, *A Little Nut-Brown Man*, 1968.
Francis Williams, *Dangerous Estate*, 1957.
——, *A Prime Minister Remembers*, 1961.
Charles Wintour, *Pressures on the Press*, 1972.
Alan Wood, *The True History of Lord Beaverbrook*, 1965.
Kenneth Young, *Churchill and Beaverbrook*, 1965.

Index

Index

Karr, David, adviser to Beaverbrook, 93–4, 178
Keeble, Harold, 27
Keys, Bill (SOGAT general secre-
tary), and Goodman, 146; at
Bonnington Hotel meeting, 177;
relationship with Stevens, 183–4;
receives Harmsworth letter, 185;
quoted *S. Telegraph*, 186; and
Murdoch, 224, 231, 237, 239
King, Cecil, 46, 57–8; ousting from
IPC, 124
Kirby, Louis, deputy editor *Mail*,
74; editor *News*, 101; talks to
Jenkins about merger, 135;
Harmsworth sees as editor of
merged evening paper, 136; letter
to Rothwell, 157; produces paper
during NUJ strike, 169
Kirkby, David, 105
Knightley, Phillip, 153

La Capponcina, Beaverbrook's villa
at Cap d'Ail, 11
Lamb, Larry, 237
Law, Bonar, 17
Lawrence, Brian, 105
Levi, Jim, 182
Levin, Bernard, libel action on story
about Associated, 74
Lloyd George, David 1st Earl, 17
Lloyd's Bank, 13, 14, 51, 147
Lockhart, Robert Bruce, 31
London Boat Show, 11–12, 84
Lonrho, interests, 197; proposal to
acquire Beaverbrook with Caven-
ham, 198–9; offer improved, 208

McColl, Ian, editor, *Daily Express*,
50, 58
McGill, Angus, 83
McLoughlin, Bill, 177
Mander, Michael, 72
Marks, Derek, editor *Daily Express*,
42–3, 50
Matthews, Victor, interest in *Stan-*

dard building developments, 61;
early talks with Stevens, 61–2;
Rothschild outlines Beaverbrook
situation to him, 209; career and
character, 221–2; formal Trafalgar offer, 230; raises offer, 235–
236; Sally Hardcastle interview,
238–9; and newspapers, 241
Millar, George, 220
Miller, Russell, 44, 56
Monopolies Commission, 224
Monteith, Cynthia, Max's first wife,
32, 68
Morgan Grenfell, merchant
bankers, 231
Morgan, Ken (NUJ general secretary), views on merger, 145–6;
and *News* strike, 169, 176, 177,
180
Murdoch, Rupert, 50, 88; bidder
for *Observer*, 90–1; interest in
Beaverbrook, 213, 216; papers
owned, 214–15; character, 215;
outline deal emerges, 216–17;
contact with unions, 223; plans
for Beaverbrook management,
223; sees Robens, 224; sees Maxwell, 225; £1.4m. cheque to Max,
227; formal offer, 231; Beaverbrook board unfavourable to
offer, 232; still hopeful, 233;
option discussed by Foundation,
236–7
Murphy, Michael, 79

National Coal Board, pension fund
buys Beaverbrook property, 121
National Graphical Association
(NGA), 127, 164
National Society of Operative
Printers, Graphical and Media
Personnel (NATSOPA), 127
National Union of Journalists
(NUJ), 127; letter to Hattersley,
129; Associated and Beaverbrook
chapels do not show solidarity,
130–1; delegate meeting, Ilkley,

252

SOCIAL SCIENCE LIBRARY

Manor Road Building
Manor Road
Oxford OX1 3UQ
Tel: (2)71093 (enquiries and renewals)
http://www.ssl.ox.ac.uk

This is a NORMAL LOAN item.

We will email you a reminder before this item is due.

Please see http://www.ssl.ox.ac.uk/lending.html
for details on:

- loan policies; these are also displayed on the notice boards and in our library guide.

- how to check when your books are due back.

- how to renew your books, including information on the maximum number of renewals. Items may be renewed if not reserved by another reader. Items must be renewed before the library closes on the due date.

- level of fines; fines are charged on overdue books.

Please note that this item may be recalled during Term.

WITHDRAWN